Making War, Making Women

Making War, Making Women

Femininity and Duty on the
American Home Front, 1941–1945

Melissa A. McEuen

The University of Georgia Press   *Athens and London*

© 2010 by the University of Georgia Press
Athens, Georgia 30602
www.ugapress.org
All rights reserved
Set in Minion Pro by Graphic Composition, Inc., Bogart, Georgia

Most University of Georgia Press titles are
available from popular e-book vendors.

Printed digitally

Library of Congress Cataloging-in-Publication Data
McEuen, Melissa A., 1961–
    Making war, making women : femininity and duty on the
American home front, 1941–1945 / Melissa A. McEuen.
        xiv, 270 p. : ill. ; 23 cm.
        Includes bibliographical references (p. [219]–261) and index.
        ISBN-13: 978-0-8203-2904-8 (hardcover : alk. paper)
        ISBN-10: 0-8203-2904-5 (hardcover : alk. paper)
        ISBN-13: 978-0-8203-2905-5 (pbk. : alk. paper)
        ISBN-10: 0-8203-2905-3 (pbk. : alk. paper)
        1. Women—United States—History—20th century.
    2. World War, 1939–1945—United States.
    3. Femininity—United States—History—20th century.
    4. Advertising—Cosmetics—History—20th century.
    5. Advertising—Clothing and dress—History—20th century. I. Title.
        HQ1420.M383 2010
        305.40973′09044—dc22   2010020412

British Library Cataloging-in-Publication Data available

For Ed

CONTENTS

LIST OF ABBREVIATIONS

AAGPBL	All-American Girls Professional Baseball League
FDA	U.S. Food and Drug Administration
JWT	J. Walter Thompson Advertising Agency
LHJ	*Ladies' Home Journal*
NAACP	National Association for the Advancement of Colored People
NUL	National Urban League
OPA	U.S. Office of Price Administration
OWI	U.S. Office of War Information
SPAR	Semper Paratus Always Ready (Women's Coast Guard)
USMCWR	U.S. Marine Corps Women's Reserve
USO	United Service Organizations
WAC	Women's Army Corps
WASP	Women Airforce Service Pilots
WAVES	Women Accepted for Volunteer Emergency Service (Women's Navy)
WB	Women's Bureau, U.S. Department of Labor
WMC	U.S. War Manpower Commission
WPB	U.S. War Production Board

PREFACE

Several years ago, on a visit to the Women's Memorial at Arlington National Cemetery, I was struck by the faces and poses of women in photographs from World War II. Their smiles and other gestures conveyed a confidence and ease that set them apart from women pictured elsewhere in the gallery. As a historian of photography, I knew what their generation thought about cameras, snapshots, and the bevy of picture magazines available on American newsstands; they had witnessed the growth of a visual culture in the United States and understood the influence of photographs in daily life. But I wondered how these wartime women wanted to be seen and whose rules dictated their appearance.

The hours I spent at Arlington brought into focus an earlier, more intimate exchange, prompting further questions about women, appearances, and power. After I had my long blonde hair bobbed, various family members reacted with shock and dismay. My distraught mother exclaimed, "But your hair was your trademark!" I wondered if, as a published historian and recently tenured professor, I needed or wanted such a "trademark" to represent me. To loved ones, I had too nonchalantly dispensed with a traditional symbol of femininity and altered my identity as the woman (more aptly, the girl) they knew. I thought, "If this could happen now, in a new century and a new millennium, what must it have been like for a woman to challenge expectations in the 1940s . . . to don trousers, a military uniform, or a two-piece bathing suit for the first time, to cut her hair, to take up a 'man's job' in a factory, to undo or turn her back on what had marked her or had been marked out for her?" Could she mollify her critics by claiming it was all for the war effort? Or would this invite even more criticism? How would refashioning herself meet political needs, social obligations, or personal desires?

These experiences coincided with an observation that more and more of my students understood the Second World War through popular histories and other media celebrating the "Greatest Generation." The various fiftieth-anniversary commemorations of the war in the 1990s had helped to promote a huge industry captivating millions of readers and viewers. But the accumulating stories seemed to narrow the past in two ways—by over-masculinizing the war years with bands of brothers and citizen soldiers, and by reshaping the American narrative largely according to participants' memories. In 1997 historians Judy Barrett Litoff and David C. Smith wrote that American women's stories had "yet to be fully incorporated into our collective understanding. Moreover, women's active participation in the war effort is still not accepted as part of the World War II canon."[1] Their comment challenged me to revisit wartime women by returning to the 1940s to hear their voices, to read their words, to see their faces, and to study their habits, their aspirations, and their relationships—with each other, their families, and their nation.

I'm grateful for the support of many institutions, organizations, and people who responded with enthusiasm to this project. Transylvania University provided generous financial support, including two Jones Grants for summer research and a Kenan Sabbatical Leave Grant that allowed me to spend several months at the National Archives and the Library of Congress. I'm fortunate to have in William Pollard an academic dean who deeply respects the scholarly enterprise and finds ways to secure time and support for his faculty to pursue their research programs. The John W. Hartman Center for Sales, Advertising and Marketing History at Duke University awarded me a travel grant to complete my work in the J. Walter Thompson Advertising Agency Archives. A fellowship from the Institute for Southern Studies not only provided everything that I needed to conduct research in the University of South Carolina's rich African American history collections, but it also included residence in a charming faculty house on Greene Street; Walter Edgar and Thomas J. Brown welcomed me to Columbia with the full measure of southern hospitality.

I appreciate the attention of thoughtful archivists and librarians, including those who assisted me at the National Archives, the Library of Congress, the University of South Carolina's Cooper Library, and the University of Kentucky's Young Library. I extend special thanks to Jacqueline Reid and the helpful staff at the Hartman Center in Duke University's Rare Book, Manuscript, and Special Collections Library. I'm grateful for the good will of the Lexington Public Library staff members who lifted and loaded *LIFE* magazine volumes for me day after day. I owe more than gratitude to everyone at the Transylvania University Library—Stephen Leist, Lisa Nichols, and Phil Walker never grew impatient with my countless interlibrary loan needs and deadline extensions; and director Susan Brown showed a sustained interest in this project, informing me about relevant databases and other developments in the complex world of information science and technology.

I've benefited from the wise counsel of several historians and other scholars who read all or parts of the manuscript. I'm grateful to Tom Appleton, Devin Brown,

Elizabeth Corsun, Ellen Cox, Martha Gehringer, Melinda Groff, Kandace Hensley, Julie Human, Judy Barrett Litoff, Amy McCandless, Leisa Meyer, Jeffrey Sklansky, Mary Jane Smith, Meghan Winchell, and an anonymous reader for the University of Georgia Press. Fellow panelists and audience members at the 2004 American Studies Association Annual Meeting, where I first presented parts of the argument, helped me to clarify and shape ideas that still lived primarily in my imagination. Any errors or lapses in judgment remain mine alone.

Teaching at a liberal arts college allows me the good fortune of close exposure to a variety of academic disciplines, some with methodologies quite different from mine; as a result, my community of scholars prompts me to think creatively and to take risks. For their probing questions and timely comments at various stages of this project, I thank Chris Begley, Martha Billips, Simona Fojtová, Peter Fosl, Kurt Gohde, Tasha Howe, Kim Miller, Belinda Sly, Bryan Trabold, Ingrid Walker, Scott Whiddon, Nancy Wolsk, and my devoted colleagues in the history program—Gregg Bocketti, Frank Russell, and Ken Slepyan. My students keep my eyes wide open with their candid responses and new angles on timeless questions. I'm grateful, in particular, to the stalwarts in the women's history classes and the Second World War classes. Every once in awhile the stars align in an exquisite pattern: as my writing schedule became more grueling, I was blessed with a cadre of extraordinary history students in the class of 2009. They not only cheered me on in my work but provided models of excellence with their own ambitious research agendas; their spirit and verve permeate every page of this book. I could not have completed it without Jessica Sullivan's research assistance and good humor. Katie Banks, our administrative assistant in Haupt Humanities, helped me with all kinds of technical challenges, as did Barbara Grinnell, whose gifts of time, patience, and expertise ensured that the book would indeed contain visual images.

I'm grateful to everyone who sent clippings, told me their families' stories, and shared other precious sources. Early in the project, Jack Girard gave me a pristine copy of a 1942 *Woman's Home Companion Cook Book* that he had found in an ancestor's attic. Jeremy Popkin presented me with a lovely first edition of his grandmother's popular novel, *The Journey Home* (1945), which became the frame for my argument. Perhaps no one took as deep a personal interest in this work as Rose Stanton, my beautiful mother-in-law, who called weekly from her Southern California home to check on its progress. A new bride in October 1941 and a new mother thirteen months later, she experienced so much of the past that I explore here. She shared my excitement and relief the day I mailed the manuscript to the press, knowing the project was complete; she died four weeks later.

I appreciate the support of my dear friend Sharon Brown, who listens with genuine interest to my theories and opinions, shares my love of travel and adventure, and accepts the fact that I simply cannot do a four-mile run before breakfast (or any other time). She is kindness incarnate.

Since I began writing this book, two exceptional women and two wonderful girls have joined the McEuen family. Susie, Megan, Liz, and Mina fill our homes with laughter and delight, and they have taught me more than they realize about femininity in the twenty-first century. I wholeheartedly thank my brothers, Kevin and Kelly, for bringing these women into the fold.

Finally, I'm fortunate to be able to spend every day and night with the great love of my life, Edward Stanton. There aren't enough superlatives in the English language or any other to describe him. He encourages me at every turn and, by his example, reminds me that "joy's soul lies in the doing." For his passion and all else, I dedicate this work to him.

Making War, Making Women

INTRODUCTION

Zelda Popkin's 1945 novel, *The Journey Home*, opens with Lieutenant Don Corbett plotting to spend his twenty-one-day leave on liquor and women. In a Miami bar, he realizes that his months-long obsession with *"American Girls"* had imprinted on his mind's eye "one single person, one face, one body, one voice." He is surprised to find much greater variety in the women he observes than his war front imagination had allowed.[1] What led the fictional Lieutenant Corbett to envision American women so narrowly? And what of millions of Americans who entertained a similar image? *Making War, Making Women* attempts to answer these questions by examining *ideal* womanhood on the U.S. home front during the Second World War. It probes the relationship between gender and patriotic duty, attempting to illuminate the ways in which archetypes of femininity jostled the lives of actual women at a decisive cultural moment in the American past.

The total war effort provided many women opportunities that loosened traditional means of control over their lives. They could more easily take jobs in previously all-male fields; they could enjoy the personal satisfaction and independence afforded by regular paychecks; they could move away from home, perhaps even hundreds of miles, to serve the war effort and enjoy its off-hours perquisites. During the war years, more than 7 million women who had not previously worked for wages joined the 11 million women already in the U.S. labor force; 350,000 volunteered for military service.[2] They came under closer scrutiny than their female counterparts who had not made similar choices. Washington war agencies, Madison Avenue advertising offices, and Main Street America promoted images of ideal womanhood to circumvent the dramatic social and cultural changes afoot on the home front.

Although Norman Rockwell's image of a muscular, cheerful Rosie the Riveter in overalls and welding goggles may very well be our generation's favorite icon of the Second World War, she and others like her appeared infrequently in print, while thousands of hyperfeminized women touted everything from soft drinks to carbon paper to protective headgear. The Rosie image breaks down further when we look at the actual work world since many more women were needed to do laundry and take dictation than to build airplanes. The U.S. Employment Service urged women to take any available job, claiming that all wage labor could be designated "war work." *Making War, Making Women* examines the ways that women from diverse backgrounds who worked in a variety of fields were viewed in relation to the U.S. government's and corporate America's prescriptions for them. Historian Robert Westbrook defends the use of prescriptive evidence for historical study, arguing that in World War II, "American propagandists—especially those working for private corporations—appealed to attitudes and convictions they believed (or their research told them) were widespread in their audiences." This assumption undergirds my argument and the evidence marshaled to promote it.[3]

Women's concerns and choices about their appearance—how they colored their lips, brows, and skin, and how they sanitized, deodorized, and adorned their bodies—tell us a great deal about their wartime world. According to some of the advice dispensed, they needed to make themselves into something worth fighting for. If they did, their efforts would be noticed, therefore qualifying them as good citizens and team players. Their postwar rewards would be consequential, they were told—comfortable homes for some, social equality for others, and male companionship for any who worked hard enough to deserve it. From U.S. government appeals to corporate America's advertisements to comments made in committee meetings and on factory floors, the conglomerate of home front words and images vividly reveals how women were wheedled, begged, and adored on one hand, and caricatured, criticized, and discounted on the other. Some women felt overwhelmed, while others were amused. Many found the assorted images to be means of empowerment. A web of subtle hints, direct instructions, and sensational warnings offered them guidance—to take or leave at their own or their nation's peril. And although radio and movies no doubt influenced them, this study focuses on print media. The faith placed in print by both government and business was evident in their expenditures on millions of flyers, pictures, pamphlets, posters, pin-ups, billboards, and other designs in magazines and newspapers.

Cultural products are as much about their creators as their consumers, as much about the agencies, the committees, and the decision makers as those whose lives they shaped. When the U.S. Office of War Information (OWI) Graphic Arts Victory Committee sent a memo encouraging members to study the "hag rags," it said more about the guys in the office who generated it than about the subject of the reference, since as they claimed, "Reading the 'hag rags' (pardon, *Ladies Home Journal, Women's Home Companion, McCall's, Good Housekeeping*, et al) doesn't make you a sissy . . . and you'll be well armed with information you can turn into selling ammunition pertinent to the National Nutrition Program and Victory Gardens." A tenuous relationship between business and government had existed since the moment war was declared, making each entity suspicious of the other's power.

On October 29, 1942, the Association of National Advertisers warned its members in a "Confidential" newsletter, "*Watch your copy*. There are rumblings in Washington that there is too much bragging going on about production of war goods, too much 'useless' spending on advertising." These tensions would not cool during the war but would grow even more heated.[4]

War agency administrators and field workers wrangled with one another as well as with American advertising's managers in their efforts to understand women, to portray them, and to convince them of the nation's needs. This work brings these constituencies together, with the argument juxtaposing records of several Washington agencies and departments against stories and advertisements published in *Advertising & Selling, Crisis, Ladies' Home Journal, LIFE, McCall's, Negro Digest, Opportunity, True Confessions, Vogue*, and several other publications.[5] The study also stands on the vast archives of the J. Walter Thompson Advertising Agency (JWT), the most influential voice to female consumers during the war. Not only did JWT have a long history of marketing personal products to women, but its executives and designers were responsible for many campaigns to recruit women for war work, enlist them in military service, and foster their cooperation with numerous U.S. government initiatives.[6]

Making War, Making Women is supported by a critical feminist framework. Deborah McDowell's claim that the body itself is a "battleground," a "site of cultural conflict and contestation in particular time and space" infuses this study, as does Elizabeth Grosz's view that the body as a "cultural product" has political demands written on it. The work of Susan Bordo, Judith Butler, and Patricia Hill Collins assisted me in explaining how and why women took certain steps to try to create desirable bodies. Collins's words also encouraged me to make this book accessible to a broad readership. She writes, "Unfortunately, many of us who possess the specialized language of academia often do not even try to translate what are excellent ideas into a form that makes them understood by others. . . . [T]o read on a high level of abstraction is itself a luxury. Privatizing and hoarding ideas upholds inequality."[7] While *Making War, Making Women* grapples with the web of political and social meaning, it also revels in what Americans saw and read in print in the 1940s. The excellent groundwork laid by a number of historians inspired me to probe the complicated intersections of consumer capitalism, political crisis, and gender definition, and to bring them into conversation with my own archival discoveries and interpretations.[8]

Grounded in the archives, supported by feminist theory, and narrated for a variety of audiences, *Making War, Making Women* explores sites of judgment important in the discourse of wartime femininity. Chapter One, "All-American Masks," while focusing on faces and cosmetics, is largely about the meaning and manipulation of whiteness in the United States. Criteria defining female beauty shifted at different points during the war, depending on the nation's most immediate needs and the culture's fluctuating desires. Chapter Two, "Tender Hands and Average Legs," highlights the fetishization of these extremities in mainstream advertising and the expansion of the "pin-up" genre. Prompting the sexualization of middle-class women's bodies on an unprecedented scale, these processes brought erotic images not just into barracks overseas and stateside but into offices and living rooms on the home front as well. Chapter Three, "Pleasant Aromas and Good Scents," takes hygiene as its starting point, showing the difficulties women faced in the struggle to cleanse their bodies enough to be considered feminine. Chapter Four, "Proper Attire and Streamlined Silhouettes," examines the relationship between women's clothes and their flesh, and how materials rationing, industrial safety, and American design affected women as decorative subjects. Chapter Five, "Sacrifice and Agreeability," probes the attitudes desired in the ideal wartime woman, among them patience, cheerfulness, and fidelity. These preferred ways of being were interpreted overwhelmingly through the lens of domesticity, which was supposed to govern all aspects of a woman's life.

The work's title pays homage to Mary Ritter Beard. In June 1945, as she finished the book that would forge a new path in an old field, she wrote: "Women have been a force in making all the history that has been made." Several decades have passed since that summer day in Connecticut and since the end of the Second World War. Women's history has flourished as a discipline in the last forty years, spurred on by political activism, a slightly more flexible academy, and the flowering of cultural studies. Contemporary scholars who believe that they first introduced the term "agency" regarding women and "others" were preempted by Beard, who suggested to her editor in 1944 that her forthcoming book be titled *Woman as Force and Agency in History*. Along with Beard's legacy, Gerda Lerner's approach to women's history inspires my own. As she has shown, women confronting social structures and identity politics lead complicated lives, even more so during national crises.[9]

By delving into the daily pressures, the cultural challenges, and the range of choices and constraints women faced in the 1940s, *Making War, Making Women* seeks to restore a past that is more human than mythic. The evidence will fascinate, amuse, and repulse. Readers who recognize the influence of today's advertising will understand the techniques employed during an earlier era of global crisis. They may notice choices similar to their own in emulating contemporary archetypes, even those requiring painful injections, cuts, stitches, straightening, bleaching, or starvation. I hope this work prompts readers to think about other American home fronts and similar issues that need regular and thorough scrutiny—the connection between decisions made in Washington and negotiations in corporate headquarters; the role of symbols in shaping thought; the use of subtle intimidation to circumscribe behavior and how Americans grapple with it. Home fronts usually become sites of rapid social and economic transformation; in efforts to slow down or halt such change, people find solace in managing gender and sex along traditional lines. Those targeted to be "managed" find creative ways to empower themselves with the directives. In the 1940s, while the United States made war abroad, strong forces also attempted to "make women" at home. This is their story.

ONE

All-American Masks

Creaming and Coloring the Wartime Face

Late in 1942 the *Jackson (Miss.) Clarion-Ledger* headlined a story, "Cosmetics for Girl Workers Boosting War Production." It recounted a *Vogue* magazine feature about a New York factory that had recently installed large mirrors in its women's restrooms and offered employees free cosmetics—changes linked to favorable results on the factory floor. Stressing the importance of personal appearance to women, the Jackson paper compared those who had answered the nation's call to their female counterparts in mental hospitals, concluding, "[w]omen remain women, cherishing vanity, even when they have become more or less insane or when they take hard jobs in war factories." In this seemingly awkward comparison, the journalist nevertheless recognized the ties between women's emotional and physical health and the nation's wartime needs.[1]

The psychology of cosmetics use among women had assumed greater import after the United States declared war in 1941. Following reports by doctors outlining beauty products' "positive physiological effects" on women, Martin Aircraft and Lockheed Corporation provided cosmetics to their employees. In determining the "essentiality" of materials to be reduced or eliminated from the domestic economy, the U.S. War Production Board (WPB) stepped lightly, deferring to psychiatrists' research results about cosmetics' ability "to counteract fatigue" among working women. Grappling with evidence that British women "came flocking" to war industry after the British government erected beauty stations in its factories, the WPB pondered an advisory committee's recommendation that the U.S. government follow suit and define American women's desire for cosmetics as "essential" in the current crisis.[2] While many mobilization success stories circulated in the press during the war, those addressing the "made-up" face often went beyond the confines of human interest to address a nagging social worry: that women's greater presence in the paid workforce might erode standards of femininity.

A genuinely "feminine" face was dictated by racial meanings and age in the United States. But the women considered most likely to possess or have the ability to create one were middle-class housewives and mothers, along with their young unmarried counterparts who presumably yearned to join their ranks. In the Depression decade, traditional womanhood had been lionized in regional cultural celebrations as well as in Hollywood movies and popular magazines. The mass media offered carefully crafted scenarios detailing a feminine ideal that was found or nurtured overwhelmingly in domestic environments. The persistence of this model revealed itself in September 1941, when *LIFE* magazine featured a thirty-two-year-old mother of three from the Midwest, Jane Amberg. *LIFE's* biopic suggested that Hollywood movies and women's magazines had so widely portrayed the modern housewife "as the sort of woman who keeps her figure, her husband, her makeup and her humor no matter how tough the going" that the archetype had become a real living presence in many American households. Referring to the "constant propaganda" influencing "millions of U.S. women" to follow its dictates, the *LIFE* story attested to the force of popular culture, especially modern advertising.[3]

That a woman's "makeup" took an equal place alongside her "figure" and her "humor" marked her face as a consequential site of judgment. The mask of her own design—her constructed face—mattered. How a woman applied creams, lotions, oils, soaps, and colors determined whether she was likely to maintain a level of femininity projected by models, movie stars, and other icons of prescribed beauty created by the American advertising industry and embraced by the larger society. The advent of war rearranged priorities for many people, including middle-class women like Jane Amberg, but to what extent did cultural standards of beauty shift after the United States became directly involved in the conflict? And what was the nature of these changes? When women saw their faces reflected in powder room mirrors or shop windows, what were they supposed to see? In a political atmosphere dripping with the rhetoric of patriotism and sacrifice, what did the ideal wartime face look like and how could a woman attempt to compose one? What rewards awaited her if she created it day after day?

This chapter explores these questions by examining the intersection of three bodies of evidence: several high-profile ad campaigns for facial products, official propaganda to recruit women for war work and the military, and the faces of real women featured in popular magazines. Taken together, the creative choices by editors, artists, graphic designers, and agency bureaucrats, and American women's responses to them tell us a good deal about shifting beauty standards in the 1940s. Over nearly four years of war, the ideal "look" coincided with the nation's changing expectations of its female citizens. What the United States and its local communities demanded from women—whether in their homes, in industry, in the military, or as volunteers—could be seen on idealized female faces. They expose the opportunities, expectations, pressures, and boundaries that American women encountered during the Second World War.

Amid the variety of messages aimed at women regarding an ideal wartime face, a common theme resonates—that the most admirable looks exude an authentic

American heritage blending middle- to upper-class life, work and leisure pursuits, and relative "whiteness." A woman in the 1940s could tinker with some elements of this heritage, working to change them or to manage an *appearance* of something different in order to attain a preferred look. To the extent that she could create a favored wartime face, drawing the lines of her mask appropriately and coloring inside currently prescribed boundaries, meant that satisfying rewards awaited her. Frequently those prizes took the form of attention from a popular or accomplished man, an engagement ring or promise of marriage, a step up from her family's economic condition, or social acceptance in a wider community—each projecting an imagined peace that women supposedly longed for in the midst of tense and uncertain days. A few unobjectionable variations surfaced, but the standard for combining patriotic contribution and a desirable appearance from the neck up remained the purview of young, impressionable women, who were led to believe that the nation's health and ultimately its peace would depend on their efforts.

Since the late nineteenth century American women had expected the most closely scrutinized aspect of their bodies to be their faces. For decades, advertisements for lotions, creams, and powders had promised to help women achieve "beauty" and its attendant rewards—a successful betrothal, a faithful and adoring husband, or a proud mother-in-law. Women of color could also use facial products to expand their opportunities to "pass" in the Euro-American community. In the 1920s, as the image of the New Woman reveling in greater physical freedom (and presumably more sexual freedom) gained currency, the female body began to garner more attention in print. But this emphasis failed to transplant the historic focus on the female face; instead, the post-suffrage generation invited new scrutiny of women's eyes, cheeks, and lips. The New Woman's face, not just powdered as her mother's had been but "painted," became a more complicated site of judgment.[4]

As advertising itself changed in order to stimulate a consumer ethic based on glossy appeals and prestige elements, copywriters such as J. Walter Thompson Company (JWT) executive Helen Lansdowne Resor began using "society women" and members of European royalty as product endorsers. The appeal of upper-class women gave low-end cosmetics, especially facial care preparations, the kind of cachet already attached to the more expensive products offered by gurus Helena Rubenstein and Elizabeth Arden. Women of color saw African American success stories in cosmetics promotions designed by the well-known Madam C. J. Walker Company. These inspirational messages pitted a national name brand against widely sold homemade creams and lotions in the black community. Not until 1938, when the U.S. Food and Drug Administration (FDA) began to regulate such products, did the competitive edge of homemade goods begin to soften. But the most stunning transformation in the American cosmetics scene was well in place by the end of the decade: advertisements now lured customers by promoting a circumscribed feminine beauty based on psychological appeals rather than individual achievement. Cultural historian Kathy Peiss concludes that "marking and coloring the face" came to be seen as a clear sign of a woman's "personality" and ultimately of her "individual self-development."[5] In this atmosphere, the lucrative business of cosmetics advertising met one of its greatest challenges: to continue selling the importance of a made-up face to millions of women confronting an array of new problems and opportunities in a nation at war. At worst, most women faced the prospects of disrupted family lives, shift work, lack of food, and childcare challenges; at best, they might revel in unforeseen chances, greater mobility, and personal independence.

In the opening weeks of the war, Audrey Druhmel's face appeared in more than a million places. In beauty salons, workplace lunchrooms, and middle-class parlors, women perusing issues of *Vogue*, *LIFE*, *McCall's*, *Mademoiselle*, and the *Ladies' Home Journal* saw Druhmel smiling as the featured "Bride-to-be" in a full-page Pond's Cold Cream advertisement. Linking her successful betrothal to a complexion "fresh as rain" and "soft as a baby's," Druhmel gave Pond's its due credit. Her endorsement of the product marked the first in a long line of similar wartime stories directly connecting Pond's use with romantic triumph. Yet the ads went well beyond this link and the requisite "glamour care" instruction. Viewers who took time to read Druhmel's story discovered that her engagement ring featured an "heirloom jewel" belonging to her fiancé's grandmother, that the marriage would unite two New Jersey families "of Colonial lineage" and, perhaps to balance these rather staid signs of social prestige with a bit of modern flair, that the two rubbed elbows with big band leaders at the Rainbow Room in New York City's Rockefeller Center. If the mainstream reader could not identify with such a privileged life, perhaps she could identify with a more personal worry Druhmel expressed about her self-described "olive-brunette" skin: "I have to keep it spandy clean or it gets *dark looking*."[6] The concern with her skin color or the impression it might give, even if temporary, connected Audrey to women all over the nation who knew that various shades and tones indicated status levels and power in American society. In populations of all represented races in the United States, lighter-hued skin counted highly. It and the larger notion of "whiteness" would reveal the function of race as written on the female face, and both would be tested as the nation rapidly mobilized its population for a total war effort.

Although more than a generation had passed since Euro-American imperialists and their intellectual counterparts had impressed theories of racial hierarchy on a willing public, what remained in the United States in 1941 were its well-entrenched cultural remnants. Ever-present physical reminders segregating blacks in the South,

Asians in the West, and Indians nearly everywhere, combined with daily cruelties throughout the nation to perpetuate notions about race, which many Americans understood in terms of skin color—specifically relative darkness and lightness. The European war, initiated and sustained by tenets of race-based nationalist ideology in Germany, had heightened awareness of similar prejudices and preferences among Americans in the late 1930s. Polls showed widespread anti-Semitic sentiments in the United States, including a Roper poll where more than 50 percent of the respondents claimed Jews should be restricted in "business and social life" since they were "different from everyone else."[7] Black–white tensions increased in 1941 as antidiscrimination measures in the military and workplace were debated.[8] The Asian war prompted swift and official race-based action in the spring of 1942, when the White House announced orders to move West Coast Issei and Nisei to locations far from the areas where they had resided for decades. Racial profiling followed the "one drop" rule, with the most taut justification articulated by the U.S. military official in charge of evacuation: "The Japanese race is an enemy race and while many second and third generation Japanese born on United States soil, possessed of United States citizenship, have become 'Americanized,' the racial strains are undiluted." Negative portrayals of the Japanese had circulated before the Pearl Harbor attack, but as they became "more numerous and vicious" in the succeeding weeks, certain racialized images of the enemy would penetrate American culture.[9] The U.S. government's mobilization of ideology—and millions of people for combat, work, and other services—not only sanctioned but fertilized xenophobia and intolerance among Americans, thus heightening racial tensions during the war.

In an environment permeated by questions of opportunity and patriotic duty, race, and world war, American advertisers played on consumers' doubts and anxieties. If Audrey Druhmel, a socialite who seemingly had everything a woman could wish for, worried about "dark" skin, how might a woman in humbler circumstances have her own anxieties intensified by similar concerns? Corporate America and the U.S. government managed in a moment of heightened patriotism to conflate skin color and care with social status, national devotion, and, in some places, even democracy itself.

This well-publicized mixture resulted from the close relationship between the advertising world and Washington's wartime bureaucracy throughout the early 1940s. Forged immediately following the U.S. declaration of war, the relationship was the brainchild of a few advertising executives who dared to circumvent government control of the communications industries (and businesses that relied on them), as had happened during the First World War. At a quickly called meeting in late December 1941, these executives agreed to organize corporate advertising for the war effort free of charge. In the ensuing years, their organization, the War

Advertising Council,[10] would amass millions of dollars worth of "savings" for the U.S. government, using their current accounts as "volunteers" to spread the word about everything from food rationing to war bond sales to the desperate need for military nurses. One writer at the time called it "the most ambitious missionary effort in the business history of the United States." The brain behind much of this integrated private–public enterprise was JWT vice president James Webb Young, who not only helped found the Ad Council but also chaired it in the opening months of the war.[11] That his own advertising company was assigned the duty of mobilizing women for war work meant its creative designs would bridge American business with government interests. Female readers of certain magazines soon saw the tight bonds between doing one's patriotic duty, putting on the right face, and enjoying the rewards in their personal lives. Advertising narratives and images would dramatize women's anxieties in a wartime context, turning seemingly mundane tasks—choosing and using cosmetics—into decisions of political import.

A couple of months after the bombing of Pearl Harbor, American women began to see and read advertisements integrating wartime themes and beauty culture. As early as February 1942 the "She's Engaged! She's Lovely! She Uses Pond's!" campaign introduced a New York woman engaged to a military officer in training (fig. 1). The ad copy also foreshadowed a coming trend in the war years—whirlwind romances based on chance meetings and quick post-wedding separations. The couple whose story stimulated the imaginations of McCall's readers had met at a party and four days later were engaged. Similar narratives would become commonplace on the American home front, the romantic tale shared by innumerable men and women, those coming from modest as well as privileged backgrounds, from urban and rural areas, from the Atlantic coast to the Pacific. But in this particular advertisement, the couple could certainly not be classified as ordinary. As in the January Pond's "She's Engaged!" promotion, the February feature emphasized the heritage of the pair. Although not identified by "Colonial lineage," as Audrey Druhmel and her fiancé had been in the earlier issue, the February couple nevertheless exuded good breeding. A photograph of the two standing together in jodhpurs connoted their participation in a hobby long synonymous with the landed American aristocracy: horseback riding. The prospective bridegroom had even found time amidst his military training to design his fiancée's star sapphire and diamond engagement ring. The "exquisite" bride-to-be, Eugenia Loughlin, stood apart as a result of her complexion, described in the ad text as "fresh, sweet, pink and white as apple blossoms!"[12] The allusion reinforced the highest standard of American beauty as a very light skin tone, marked only by the blush of health, and likened to something delicate found in nature. The "She's Engaged!" wartime campaign would take shape from here, integrating the importance of men in uniform, while continuing the

Figure 1. Pond's advertisement for *McCall's*, February 1942. JWT Archives, Hartman Center, Duke University.

proven method of "transferring prestige," a strategy that had made Pond's one of JWT's most successful accounts.

Advertising executive James Webb Young had explained as early as 1934 how his company had used the prestige factor to appeal to its customers. It depended on heritage, which may or may not have delineated a person's socioeconomic status in the United States. In a lecture Young explained, "[I]n this country it is well known that we don't take much stock in pedigrees, so we have a Mayflower Association, Daughters of the American Revolution and Daughters of the Confederacy, and I think none of us would disclaim a signer of the Declaration of Independence. And so we are interested in pedigrees in an indirect way and therefore, when products can be given prestige through something which has some prestige, it increases our satisfaction in owning them."[13] Young distinguished between traditional pedigrees, presumably European, and an American brand of lineage classification. He seemed to deny any American interest in family lineage based on class status, while he identified several groups whose membership depended on family ties. In fact, for each group he named, membership relied solely on producing sufficient paperwork to prove one's connection to a soldier (in the case of the DAR and UDC) or to a Protestant settler. However "indirect" the interest among Americans, status mattered and was conferred by those who made it their business to approve or deny entry into their enclaves. In Europe, pedigrees and their titles were assumed as a function of birthright or marriage or, every once in a while, a good sale or a nod from the royal family. In the United States, comparable standing was by invitation or confirmation after one's ancestral authenticity had been scrutinized. So the testimonial support of European aristocrats for Pond's Cold Cream ads may have piqued different interests than the American heritage appeals that took shape in the 1930s and 1940s. JWT copywriter Helen Resor's protégée, Ruth Waldo, shaped the wartime Pond's "She's Engaged!" campaign to reflect immediate social and political issues on the home front. Waldo and other copywriters would perfect the most operative component of "prestige" advertising during the war years, convincing women of a product's role in the "achievement of personality." Since Waldo had spent years in applied social sciences before entering the ad business, her experience provided the perfect apprenticeship for bridging modern psychology and national sales.[14]

Alongside Audrey Druhmel and Eugenia Loughlin in 1942 were other Pond's Cold Cream users who, having met essential criteria, were selected as brides of distinction. "Dainty" Jane Drury of Massachusetts was described as an "adorable, modern daughter of a distinguished New England family." Sallie Hamilton's story, presented in a May issue of *LIFE* magazine as well as the June issue of *McCall's*, was slimmer on an already-established family heritage, but the tale emphasized another means of status building that would appeal to many young women in the coming months: the advantage of "a military wedding." Marrying an officer in "the famous West Point Chapel" could enhance nearly any woman's sociopolitical standing in the early 1940s, but Hamilton possessed something more crucial— "delicate white skin, as fresh and dainty as sweet-pea blossoms." Situating her inside the boundaries of the feminine ideal, her skin tone also gave her an air of privilege in a nation increasingly more attuned to racial difference and demonization. Likewise, New Englander Jane Drury's "fresh-as-wild-roses complexion" and "honey-blonde" hair made her a model of mainstream female beauty on the home front. Viewers saw the faces of these prospective brides in full-page formal portraits, a design element understood by cosmetics salespeople to elicit the "beauty plus prestige" appeal that would work psychologically on their customers.[15]

But how effective could such appeals be to the average American woman? In the 1920s and early 1930s, women claimed they were not influenced by patricians touting the wonders of certain creams and powders. Research survey results showed that neighbors and local retailers were more likely to affect a woman's cosmetics choices. Based on this evidence, Kathy Peiss has shown that the advice shared between people who trusted each other mattered more than slick advertisements touting nearly impossible standards of beauty, especially if the ads turned on the premise of attracting and keeping a man. Peiss concludes that cosmetics use "often underscored women's ties to other women, not to men."[16] But could engagement in world war have altered this, and if so, to what degree?

In 1942 a sense of urgency permeated all mobilization efforts, from the military to industry to agriculture. Although a peacetime conscription had been in effect since the fall of 1940, the nature of the draft changed after the Pearl Harbor bombing, widening the pool of men subject to military service by extending the age range and removing the ban on service outside the Western Hemisphere. Men as young as eighteen and as old as forty-five could now be drafted, cutting well into the population of eligible males for romance and marriage. Although the rumored "man shortage" would not begin to be felt until midway through the war as casualty figures steadily mounted, the "bridal terror" had begun in earnest in 1940.[17] Two years later, with a burgeoning number of men headed off to training camps, unmarried women all over the country felt their chances for matrimony drop considerably. In small isolated towns where the absence of young men was particularly noticeable, or in major cities or camp towns where soldiers and sailors congregated before deployment, the urge to send men away happy meant numerous intimate liaisons, quick marriages, or both.[18]

The Pond's "She's Engaged!" wartime series worked off these fears, desires, and competition, with ad copy designed to entice particular target audiences. In addition to the earlier series featuring American socialites, a second series depended on fictional narratives about less affluent single women. Aimed at fans of newspaper comics, the stories continued to pivot on the leading gauge of female beauty: a fair complexion. In a typical promotion, the betrothal announcement of a Washington, D.C., woman was relegated to a small corner of the ad, while the fictionalized story took center stage. A young woman named Betsey worries aloud about her fair hair after her roommate announces, "Look . . . Here's Nan's bridal picture! I adore jet black hair and white skin like Nan's!" Assuring Betsey that her blonde hair is not the cause of her romantic failure, the roommate advises Betsey to "sweeten up" her complexion instead. Here sweetness is equated with softness and smoothness but not directly linked to color. Whiteness, having been established clearly in the first frame of the narrative, is only implied as the story unfolds. The result of Betsey's Pond's Cold Cream regimen is a new face with a complexion that looks "like peaches and cream." Her wise friend takes pride in the success of the skin project, measuring it at a party where a guy named Tom "can't take his eyes off" Betsey and again after the two announce their engagement. The last panel in the strip focuses on the protagonist's face, set cheek-to-cheek against her fiancé's face.[19] While she may not have matched the original model—with jet-black hair and white skin—Betsey put her energies into perfecting the area that seemed to matter more in the struggle for romantic success—her skin.

Advertisements like these reached several audiences and had the potential to bridge different classes of working women. More than their pink-collar counterparts, those vying for the "heavyweight purchasing crown" were female factory workers who enjoyed "higher hourly rates, longer work weeks, [and] fatter pay envelopes." One consumer analyst noted, however, the absence of "Miss Factory" in wartime advertising: "[S]he can't understand why a clerical worker or Amateur Miss America should adorn an advertisement for hand lotion or skin cleansing cream when any thinking advertising man would ascribe the greatest need for these items to women who work in an atmosphere of dust, lint, metal filings and soot." Where "Miss Factory" and her office counterpart similarly aspired and strived was in the field of "matrimony." As long as marriage was viewed not merely as a step up for working women, but perhaps the last important step they would take in their lives, the prospect of engagement would continue to drive beauty product promotions, inspiring the ideal wartime face. And this tied women across classes together, mainstream advertising insisted. As Jennifer Scanlon argues, products "became women's common denominator" in modern America, with consumption the one activity they shared in defining "woman's true realm."[20] Armed with their own paychecks, women arguably could become even greater consumers than they had been in recent decades and, with a war on, better citizens as well. Suggestions on how to accomplish these feats abounded, as defining femininity became an art form on the home front.

Early in 1942, the ideal American female appeared even in advertisements directed at young teenagers, published in serials such as *Forecast*, a home economics journal. In a set of lessons entitled "How to Become a Dream Girl," a full page of "do's" and "don'ts" directed young women toward their goal. Like their slightly older male counterparts, who were learning and refining military tactics in training camps, young women received instruction about swift movement, covert action, the ability to recognize and quell distraction, and finally, how to overcome the enemy—all explained in martial language. The candidate in training was to concentrate regularly on "maneuvers with Pond's Cold Cream." On the battlefield, here depicted as a formal social occasion, the Dream Girl did not aim her "ammunition" directly at her Dream Man; instead, she had to employ subtle cunning in order to gain ground, lining up "a couple of other conquests for decoy." Her position could be weakened in several situations—by getting stuck in a dark corner, by offering herself for comparison with her competition, or perhaps worst of all, by neglecting her own skin and therefore leaving herself exposed to derision and defeat. In the end her vigilance and training in developing "lovely" skin would carry her through to the end of the battle, in this case, to "the all-important goodnight" scene. Her war would continue until she had secured a promise of marriage.[21]

The full-page promotion in *Forecast* actually had two audiences—teenaged girls and their teachers. The directions aimed at the adult audience impressed upon them the need to encourage and develop femininity in their young charges. The language defined behavioral boundaries, setting up gendered opposites in the declaration: "She may have started her teens a tomboy—but she's soon longing for beauty." How could a girl be a tomboy yet also want to be beautiful? An impossible combination, the message implied. Pond's Cold Cream's "softening, smoothing, cleansing skin care" would help eradicate such undesirable adolescent behavior by polishing harsh edges. Yet a few scrubs would not permanently rub off hints of boyishness or masculinity; the action had to be done daily, so that femininity was continually restored and maintained. The information for teachers also contained subtle hints about nurturing sexuality among their female students to prepare them for "romance." Six months later, the president of Weinberger Drug Stores noted that cosmetics advertising had changed considerably in the previous few years, especially in appeals to teenagers. Identifying "the young girl of today" as "not more sophisticated but rather more mature for her years," Weinberger claimed that many cosmetics manufacturers had "changed the pace of their advertising appeals to keep step with this trend."[22] Many of the young women who matured earlier than previous generations would join a workforce centered on efficient and fast-paced war production.

The nature of the new American workplace challenged the notion of ideal womanhood, with the struggle playing out in popular print culture in the early months of the war. In March 1942 *LHJ* reported responses to a survey in which American men in uniform were asked, "What Is Your Dream Girl Like?" Beyond their mention of personal attributes such as "figure and disposition," most men claimed to prefer a woman "devoted to her home and children" who did not seek paid employment. The Dream Girl survey unequivocally identified the ideal American woman as one of a certain class, whose single household income (earned presumably by her husband) allowed her the privilege of staying home with her children rather than working for wages. The sentiments that emerged in the survey were widely understood by the U.S. War Manpower Commission (WMC), whose initiative to target "housewives" in "Critical War Areas" faced resistance from mainstream America. Recognizing possible obstructions to the nation's mobilization goals, the WMC directed all recruitment efforts "to remove social stigma attached to the idea of women working."[23]

Print media played a vital role in the process. Research surveys revealed that in addition to newspapers and comic books, younger working women's magazine choices included *Photoplay, True Experiences, True Love,* and *True Romances.* Whatever their marital status, they saw or read copies of the wildly popular *McCall's* and *Ladies' Home Journal.* If aspiring to situate themselves in a higher socioeconomic class or merely to fantasize about its accoutrements, they likely picked up issues of *Harper's* or *Vogue.* In all of these magazines, advertising underwent subtle changes to show the necessity of accepting women into certain workplaces, especially heavy industry. In addition, the advertising community debated how to approach women as consumers, whether to appeal to them in different ways than to men since women had acquired a new status in the wartime emergency. One writer boldly suggested that women be addressed simply as "people." She criticized advertisers for trying to communicate in a "strange female language," arguing that women resented "being talked down to" and would resent it even more in the current crisis. She concluded, "There are all kinds of women and many types of men, each with characteristics common to both. There is too much loose classifying of men as 100 per cent masculine in their way of living and of women as purely feminine."[24] Not quite a year into the war, the challenge for Madison Avenue and Washington would be to inspire women to participate fully in the war effort without compromising their femininity. Here, faces mattered.

The Pond's Cold Cream "She's Engaged!" campaign took a turn in late 1942 to reflect the realities of home front mobilization efforts. The ad writers initiated what they called "New War Worker Advertising" in order to maintain the product's "front-line position." Described as "full of human interest," the campaign ads made "a direct appeal to women to take part in the war effort." The brides-to-be in the "She's Engaged!" texts were no longer featured in traditional portrait poses, but instead were pictured in action—taking on the kinds of workforce responsibilities that the U.S. government strongly urged American women to assume. The accompanying narratives and photo captions also shifted in order to highlight the featured individual's dedication to the larger cause. But certain earlier themes retained their places in the new ad copy.[25]

"Whiteness" continued to resonate in the stories. One of the earliest advertisements in the New War Worker series appeared in *LHJ, LIFE, McCall's, Vogue,* and *Woman's Home Companion* in November 1942 (fig. 2). In the ad's principal photograph, Martha Gaffney sits in a laboratory, pondering a current experiment. To make her work at a U.S. Army field lab understandable to a wide female readership, Gaffney emphasizes that they are looking for "harmful bacteria" that might "cause illness among the boys at the camps." Her "skilled hands" and "highly trained mind" are matched by "a particularly lovely complexion—creamy smooth and white." That Gaffney, a South Carolina native, hails from a "fine Southern" family contextualizes further her physical attributes. Not likened to wild roses or peach blossoms, her skin is "white," period. This provides her an unquestionable pedigree among white southerners, one that is elevated further by her identification as "the great, great, great grand-daughter of the eminent statesman, John C. Calhoun." If someone of Gaffney's background could cross the threshold into the paid labor force, any American woman could do it without fear of ruining her reputation, the ad implied. Even more subtle was the underlying hint that most other women would not be in as much danger as Gaffney, who put her family's bloodline at risk each day she handled dangerous biological materials.[26]

While they celebrated working women, the Pond's New War Worker campaign ads also confronted elements considered damaging to traditional femininity—physically demanding farm labor, jobs that required uniforms, even personal drive and ambition in the workplace. As a result, the combined themes of heterosexuality and whiteness figured prominently to ease Americans' potential fears about certain women entering the workforce for the first time. Carolee Arnold, who had learned to run farm machinery with "masculine ease—and feminine charm" possessed "azure blue" eyes and a "wild-rose sweet" complexion; Jacqueline Proctor's "soft fair Pond's" face complemented a "becoming deep brown uniform" she wore as a Massachusetts Women's Defense Corps member; and Hope Bulkeley's beauty was enhanced by her decision to give up her stage career in order to contribute "something *specific*" to the war effort. A productive war bond saleswoman could

MARTHA AND FIANCÉ on campus of Clemson College, S.C., last spring before Niles became an Aviation Cadet, and she went into training for her mobile laboratory work. She's as sweet and feminine looking now in her crisp lab uniform, so flattering to her soft-smooth Pond's complexion.

GUARDING HEALTH OF BOYS AT ARMY CAMPS while her fiancé flies for Uncle Sam, Martha is at Fort McPherson now in the Field Laboratory of the Fourth Service Command.

MARTHA'S RING is unusually beautiful—a 2-carat diamond in an exquisitely simple platinum band.

She's ENGAGED!

. . . . *MARTHA GAFFNEY'S engagement to Henry Niles Nelson, Jr., unites two fine Southern families. She is the great, great, great grand-daughter of the eminent statesman, John C. Calhoun*

MARTHA'S HEART is with her aviator fiancé—but her skilled hands and highly trained mind are given to her important war job with the Fourth Service Command's mobile laboratory.

This is the first large mobile laboratory to be used by the Army—and Martha is proud to be part of it. "We work like mad," she told us. "We do blood and disease tests regularly, of course—and test about everything in sight as well—water, milk, ice cream—anything that might contain harmful bacteria and cause illness among the boys at the camps."

Martha has a particularly lovely complex-ion—creamy smooth and white. She says: "My lab work makes me an absolute stickler for cleanliness. That's why I'm so fond of Pond's Cold Cream. It *cleanses* so thoroughly —and leaves my skin feeling *soft* and *dewy.*"

• • •

Use Pond's Martha's way, *you'll* love it, too. First —pat Pond's Cold Cream on your face and throat—gently, quickly. Tissue it off well. See how it softens and releases dirt and old make-up.

"Rinse" now with a *second* lovely Pond's creaming. Tissue off. Your face will feel fresh as a flower!

Do this *every* night—for daytime clean-ups, too.

You'll see why war-busy society women like Mrs. W. Forbes Morgan and Mrs. Ernest du Pont, Jr., use Pond's—why more women and girls use it than any other face cream.

Ask for the *larger* sizes when you buy Pond's Cold Cream—you get even *more* for your money. Popular in price, at beauty counters everywhere.

Yes—it's no accident so many lovely engaged girls use Pond's!

She's Lovely! She uses Pond's!

85

Figure 2. Pond's advertisement for *LHJ, McCall's, Vogue, Woman's Home Companion,* and *LIFE,* November 1942. JWT Archives, Hartman Center, Duke University.

attribute her success to "breath-taking eyes and a complexion smooth, cool and fine as alabaster," since her own initiative would be too unwomanly an explanation for the sizable receipts she bagged. Since all of these New War Workers in 1943 were safely circumscribed by their physical attributes and their betrothals to men, work would be less likely to ruin their femininity.[27]

The New War Worker campaign also subtly addressed the controversial issue of women working late shifts. The wartime waiver of many state night-work laws for women heightened the specter of nighttime wandering and increased sexual activity once work shifts were over. Since female bodies had come to be identified in home front culture as disease spreaders who could weaken male soldiers and sailors, the sooner they returned from work to the confines of home, the safer both men and women would be. One striking Pond's ad featured a third-shift worker emphasizing her need to be "extra fussy" about her appearance because she had to rise at 8:30 in the evening to begin her day. She spent more time than usual with Pond's Cold Cream: "to help smooth away tiredness" due to her extraordinary schedule, the ad suggested. Industrial workers attributed "lost" complexions and bloodshot eyes to irregular sleep due to shift work. While churches and YWCA chapters provided "after-dark toilers" with many opportunities for wholesome relaxation and fun, including "early morning tournaments of badminton, swimming, and ping-pong," Pond's ads contributed to setting the proper boundaries for women whose ever-widening opportunities in 1943 had extended the lines in place before the war. If women working night shifts devoted more time at home to their faces, they would be less likely to compromise their bodies or their reputations.[28]

The Pond's "She's Engaged!" campaigns took another significant turn in 1944, the year that discussions in several Washington war agencies began to focus on the postwar era. American military success on the European front in the spring and summer of 1944 had made such discussions possible, but the human costs in those military campaigns stimulated a new sense of urgency among young American women. The "bridal terror" that had surfaced in 1940 with the peacetime conscription and solidified after Pearl Harbor intensified as casualty figures rose and unmarried women realized that their chances for marriage were shrinking. Two effects of the scare worked their way into Pond's magazine ads: an emphasis on the crucial need for female nurses and a prescription for hyperfemininity to help women increase their chances of finding husbands. In emphasizing the field of nursing in its 1944 advertising, Pond's campaigns took a step away from their earlier focus on industrial work.

Since JWT was responsible for both the Pond's account and U.S. Cadet Nurse Corps recruitment, it could mix and match the appeals it presented to American women. JWT helped to create society's image of nursing during World War II. Of all working women, nurses received the highest sociopolitical approval ratings in the United States, viewed as "heroines, achieving distinction while maintaining a feminine image," writes historian D'Ann Campbell. By December 1944 the ideal Pond's bride-to-be would not stand on duty in a tailored nurse's uniform, but instead would sit enveloped in a costume harkening back to an earlier age when "angels of mercy" rolled bandages for wounded men on the front (fig. 3). Mary Florence McKenna's purity was suggested by her attire in the small inset photograph and reinforced by a caption noting that her veil served as "an immaculate frame for her flower-fresh face." These signs made her a vision of the hyperfeminine ideal, marking both the cultural and the *actual* shift away from industrial work as a permissible option for women as the war came to a close. Hints of the impending postwar female archetype appear in the adjacent portrait of the angelic figure, demure and innocent in white chiffon and tulle. By war's end, the Pond's "She's Engaged!" campaign would fully embrace a theme that portrayed the characteristic bride-to-be as an expert in domestic activities rather than a whiz at mechanical or scientific challenges.[29]

Pond's engaged women were blondes and brunettes from various regions in the United States, carrying out a variety of wartime responsibilities, but none was African American. The wide circulation of the ads, however, meant that these were the two-dimensional faces that black women saw most often. *LIFE*, the weekly magazine of choice for African Americans during the war years, featured women once or twice a month on its covers, but no woman of color appeared in any of these photographs. The dearth of glossy picture magazines targeting black audiences during the war, as well as *LIFE's* popularity in the African American community, led Chicago publisher John H. Johnson to create *Ebony* late in 1945. He wanted to satisfy a picture-hungry African American community that had read his own wartime creation, *Negro Digest*. A compendium of excerpted fiction and news stories of interest in the black community, *Negro Digest* contained relatively few advertisements and no ad campaigns driven by glossy photographs or similar graphics. But it filled a huge gap from 1942 to 1945, countering as Johnson said, "an almost total White-out on positive Black news in White-oriented media." When it came to revenues, black newspapers particularly felt the pinch as they accounted for only 2 percent of total advertising shares in American newspapers.[30]

Intensifying the characteristic absence of blacks in mainstream media was the perpetuation of stereotypes, where commercial advertising proved a serious offender second only to the film industry. African American women most often appeared as prostitutes, "overbearing and aggressive" wives, or domestic servants. The domestic was "portrayed as a fat, dark-skinned woman wearing a head wrap" and "never situated in a context that would encourage viewers to see her as a

She's Engaged!

Her Ring—a beautiful diamond with baguette on each side. It is set in a platinum band.

Mary Florence McKenna of Chicago, engaged to Lt. John Christopher Mullen. *Marine Corps Flyer*

At Barat College Mary folds bandages each week—the veil an immaculate frame for her flower-fresh face. Bandage quotas must be filled. Work with the group in *your* community!

She's Lovely!

Mary's dream-sweet face has the shining, unsophisticated beauty of the first spring snowdrops.

She is another engaged girl with that soft-smooth "Pond's look" about her.

"I have ever so sensitive skin," Mary says, "and Pond's Cold Cream seems to be just what I need—it's *such* a fine, soft, lovely cream, it just makes my face feel *grand*—so clean and so smooth."

Mary's Beauty Care with Pond's

She *slips* Pond's luscious Cold Cream all over her face and throat and pats on briskly to soften and release dirt and make-up. Tissues off.

She *rinses* with more Pond's Cold Cream—going over her face with little spiral whirls of her white, cream-coated fingers. Tissues off. "I adore the nice *extra* clean, *extra* soft feeling this gives my skin," she says.

Use *your* Pond's Cold Cream Mary's way—every night and morning—for in-between clean-ups too! It's no accident so many more girls and women use Pond's than any other face cream at any price. Ask for the luxurious big jar—and help save glass. You'll enjoy it more, too, because you can dip the fingers of *both* hands in this wide-topped big Pond's jar.

Mary Florence McKenna—adorable young Bride-to-Be of Marine Corps Flyer

She uses Pond's!

A few of the Pond's Society Beauties

Mrs. Ernest du Pont, Jr.

The Countess of Carnarvon

Mrs. Charles Morgan, Jr.

Mrs. A. J. Drexel, III

The Lady Tennyson

POND'S

Figure 3. Pond's advertisement for *Good Housekeeping*, December 1944. JWT Archives, Hartman Center, Duke University.

beauty," writes Maxine Leeds Craig. All three stereotypes reinforced the notion that black women could be "asexual, out-of-control, or oversexed but never beautiful." A wartime survey conducted by Columbia University's Bureau of Applied Social Science led the Writers' War Board to conclude that in the consumer marketplace, advertising was "openly and self-admittedly addicted to the Anglo-Saxon myth because of reliance on 'snob appeal.'"[31] While the myth and its central feature of whiteness were prominent on the pages of weeklies such as *LIFE* and women's magazines such as *McCall's* and *Vogue*, a variation on the myth could be found as well on the covers of prominent African American publications during the war. Snob appeal functioned across the color line to serve the political purposes of African American elites.

Although the most popular publications directed at black audiences carried fewer glossy advertising photographs than the mainstream American magazines, the visual images that did appear in feature stories and on covers demonstrated the inextricable bonds between class, color, and respectability. The "bourgeois race woman," a mainstay in the black media since the early twentieth century, prevailed during the war. Celebrated by successful African Americans living primarily in urban areas, the face of black femininity belonged to a college-educated, middle-class matron or matron-to-be who strove to create an aura of respectability for those in her station and a recognition of humanity for those below it. The literal face of this femininity possessed features more European than African, with light skin a prominent characteristic. The creation and persistence of this image may be attributed, in part, to the strength of the NAACP, which clung to the moniker "colored people," a phrase "preferred to 'Negro' or 'Afro-American' by many light-skinned and affluent blacks because it evoked their connections to white America." In visual terms, their argument was made regularly in *Crisis*, the organization's monthly magazine that circulated widely beyond its subscription numbers and reflected the larger black news media. Cover photographs were as highly stylized as those produced in any American magazine during the war. *Crisis* used portraits of light-skinned African American women to perpetuate class divisions and reinforce the idea that racial integration could only be accomplished by emphasizing African American whiteness or assimilation of middle-class goals and values. For young women of color, this meant strict cultivation of "[e]ducation, talent, fashion, and grooming."[32]

The intersections of color, caste, and opportunity had generated heated debates in the African American community for decades. The debates hit a literary zenith during the Harlem Renaissance, then moved out of the exclusive realm of art into cities and towns where larger audiences of strivers lived and worked during the war. War correspondent Roi Ottley spoke forthrightly about the black upper class, especially in the South, who wished "to maintain a caste based on color." He exposed organizations where "the blackball is rigorously employed against any crasher whose coloring is deeper than high yaller." He identified light-skinned women as "the props of Negro society" who, because they met "Caucasian standards of beauty," held the most "enviable positions in the Negro community." Sociologists Horace Cayton and St. Clair Drake reported similar findings in their study of Chicago's "Bronzeville" in the 1940s. They heard rumors but could not prove the existence of "blue-vein" clubs and associations, where membership depended on whether one's skin was "light enough for the veins to show through." Bronzeville residents did refer to a habit of being "partial to color" or as the sociologists concluded, "'partial to *less* color' — to light color."[33]

Partiality to "less color" manifested itself in the marriage market, the employment arena, and club membership. Darker women seemed to fare worse in all three areas, according to Drake and Cayton's findings in Chicago. One man considered lighter-skinned women not only "more attractive" but also "more affectionate, lovable, and understanding," as well as "more intelligent." Such opinions meant that certain women were more likely to secure office jobs and paraprofessional work. Government photographer Jack Delano featured successful hat shop manager, Selma Barbour, in his 1942 series on Bronzeville. Situating her among exquisite hats on display in a milieu of glamour, Delano perpetuated the community's belief that light skin, beauty, and success were linked (fig. 4). One local restaurant owner stated unequivocally his policy of hiring "only real light girls" because others could neither attract customers nor earn tips. Identifying "a veritable cult" of lighter-skinned female beauty in Chicago's black community, Drake and Cayton pointed out that the cult most "vividly revealed" itself in cosmetics advertisements.[34]

Although many youthful female faces adorned *Crisis* covers, only one cosmetics advertisement with a "face" appeared regularly in the magazine's wartime run. First appearing in *Crisis* in December 1942, the promotion featured New York "social leader" Grace Clifford offering advice to viewers about the benefits of "a clear unblemished complexion" (fig. 5). The product, Palmer's Skin Success Ointment, linked good skin with social achievement. The Palmer's ads varied little during the war, with Clifford the singular "face" of the product and healthier skin the main emphasis. Palmer's "SKIN-SUCCESS" system, a three-product regimen, included a "whitening" cream that promised to show quick results. As a standard of female beauty in the black community, lighter-hued skin equated cleanliness and health with upward mobility. Many of the beauty queens featured in *Crisis* studied at all-black colleges, such as Fisk, Howard, Prairie View, and Tuskegee. The legendary "brown bag test" thought to be the litmus for sorority membership at these

Figure 4. "Miss Selma Barbour, manager of the Cecilian Specialty Hat Shop, 454 East 47th Street. Miss Barbour has been managing this store for one year and has been in business for four years. She was born in New Orleans and has eight brothers, seven of whom are eligible for the army. Chicago, Illinois." Jack Delano, April 1942. FSA-OWI Collection, Library of Congress (LC-USW3–001471-D), digital ID: fsa 8d03733.

Mrs. Grace Clifford, New York social leader says, "There is no greater social asset than a clear, unblemished complexion. Ugly, blotched, rough skin seriously detracts from whatever popularity one enjoys and makes it extremely difficult to gain entree to society. Those women who have unattractive complexions will find the answer to their troubles in **Palmer's** SKIN SUCCESS OINTMENT"

Mention THE CRISIS to Our Advertisers

Figure 5. Palmer's Skin Success advertisement, *Crisis*, December 1942.

institutions revealed the power of color hierarchy in privileged African American communities.[35]

African American cosmetics advertising also relied on the appeal of nonwestern exoticism, a popular approach since the 1910s. Kashmir's Nile Queen promotions had incorporated African and Asian elements and lore to attract buyers with an image of black female beauty set in a "mythic time and place." One of the most successful cosmetics lines for African American women, Valmor Products, featured cleansing creams and "vanishing" creams promoted by women with kohl-drawn eyes, red lips, strands of jewels, and elaborate headdresses. Valmor, one of Chicago businessman Morton Neumann's Famous Products' brands, capitalized on "explicitly sexualizing the sale of beauty products" to black women, a tactic that African American elites had worked against for decades in their struggle to secure an image of sexual reserve and respectability for women of color.[36] Famous Products' "Lucky Brown" advertisements displayed similar elements of sexual appeal, but the female face who promoted "Snow White Cleansing Cream" had a broader nose, slightly fuller lips, and wider-set eyes than the faces of other Famous Products.

What the promotions all had in common by the 1940s was the promise of satisfying heterosexual intimacy—romance, passion, and love—for women who regularly used the products.

These messages mirrored stories aimed at young black working women in publications such as *Opportunity*, magazine of the National Urban League (NUL). In its 1943 issue celebrating women war workers, a short story focused on a high school girl whose vision of female beauty came from European fairy tales—"fair skin and blue eyes and golden hair," she says. Lacking these characteristics, she considers herself a social failure until a new boy challenges her vision of the ideal, exclaiming, "'Who wants cold, ice-bound beauty like that?'" He likens her to the "princesses" in his favorite tales, *The Arabian Nights*. Only after their conversation does she come to appreciate what she saw in her own mirror: "smooth, brown skin" with "dancing dark eyes and black permanent curls."[37] The story's protagonist had features similar to those of women in numerous photographs illustrating the issue's nonfiction features—a Pennsylvania artillery inspector, a New York radio operator, several California aircraft welders and sheet metal assemblers, as well as ambulance drivers and army mechanics.

Black beauty culture and mainstream cheesecake culture merged during the war. The most successful 1940s brand for black women, Sweet Georgia Brown, vividly illustrated the overlap with mail-order covers that featured not just ideal faces but bodies as well. The cover models mimicked scantily clad "pin-up girls" synonymous with wartime desire in American popular culture. *Crisis* editors chose to feature swimsuit-clad Sepia Miss America contestants on its pages. In her analysis of *Crisis* covers, Megan Williams uses Lena Horne's appearances in the magazine to reveal Hollywood's influence in shaping black standards of beauty. If cleanliness and health had earlier signified middle-class American values and priorities, these themes would be overtaken by a more modern goal in the 1940s—the achievement of glamour. Elsa Maxwell wrote in the *New York Post* that light-skinned beauties such as dancer Katherine Dunham and singer Lena Horne, both *Crisis* cover subjects during the war, possessed "the most powerful of all social weapons: glamour."[38]

The force of "glamour" in popular culture drove editorial decisions about magazine cover art during the war. Early in the war the NUL's *Opportunity* did not draw color lines as deeply as the NAACP's *Crisis* did in its imagery of women, but the magazine moved closer to the mainstream on this front in two years' time. For their post D-Day issue in the summer of 1944, *Opportunity* editors highlighted two workplace success stories, both featuring African American women in war plants. Vivian Currey, an automatic screw machine operator, was named a Pin-Up Girl finalist at the New Jersey factory where she worked; Elizabeth Vernando and

Cleo Glover, a riveting team on v-1 bomb bay doors at Lockheed Aircraft in Burbank, California, won a production test by securing 104 rivets in 120 seconds. Of the three, *Opportunity* chose lighter-skinned Currey for its cover, featuring her in a "sweater girl" pose, arms locked behind her head and smiling; Vernando and Glover, both darker-skinned than Currey, were shown in a small photograph near the end of the issue, both women with hands and eyes on their work. As Maureen Honey has pointed out, Currey's pose was not as provocative as many similar circulating images of Euro-American women; yet the image does sustain the notion entrenched in the black community and larger culture as well that lighter skin signaled ideal female beauty, which by the 1940s granted license to depict women as cheesecake. Although Honey contends that the war "provided an empowering political base for African American women, one that contrasts markedly with the narrowing of that base for white women," the popular vehicles used to objectify each group differed little.[39]

Images of other African American women were available, but editors chose to use them sparingly or not at all. *Crisis* published one wartime cover featuring a rural scene: a woman behind a plow, her face shadowed by a scarf. Situated safely at a distance from the camera and identified only as "One of the Co-eds at Southern University, Scotlandville, Louisiana, doing her share in the Victory Farm Program," the woman's work, not her face, was to be judged. While university women outnumbered trade school students as *Crisis* cover subjects by "over five to one" between 1941 and 1945, very few southern black women graced *Crisis* covers unless they had been selected college beauty queens and then only in formal portraiture.[40]

Shifts in the magazine's wartime cover art revealed more urban faces as well, marking the increasing popularity of M. Smith Studios in Harlem. Dozens of young women visited the second-floor photography studio at 243 West 125th Street. Run by twin brothers Morgan and Marvin Smith, the studio provided images for models' portfolios as well as a chance for ordinary women to experience the excitement of posing under the spotlights. Although the photographers invited many women to pose for their cameras, black publications that bought the Smiths' pictures wanted women to "look as white as possible," Marvin Smith said. The Smith portraits selected by *Crisis* editors in 1944 and 1945 were identified vaguely on the magazine's covers by brief captions such as "Photographer's Model" and "A New York Secretary" (fig. 6). They were identified inside the magazine only by their names and hometowns or occupations, a departure from earlier narratives focusing on educational accomplishments, club activities, and church memberships. By 1944 such résumés seemed not to matter as much as the cover girls' physiological marks of whiteness. That M. Smith Studios had hundreds of available images re-

The CRISIS

June, 1944 • Fifteen Cents

A NEW YORK SECRETARY   *Morgan Smith*

Figure 6. "A New York Secretary." Photograph by Morgan Smith. *Crisis* cover,
June 1944.

vealing a wide variety of African American female faces with "different colors . . .
different looks" meant little to the magazine.[41]

The role of faces in the black beauty business gained ground in the 1940s. Two
successful beauty culture systems, Apex and Poro, adjusted to the wartime demands of African American women who wanted "facials, eye-brow arches, mas-
sages" and similar treatments. Although hair care remained the bread and butter
of beauty curricula in the black community, greater attention to "facial structure"
and "personalized make-up" indicated a wider spectrum in female beauty culture.
In January 1943 *Crisis* ran its first full-page advertisement for modern facial cosmetics. Inside the front cover of the issue, a photo of a young woman filled the

page, with brief text below the image touting Madam C. J. Walker's Cold Cream and Egyptian Brown Face Powder. "Discriminating women" would choose these products to achieve "soft and velvet-like skin," the advertisement claimed. Until 1943 most of the Walker franchise ads in Crisis had focused on beauty training, but during the war, products mattered even more and were tied to successes in beauty operation. Training expanded during the war as many black women chose to use their disposable income from defense work to take classes, in hopes of securing postwar financial security. A beauty training course could cost up to $185 and take five to nine months to complete. Labor representatives in the black community set a pragmatic tone when warning women that industrial jobs, even the lowest paid, would not last beyond the war years. In 1943 the Brown American asked whether the black woman worker would be prepared to take "an 'inferior' situation" again. Sociologist Walter Chivers declared, "The war has opened the kitchen door and the Negro cook is closing it behind her as she goes out." But he warned that she would again "have to seek employment in the white woman's home." A promise from President Roosevelt to the National Urban League had to be realistically considered. Would the "social and economic advantages" for which the U.S. forces were fighting "to defend *and to further*" be available to African Americans in the postwar years, as he claimed? Myriad perspectives on this question filled the pages of African American publications throughout the war years.[42]

Anticipating narrowed rather than expanded opportunities, record numbers of young black women "anxious to find work in which they might attain a certain amount of dignity, self-respect and financial security, turn[ed] to beauty culture as an attractive and sensible way out." The Franklin School of Beauty's 1942 commencement essay theme—"Beauty for Defense"—may have suggested national interests, but it also indicated self-sufficiency for the Houston school's graduates.[43] Wartime employment opportunities afforded thousands of black women a new-found sense of independence that would translate into widened visions of African American female beauty in the postwar world. But until that time, mainstream media and the black press would have the greatest influence, with the U.S. government contributing a substantial share of racialized images.

Washington's war agencies and other offices generated a variety of "color" profiles for public consumption. Faces circulated by the Office of War Information (OWI), the War Manpower Commission (WMC), and the Women's Bureau (WB) revealed a wide range of understanding about race and gender. The OWI's in-house views of women stood out in the propaganda organization's monthly magazine war guides, sent to 548 magazine editors and 940 writers. In March 1944 the organization encouraged editors to devote column space to various groups of women (fig. 7). Depicting them as caricatures, the OWI artist denied African Americans

Release on religion in women's branches to press bureaus, national wire services, etc., etc.

Release on Negro women in war.
Release on women of foreign language groups in war, especial emphasis to their groups.

Release on unusual war jobs to women's editors.

Comparison story on foreign women war workers, especially to rural, foreign language, and industrial press.

Figure 7. Illustrations in the OWI media guide, "Women in the War Campaign," March 1944. RG 208, National Archives.

and professional women marks of contemporary feminine beauty. Portrayed as the stereotypical "mammy" character, the black woman's thick lips, wide nose, dark skin, and headscarf defy standards set by popular magazines. The pondering female editor also stands apart from the ideal American woman on the home front. Her sharply pointed nose and eyeglasses paired with a modest neckline and unwavering attention to work indicate a lack of sexual attractiveness. The female war worker stands as the most desirable woman on the page, marked by bright eyes, a pert nose, long lashes, and upturned lips. In just a few pen strokes, the national propaganda pacesetter—the OWI—set its vision of women then sent it out in large format to nearly 1,500 recipients.[44]

Not all of the OWI's visual artists, however, reflected its magazine division's aesthetic sense. The photography unit, directed by New Dealer Roy Stryker until it was shut down in 1943, produced penetrating studies showing complexities in African American women's lives and experiences. In the fall of 1942, Gordon Parks turned his cameras on Ella Watson's daily activities, from her work in a government office building to her care of several grandchildren. The series later became known for its iconic image of Watson standing with a broom and mop in hand against the background of an American flag (fig. 8). Providing depth beyond caricature, Ella Watson's position came to stand for working-class black women. That she inhabited a federal government world, the venue most likely to elevate her socioeconomic status, made the images more poignant. One year later, OWI photographer Esther Bubley used a modernist vision to tell a story of Americans living and traveling in the Midwest and upper South. In her pictorial record of life on the road during the war, Bubley showed the challenges to segregation posed by large crowds and a highly mobile population. While tradition and habit worked to keep blacks and whites separate in public transportation, wartime realities blurred the boundaries. African American women in Bubley's photography appear as a normalized and integral part of wartime crowds. Both Parks and Bubley revealed signs and symbols of entrenched racism, but their decisions to foreground complexity in black life moved their imagery beyond caricatures and stereotypes prevalent in other segments of American visual media.[45]

The WMC also normalized African American women in wartime culture through its illustrations. The agency attempted to highlight women's contributions to industrial mobilization through "human interest" stories that would inspire other women to seek paid employment. Its appeals to companies nationwide yielded a wide variety of women's labor experiences at such companies as U.S. Steel, Lockheed, Boeing, Curtiss-Wright, Firestone, RCA Victor, Summerill, 3-M, Ken-Rad, Servel, and Sunbeam. Among the anecdotes featuring Phi Beta Kappa grads, "Federal grandmothers," and Pearl Harbor widows were stories of interracial

Figure 8. "Ella Watson. Washington D.C. Government charwoman."
Gordon Parks, August 1942. FSA-OWI Collection, Library of Congress
(LC-USF34–013407-C), digital ID: fsa 8b14845.

cooperation. Lockheed Aircraft Corporation extolled its record on the factory floor, boasting that "no color barrier" existed in its factories. A company publicity manager reported to the WMC that African American women were employed in highly preferred "production and assembly departments" much more than in maintenance jobs, where they represented just a "small percentage" of the workforce. Lockheed's record of "complete harmony" between workers was attributed to fairness in hiring, the company's policy of "putting democracy to work in their plants."[46] Lockheed's "face" of such success belonged to Georgia Williams, a riveter in the final assembly stage of Lightning P-38s (fig. 9). With two sons in high school,

Figure 9. Georgia Williams, Lockheed Aircraft Corporation, Burbank, California, 1943. RG 211, National Archives.

a husband in the army, previous experience in industry, and additional technical training, Williams had the profile of an ideal female employee. The WMC's publicity arm needed this kind of appeal for mobilization to work, with team spirit and smiles the most important elements in the organization's message.

Of all U.S. government agencies, none portrayed African American women as positively as the Labor Department's Women's Bureau. It expended countless field hours to highlight black women's contributions to the war effort. A 1945 Labor

Department report celebrating black women as "Trail Blazers for Uncle Sam" illustrated its argument with photographs provided by the Department of Agriculture, the navy, Boeing Aircraft, New York Central Railroad, and *LIFE* magazine. From rigorous manual labor to precise laboratory work, the activities of the women in the pictures reveal a variety of color profiles. Not all of the physically demanding and dirty jobs belong to "darker" women. For example, a mechanic repairing a rail car could easily have put down her tools to pose for a portrait even *Crisis* editors would have liked. To depict women engaged in their work was vital to the WB's message about black workers. All of the illustrations picture women on site with the tools of their trades rather than posed for portraits. In 1945 the bureau's retrospective look at mobilization efforts celebrated black women and warned that "their contribution is one which this Nation would be unwise to forget or to evaluate falsely. They are an integral part of America's prospect. Not only have they helped to produce the weapons of war, but their labor has been a large factor in preventing a major break-down of essential consumer services." The WB made a special plea to keep African American women employed at all levels in the postwar world. Discrimination against them would jeopardize not only their individual livelihoods, it argued, but national and international stability as well. Only fair employment would arm black women with "the best weapon against poverty and disease"—security.[47]

The WB fought against great odds, since the mobility of the American population had aggravated human relations at all levels. With strangers jockeying for standing room on buses and trains, sharing tight quarters in military camps and boardinghouses, and competing for job opportunities, tensions ran high. The African American migration from the rural South to northern and western cities spiked during the 1940s, further boosting contact between blacks and whites and revealing regional and cultural peculiarities on all sides.[48] During the war, the Women's Bureau stood in the middle to defend female workers against prejudices in other government agencies, in the new communities where they had relocated, and in the old communities where they and their families had resided for years.

How women of color were portrayed in the black media and by U.S. government agencies during the war was significant since their faces were largely absent in corporate advertising. A whiteness standard prevailed, but the criteria for it shifted; a woman's individual accomplishments took a back seat to her glamour quotient and her photogenic qualities, bringing African American female beauty more closely in line with Anglo-American standards outlined by campaigns such as the Pond's "She's Engaged!" series. Authentic American heritage could be written on female faces, but the war had complicated which women would be able to claim it. Assembly line workers might be able to, as could aspiring models and entertainers and devoted wives, but those who aggravated the delicately balanced gender/race/ class nexus entered a realm where women had rarely been seen—the U.S. military.

The owi and its affiliated agencies confronted yet another public relations challenge after Congress approved a bill to create the Women's Army Auxiliary Corps in May 1942. Would enough women volunteer to make it viable? How could they be convinced to enlist? To what extent would the American public accept women in uniform? Immediately after the women's army was formed, the organization's director, Colonel Oveta Culp Hobby, faced a press corps curious about enlistees' private lives and possible challenges to their femininity. Among other issues, reporters wanted to know if female soldiers would be allowed to wear cosmetics. Despite Hobby's serious treatment of all queries, the next day's newspapers sensationalized and debased the military project with headlines and photo captions directly linked to the culture's fixation with cosmetics. "Powder Magazines" and "Fort Lipstick" announced a women's army to Americans. A few months later U.S. House Representative Beverly M. Vincent of Kentucky argued against the creation of a women's navy, noting that women were better at "putting on lipstick and looking in mirrors." Such light-hearted derision of women's military organizations became commonplace. Humorous tales such as H. I. Phillips's *All-Out Arlene: A Story of the Girls behind the Boys behind the Guns* offered a tongue-in-cheek look at women's military experience. The protagonist Arlene, a "typical" recruit, claims to miss reading *Vogue* magazine, but she soon gets used to a new routine in which she and her fellow soldiers "go easy on the make-up." They sing their own rendition of the popular song "You're in the Army Now," indicating the incongruity of military life and beauty routines.

> You're doing duty now;
> So beauty disavow;
> Forget your complexion!
> Pull in your midsection!
> You're in the army now.

Such changes had to be difficult, Arlene's father notes in a letter, since she and other "girls" like her had previously enjoyed "lots of time for primping." Yet according to Arlene, women soldiers recognized the role of makeup in certain kinds of combat, since they referred to cosmetics as "Dry Ammunition."[49]

Recruitment literature centered on women's traditional pursuits and domestic interests in order to normalize the notion of their joining the military. One owi text linked cosmetics to the Marine Corps uniform. Not only did U.S. Marine Corps Women's Reserve (usmcwr) members "carefully match their lipsticks" to the "red cord on their caps"—Elizabeth Arden developed a shade called Montezuma Red—

but as one sergeant told the OWI, "Every girl spends lots of time on her make-up." USMCWR posters reiterated the message with touches of red in their graphic design schemes.[50] After the Women's Army Auxiliary Corps was integrated into the U.S. Army in 1943 and subsequently renamed the Women's Army Corps (WAC), the organization's recruitment literature needed, more than ever, to show an unsullied, mature feminine ideal. WAC officials had fought rumor, innuendo, and mockery for over a year, but the stakes got higher.[51] In 1944 the OWI reminded media outlets to depict Wacs as "serious" workers and to "avoid copy angles or pictures" that would "glamorize" them. The National Better Business Bureau alerted its members to observe the "different standards of good taste" when women soldiers were portrayed. Any reference to the WAC had to go to the War Department's Bureau of Public Relations "for review *prior to its release*," a stipulation that did not apply to the male army. In a challenge to entrenched cultural mores, the Ad Council instructed ad agencies to refer to female soldiers as "'women'—never as 'girls.'" Early WAC advertising had been criticized for its lack of seriousness, especially its failure to appeal to those who might see the military as a career path rather than a temporary wartime job. One expert wrote to the OWI, "Buying a career is no 'impulse purchase' for a woman. It is her future that is at stake—and that requires a great deal more thought and deliberation than spending a few cents for a new lipstick." The language and power of cosmetics infiltrated the development of the American women's military in order to safely sell it as well as control it.[52]

The "faces" used to recruit women into military service recalled Western ideas of feminine beauty linking whiteness and purity. U.S. War Department artist Jes Schlaikjer's 1944 poster for the Women's Army Corps, entitled "Mine Eyes Have Seen the Glory," echoes World War I propaganda images that defined female figures as exemplars of virtue (fig. 10). Set against the darkness of contemporary battle scenes, the silhouettes of infantrymen and airplanes in the background, the female soldier's face offers a stark contrast to the brutalities of war. With eyes turned upward, her face and neck bathed in a stream of light, the WAC volunteer is lit both from without and within, her porcelain skin glowing. The first line of Julia Ward Howe's 1862 "Battle Hymn of the Republic" infuses the design with spiritual resonance, implying an angelic symbol at the center. The most widely distributed WAC face of the war, however, was illustrator Brad Crandell's "girl with a Star-Spangled heart" (fig. 11). How many recruits it won from coast to coast is unknown, but the woman peering out from the shadow of her "Hobby cap" reveals a hint of confidence and sufficient solemnity along with a carefully "made-up" face. With painted lashes, lips, and cheeks, the model Wac stands to attract women who may earlier have hesitated to join; her image calls to the audience while simultaneously reassuring it. She embodies the U.S. government's promise to allow women to use

MINE EYES HAVE SEEN THE GLORY

WOMEN'S ARMY CORPS

ARMY OF THE UNITED STATES

Figure 10. WAC recruitment poster by Jes Schlaikjer, 1944. Collections of the Women's Memorial Foundation, Arlington, Virginia.

cosmetics while in uniform. Crandell's created face, like those he had drawn for *Cosmopolitan* magazine covers, exhibited a certain wartime style marked by arched eyebrows and a deeply colored mouth. While it no doubt matched those of many actual Wacs, the element tying most volunteers together would be a "Star-Spangled heart," the poster announced. The sentiment enhances the irony of a 1945 photograph of two new WAC recruits (fig. 12). In it, sisters Emiki and Rose Tanada set their real faces against the WAC archetype. Older sister Emiki (on the far left)

Figure 11. WAC recruitment poster by Bradshaw Crandell, 1943. Prints and Photographs Division, Library of Congress (LC-USZC4–1653), digital ID: cph 3g01653.

Figure 12. WAC enlistees Emiki Tanada (left) and Rose Tanada. January 23, 1945. RG 208, National Archives.

appears a bit more incredulous in her gaze at the image than does her younger sister. As Japanese Americans, the Tanada sisters belonged to the most heavily racialized and demonized "other" on the home front.[53]

Scorned as possible subversives and enemy collaborators, Japanese Americans had seen themselves inextricably linked to the Empire of Japan. To prove their affinity with mainstream America, incarcerated Nisei women competed in beauty pageants at internment camps throughout the nation, grappling with the strictures of racism and the limits of loyalty, all the while hoping to prove their all-American femininity behind barbed wire. The U.S. government's incarceration orders meant that most Nisei women who wanted to serve in the women's army had to wait until they could prove their loyalty to the nation. And even after they did, they were rarely used in WAC publicity, their faces off-limits to news photographers. The Tanada sisters joined the WAC and were officially photographed a full thirteen months after the first Nisei woman was inducted into the organization. Discrimination policies in the navy's auxiliary corps, the WAVES, kept out racial "others" until late 1944 when the first African American recruits took their oath. More than anything else "the color line" bound Japanese Americans and African Americans together during the war, wrote journalist Harry Paxton Howard. Since the Nisei had been "plundered of everything," they became "an integral part" of the nation's race struggle. He insisted that African Americans embrace the internment story as their own.[54]

Recruitment posters displaying Euro-American archetypes also suggested that the military was a safe place for women to combine skills they already possessed with specialized training for one of "239 kinds of jobs." As a 1944 image of a "Topographic Draftsman" shows, military work would require concentration and exactitude from women (fig. 13). The female soldier, the poster implies, has the necessary skills to do the job. She knows how to draw lines and color within them, as her perfectly constructed face tells viewers. The same kind of care and attention the draftswoman uses before her mirror at home, she can apply to maps at work. She will not likely let the pencil slip, since lives and reputations (including her own) depend upon her precision. In particular, her red lips offer a foil for the routes marked in red on the map. The former indicate the cultivation and maintenance of femininity, while the latter denote the movements of men in war, the most masculine of human activities. As male soldiers carry out their duties abroad, she fulfils her responsibilities at home. Keeping her lips colored matters as much as keeping the red lines up-to-date, even more so since she represents the greatest of America's wartime experiments—allowing women to be soldiers. But the poster works on yet another level, given its propagandistic purpose. The idealized female soldier embodies whiteness and its attendant privileges. Recruits might aspire to these. The model works indoors, presumably in a comfortable space. That she is buttoned up, cuffs and collar down, suggests her work will not require her to break a sweat. The coolness in her manner, despite intense concentration on the task at hand, suggests an even, controlled disposition, which since the nineteenth century had been an indicator of class, rank, and respectability. All of these make her a racialized figure as well, but her identity as a model Wac is further secured by gleaming golden hair and a complexion like those described in the most famous wartime face cream advertisements—"peaches and cream" cheeks and "delicate white skin, as fresh and dainty as sweet-pea blossoms." Thus a "woman's place in war" was occupied by figures whose femininity, properly overseen, remained intact. The military could then be viewed not only as a safe place for women, but perhaps more importantly, as the poster suggests, a haven for white American womanhood.[55]

Local community support could help military women uphold standards of femininity and domesticity. The government sought help from department stores, women's organizations, and hospitality groups such as the United Service Organizations (USO). It encouraged private citizens to provide gender-specific comforts for women in uniform—kitchens where furloughed soldiers could cook, afternoon tea parties where they could relax and socialize, and places "to freshen up after a long train trip." Photographs of Wacs powdering their noses and applying

Figure 13. WAC recruitment poster created by the Office for Emergency Management, OWI-Domestic Operations Branch, Bureau of Special Services, 1944. National Archives (44-PA-260A).

lipstick accompanied stories about women's adjustments to military life. Wartime writer Mercedes Rosebery pointed to the "radiant" faces of enlistees in the WAC and WAVES, who became the new cover girls on popular magazines. Such images suggested to viewers that women in uniform had normal desires and posed no social threat. But sympathetic groups were still needed to assist them in counteracting the notion that men disapproved of women in uniform. Male GIs in particular railed against it, writing pithy opinions in their letters home. Among the many read by government censors, one man warned, "You join the WAVES or WAC and you are automatically a prostitute in my opinion," while another demanded, "Get a damn divorce. I don't want no damn WAC for a wife." Wac Aileen Kilgore knew fellow soldiers whose "overseas boy friends" had broken off their relationships. One woman, Kilgore reported, "got a letter from her husband of many years, a Captain in Italy, saying he's divorcing her because she joined."[56]

The OWI blamed the media for encouraging such attitudes and offered suggestions for improving their messages. "Women have *not* been told in national publicity that military services does not destroy their femininity nor detract from it. There has *not* been sufficient emphasis on the fact that women in the Armed Forces are respected as women, and that they are not remolded into some other kind of half-male, half-female hybrid." The OWI informed media outlets that military organizations had actually encouraged women not only "to remain feminine, but to try and become 'more so.'" All communications were to make clear that prospective recruits would be allowed to use cosmetics in the military, since all of the services wanted women "to look [their] best at all times." The Ad Council advised magazine and newspaper advertisers to include images of army handbags with compacts and lipstick cases clearly visible. USMCWR recruitment literature promised volunteers that their official handbags had sufficient pockets "for both orders and cosmetics." Tempering military life with a well made-up face—even if abstract—would, they hoped, convince skeptics and critics.[57]

For some recruits, however, the world of cosmetics was new and foreign territory. Aileen Kilgore intimated as much in her diary when describing her experimentation with a lipstick that a friend had purchased, noting that she "used it heavily to see what it's like." A few weeks later, more discussion among the women centered on "beauty treatment." Kilgore considered it significant enough to write about, noting, "[Daisy] and I bought Noxema Cream for our complexions on the recommendation of Carmen. Saturday night we used it for the first time and arose next morning with scaley faces. Daisy quit the treatment then and there. Carmen insists we need to give it a longer trial." Such initiation rites into womanhood, the group's experimentation with new cosmetics and the wise mentor's oversight, mark the WAC as a site where rituals of femininity were sustained as much as challenged. And since a large majority of Wacs were younger than their WAVES or Marine counterparts, they were more likely to be uninitiated in beauty rituals. Nearly half of WAC enlistees were from small towns and rural areas, where conservative social values and community oversight of individual behavior had traditionally restricted cultural influences targeting young women. For some soldiers, then, the army offered worldly experience they might not have gotten as early, if ever.[58]

Military women who faced the least cultural resistance were nurses. Working in an already feminized profession, they could don the pins and colors of the U.S. Army and U.S. Navy because their reputations as "angels of mercy" preceded them. Ruth Haskell, a thirty-three-year-old divorced mother from Maine who served in the U.S. Army Nurse Corps, entitled her 1944 memoir "Helmets and Lipstick." Determined to attract other women to war front nursing, this "self-initiating" and "confident" woman thought that putting on a face every day boosted her morale. She wrote, "A fresh application of lipstick, my helmet at a jaunty angle, and I was ready for anything."[59] As early as February 1943, *Crisis* had put a military nurse on its cover, publishing her contact information in order to "save the time and postage of the men who always write for addresses of our cover girls." Editor Roy Wilkins concluded his accompanying story on black nurses: "It seems unnecessary to add, especially in view of the pictures accompanying this piece, that 'our boys' will feel better, too, the minute these clear-eyed, efficient young women step off a boat somewhere on the other side of the world." Efficiency and professionalism combined with the need to make the magazine's cover girls available to male viewers, particularly black soldiers. Copies were passed around, sent overseas, and circulated more widely than ever before. By placing more and more young women on its covers throughout the war, *Crisis* sanctioned their objectification. These women who had chosen the most feminine of military pursuits and the most acceptable feminized vocation could serve a larger purpose in satisfying the male gaze. As more photographs of black nurses circulated in the African American press in 1944, many more women of color joined the forces. Finally, in January 1945, they were integrated throughout the various military nursing corps, a process made possible by the convergence of several factors, not the least of which was an escalating American casualty rate.[60]

On both the European and Pacific fronts, the heightening wartime crisis made nurse recruitment even more urgent. In the spring of 1945, as American combat casualties increased daily, overseas hospitals "filled to capacity," and VA facilities held more than a hundred and twenty thousand veterans requiring "permanent or recuperative" treatment, the appeals for nurses reflected an urgency not seen on the home front in the previous three years. The army estimated its "immediate" need at six thousand new nurses, with ten thousand more to follow throughout the year. The navy hoped to bring in five hundred nurses each month through the spring and summer. The Veterans Administration urged another three thousand nurses for its hospitals, while the Red Cross needed eighteen thousand new instructors. It was projected that nearly eighty thousand new Cadet Nurses would be needed by mid-1946 in addition to three million home nursing students. These numbers did not include nurses' aides and WAC hospital technicians. In this state of emergency, the National Retail Dry Goods Association and the American Red Cross cosponsored a program to set up recruitment stations in department stores. To encourage enlistment in the various military nursing corps, stores were urged to give door prizes at in-store parties and to offer incentives such as merchandise certificates to early enlistees. The program planners recommended that every woman who signed up for nursing be given "a cosmetic kit." The campaign proved successful, because six weeks later "the Navy was turning away applicants, the Army was adequately staffed, the Cadet Nurse Corps was continuing to meet its quota, volunteers were being turned away from the WAC Hospital Technicians, and it was impossible to train all the numbers applying for the Nurse's Aides and the Home Nursing Classes."[61] Make-up had worked.

Wartime cosmetics kits included a variety of goodies, from powders to paints to fragrances, but in the end, American women considered one item their most vital tool in constructing a home front face: lipstick. The cylinder filled with a small block of paraffin available in hundreds of colors established, confused, and unmoored female identities unlike any other cosmetic in the 1940s. Lipstick's force radiated in many directions. Perhaps more than any item made for the face, it allowed American women to "assert themselves, critically and as sexual beings, into the body politic" during World War II, writes Page Dougherty Delano.[62] While men carried weapons on battlefronts, women commanded riveting guns, welding torches, and other heavy equipment marking their forays into masculinized territory; others entered male white-collar enclaves, signing contracts and accounts at an unprecedented rate and accruing power in places not previously open to them. Women's use of cosmetics helped to mediate the subsequent conflict that arose from the literal challenge to traditional gender barriers in male workspaces. No single item in the "make-up" arsenal accomplished this negotiation more successfully than lipstick. It highlighted and reasserted what was both female and feminine on the U.S. home front, thus confusing gendered power arrangements. Touted in advertisements as "a symbol of democracy and freedom," lipstick held a prominent place in American women's daily routines.[63] When asked, they would not give it up.

In the spring of 1942, as the War Production Board sought to curtail domestic use of essential materials, it convened a Cosmetics Industry Advisory Committee to help determine conservation measures. In a few weeks the committee's research determined that 175 of 800 "different raw materials" used in toiletries and cosmetics were deemed "of major importance to the industry." Early WPB measures had already restricted 20 of these 175 critical materials, but additional restrictions would be necessary, the committee determined.[64] Recognizing both consumer desire and business health in their deliberations, the committee sponsored a series of surveys among middle-class American women. The written survey opened with a stark declaration: "Most of the ingredients used in cosmetics are critically scarce. This questionnaire is circulated to ascertain, if cuts are necessary, what items consumers could best do without." In one of the control groups, 201 female employees in the Office of Price Administration's Consumer Division were given a list of 34 toiletries and cosmetics items to classify in one of three ways: "those items most important to you," "those items next in importance to you," or "those items you can easily do without." The results revealed the overwhelming popularity of lipstick among women of all ages. One hundred eighty-four of the 201 women surveyed, nearly 92 percent, identified lipstick as a "most important" item, with only 6 individuals claiming they could "easily do without" it.[65]

No other product received such overwhelmingly uniform responses. Face powder came in second place for most women, with "rouge" a close third. No woman over forty admitted that she could "easily do without" face powder. The only products to vie with face powder and rouge were deodorants and antiperspirants, which ranked highly among just one group of women, those younger than forty. All groups gave eye shadows, mascaras, and eyebrow pencils low marks as primary or secondary needs. The gravity of the national crisis in the months following Pearl Harbor had made sacrifice the touchstone in American consumer culture, yet the WPB survey results reveal that respondents considered their faces off-limits to full U.S. government regulation. Even the loaded opening statement on the cosmetics questionnaire seems not to have budged women who considered their faces sites of individual expression and autonomy. If they had to relinquish a facet of their constructed masks, they would forfeit their eyes. But they wanted tools to enhance skin tones and colors, and they unequivocally demanded lipstick.

The WPB's Toiletries and Cosmetics Committee waxed and waned according to the dictates of lipstick. Through the summer and fall of 1942, WPB committees determined the "essentiality" of hundreds of products. Lipstick ended up on a list of cosmetics that required few or no "critical materials." But the list was determined, as reports indicated, by public opinion surveys as well as judgments of "beauty editors and advertising agency experts." Taking age, race, and women's new responsibilities in the work world into consideration, the committee produced a long list of items "most needful to women." While lipstick took its place among nearly fifty other products, in due time it would stand out as the most widely discussed facial cosmetic in Washington. For a brief moment WPB policy makers enjoyed the freedom of determining "the number of shades" they would allow in each cosmetics category, but their power was short-lived. WPB limitation orders came to focus on conservation measures in packaging rather than in the products themselves. A castor oil shortage had encouraged lipstick makers to experiment with substitutes such as peanut oil, but their research proved unsuccessful, so deliberations over sample sizes, holiday gift sets, and special cardboard displays for products took precedence at committee meetings. By mid-1943 the all-male Toiletries and Cosmetics Industry Advisory Committee engaged in serious deliberations about standardizing lipstick cases. They debated the virtues of "screw lifts" and "swivel cases" and "push-ups," all the while confirming that companies had spent years and lots of money establishing "individuality" in the market. The gravity of the challenge motivated the creation of a "lipstick task group" whose research concluded in a mere six weeks with the announcement: "[A] state of emergency exists with respect to the quantity of lipsticks now available to American women."[66] Production would increase rather than decrease over the next year and a half, with lipstick advertisements projecting greater political and cultural import than ever before.

As early as December 1941, American women had been encouraged to put "a bright inviting flash of color" on their lips as an appropriate response to the Pearl Harbor attack. A *New York Times* fashion reporter advised that "experts" recommended "strong and red" lipstick hues. Advertising played on women's duty to beauty as an appropriate national morale-builder. By mid-war, after millions of American women had entered the paid workforce, the House of Tangee initiated its "War, Women, and Lipstick" campaign, reminding female citizens of their "right to be feminine and lovely." Tangee's lengthy ad narratives exclaimed to *LHJ* readers: "It's a reflection of the free democratic way of life that you have succeeded in keeping your femininity—even though you are doing man's work!" Fan magazines with younger, working-class target audiences, such as *Photoplay–Movie Mirror*, "linked lipstick with courage and emotional fortitude," argues Jane Gaines, while they also "held at bay the fear that the new 'tough girls' might be lesbians." All-American Girls Professional Baseball League players, who met Helena Rubenstein Beauty Salon representatives at spring training, were urged to embrace "the artistic part" of "creating a lovely mouth." After receiving instructions on how to apply lip colors with brushes, each player carried her own "beauty kit" on road trips. Femininity, respectability, and heterosexuality were tied inextricably to "an attractive and pleasing mouth."[67] Lipstick use, it appeared, could circumscribe women who might need boundaries.

Containment strategies also relied on lipstick's relationship to sex appeal. The Chesebrough-Pond's wartime "LIPS" series highlighted this relationship. In a 1943 ad targeting young women, appearing in magazines such as *Mademoiselle*, a male sailor shouts, "There's my girl with the New Pond's 'LIPS'—and half the Navy!" But by late 1944 as a postwar world seemed to be edging closer, the same Pond's series focused on monogamy as its principal selling point. Keeping one man rather than attracting many was what women should aspire to, the ads suggested. In each three-frame graphic, time and seasons pass while a man and woman passionately kiss. The most illuminating cartoon in the series features a sidewalk scene, where the growth of a family business provides the backdrop for a postwar dream of prosperity (fig. 14). Pond's "LIPS" spoke directly to the private interests for which many Americans thought the war was being waged. The lipstick's staying power connoted the woman's steadfastness as well, despite any wartime changes or personal temptations that may have altered her world or her worldview.[68]

The trajectory of the Pond's "LIPS" series over time indicates the suggested plot changes for the ideal woman through the war years. "Bright" lips seemed preferable at the beginning of the war, when home front culture was not yet established. But after millions of women took men's jobs, entered female military forces, and experienced greater overall independence, sharper emphases on femininity inside domestic tradition seemed culturally necessary if social order were to hold. The girlfriend who could attract half the navy enjoyed a brief moment when her appeal was politically appropriate. By late 1944, with victory in Europe in sight and postwar planning going full steam, mainstream advertising relied more heavily on the faithful girlfriend or wife. She who literally "sticks" to her man throughout the years becomes the all-American female icon, the right kind of woman. Having found or been reunited with her partner, the woman's own security lies in the locked kiss. And ultimately, she would be responsible for the stability of the union.

While lipstick signaled flirtatiousness, exertion of femininity or heterosexuality, and display of emotional strength, it also could indicate danger. U.S. government posters warning against venereal disease provided the icons of such horror: female faces reminiscent of the "public" or "painted" woman of years past, similar to the "stereotypic no-good women of the silent film" whose "heavy eye makeup and lip paint" connoted their "destructive sexuality." Yet by the 1940s Hollywood had transformed the bad woman into a "glamour girl" whose "erotic femininity" stemmed largely from her made-up face. As Susan Brownmiller observes, "the very words 'glamour' and 'glamorous' when applied to women became synonymous with the razzle-dazzle of cosmetic glaze as much as with a curvaceous figure, high heels and revealing clothes." All of which meant it was difficult for observers to determine if a woman had crossed the line from being simply flirtatious to becom-

Pond's "Lips" stay on...

and on...

and on !

Six kiss-provoking shades . . . . . Try new "Beau Bait"— rich, rosy-crimson!
The BIG case is only 49¢—*plus tax*

Figure 14. Pond's "LIPS" advertisement for magazines. May 1945. JWT Archives, Hartman Center, Duke University.

ing seriously dangerous. Although the government's purpose was to warn men in uniform, the illustrations posed one of the war culture's toughest quandaries for women—how to stay on the right side of the boundary distinguishing them as glamorous morale-builders rather than "victory girls, khaki-wackies, and patriotutes" who could be arrested by authorities. Washington's graphic artists drew on a full arsenal of derogatory monikers including "Pick-Ups," "Good Time Girls," and "Juke Joint Snipers." The heavily made-up central characters in these oversized government warnings reiterated stereotypes, with "painted" women starring in the visual narratives (fig. 15). Each poster urged viewers to believe that something sinister lurked behind the woman's deeply colored full lips and the cigarette between them. A dangerous woman could be easily identified by her smoking, the warnings implied. The "Juke Joint Sniper" (1942) feeds her habit, as do other sultry figures whose faces provided signs for soldiers and sailors to look for—darkly shadowed cheeks and eyes, but most telling, conspicuous and active lips.[69]

What complicated the seemingly easy task of identification was the wartime reality that more and more young women were becoming sexually active, some of them to fulfill a notion of availability as a patriotic duty. No longer the traditional "woman of the night," a disease carrier might just be the "girl next door," official poster art announced (fig. 16). Difficult to spot since she wore no overpainted masklike face, the wartime disease spreader could by all outward signs appear innocent. She looked much more like sweethearts portrayed in the Pond's "LIPS" series, including the woman who had attracted "half the Navy" with her lipstick, admitting, "you can't blame a girl for liking a little extra attention." Meant to be lighthearted humor at first glance, the message spoke at a deeper level to the social reality that made cultural observers and guardians of traditional values increasingly uneasy. Once-innocent girlfriends or wives who had become objects of desire for many men might just enjoy the attention and act upon it. The warning "She May Look Clean—But" denoted the discomfiting belief that old moorings had loosened and as a result, unseen risks abounded.[70]

The female culprit starring in public health poster art was part of a home front visual communications initiative uncomfortably shared by the U.S. government and American advertising during the war years. The buzz about the possible role of posters to shape public opinion was generated in several Washington offices soon after the Pearl Harbor attack. Getting corporate America to cooperate proved difficult, however, so government bureaucrats attempted to distinguish their work from advertising copy by arguing that they were not in the business of "selling" war to Americans. Instead of trying to convince consumers to buy products, government posters would "bring home the war issues to people by a more deeply felt kind of art." Hiring such artists as George Grosz, John Stuart Curry, and Norman

Figure 15. "Juke Joint Sniper," 1942. National Library of Medicine, History of Medicine Division.

Rockwell to fulfill these needs would further distance the nation's visual campaigns from those of commercial advertising, which were clouded by "the film of technique," a government spokesperson snidely remarked.[71] Their fierce competition with advertising agencies for the hearts and minds of Americans led the Washington offices to flex limited muscle with tough talk. While corporate America could merely buy space for its messages, the U.S. government had a right to "every wall, every fence, every window in the country," administrators claimed. They boasted, "Ideally, it should be possible to post America over night. People should wake up to find a visual message everywhere, like new snow — every man, woman, and child should be reached and moved by the message."[72]

Such grand goals veiled a welter of frustrations in Washington, where the strained relations between advertising and government information agencies only intensified. Ad executives' creation of the Ad Council in December 1941

Figure 16. "She May Look Clean—But," ca. 1940. National Library of Medicine, History of Medicine Division.

demonstrated their intention to maintain control over their businesses rather than have a Washington office oversee them, as had happened in the First World War. The modern corporate world moved too quickly for a government information agency to keep pace, advertisers contended. In November 1942 industry president Paul West offered an olive branch by inviting U.S. vice president Henry Wallace to give a formal dinner address at a national advertising meeting in an attempt "to bring government and business closer together." The OWI would vie for attention and credit with advertising agencies throughout the course of the war, with petty jealousies surfacing from time to time. Advertisers used their existing connections and expertise to blend product sales and wartime messages, thus couching all of their work as service to the nation.[73]

Women's faces appeared on the most widely disseminated and popular posters during the war. The earnest combined efforts of Washington bureaucrats and graphic artists, Madison Avenue ad writers, and a few freelancers yielded hundreds of poster designs that were seen by millions. In nearly every case, they were designed to sate the interests of private enterprise more than the desires of government. Yet, who created or funded or got credit for the message did not matter as much as the message itself—whether in military uniform, coveralls, bridal attire, or apron, the ideal woman wore a properly constructed face. J. Howard Miller's confident industrial worker boldly exclaimed to Westinghouse employees, "We Can Do It!" And her arched brows, shadowed lids, false lashes, rouged cheeks, and lined, colored lips made her the safest kind of female laborer on an assembly line (fig. 17). The woman who cared to create the right mask on a daily basis sent a variety of signals to herself and all onlookers—that she was more interested in her appearance than her job; that she wanted to get ahead in the world and therefore put time and effort into creating the right face; that she had embraced the wartime feminine ideal by using cosmetics to say, "I'm a safe bet, not a threat, here for the duration, gone when asked to leave." Or maybe that American advertising had indeed convinced her of the necessary link between her well-made-up face and victory. As the *Washington Post* instructed young women who had taken over the capital city's offices to type and file, time spent on their "make-up" ensured they would not "lose face before the day [was] over."[74]

Historian Leila Rupp has argued that the American public's desire to maintain traditional roles for women had long-term consequences, making the popularized "Rosie the Riveter" image a mere mask covering the more circumscribed woman of peacetime America. Page Dougherty Delano points out that many images "suggested that underneath that rough welding mask lay a carefully coiffed woman whose femininity remained intact despite the national upheaval." The *New Yorker* artist Alan Dunn astutely captured the mixed messages in a 1943 cartoon of a woman who creates a face then covers it with a metal helmet, thus illustrating a wartime paradox (fig. 18). Only she knew what her artistry meant, since it would remain hidden for hours underneath her headgear and might just melt, run, or otherwise disappear while she worked. But the efforts put forth by women like her secured their consciences in light of the political obligations and private desires

Figure 17. Poster by J. Howard Miller, 1943. Produced by Westinghouse
War Production Co-Ordinating Committee. National Archives Still
Picture Branch (NWDNS-179-WP-1563).

they sought to fulfill. As Lane Drug Store saleswoman Kate Snoderly reminded all
cosmetics sellers in 1944, "Few things are more personal—and important—to the
average woman than the cosmetics she uses."[75]

Between 1940 and 1945 retail cosmetics sales increased by 63 percent, to well over
seven hundred million dollars. Women constructed and maintained their faces
on a scale not seen before, while they spent their remaining hours building airplanes, mopping floors, and making Victory Sandwiches. They mixed, welded,
cooked, saluted, typed, danced, and entertained, all the time keeping an eye on the
mirror and society's recommendations. Embracing femininity through cosmetics use mattered on the home front, as many groups of women came to realize.

Figure 18. Cartoon by Alan Dunn. *The New Yorker*, March 13, 1943. © Alan Dunn/Condé Nast Publications/www.cartoonbank.com.

Washington, D.C., workers who lived among nearly five thousand women at the Arlington Farms housing project were thrilled to have a "line of make-up mirrors" that provided "a touch of glamour" to their residence halls. Just two years into the war, editors at *McCall's* magazine asked women which products they wanted to see after the war ended. Based on the survey results, a market research executive inferred, "With women more numerous than men after the war, competition for both husbands and jobs will promote a 'youth complex.'" Cosmetics advertisers could use this to their advantage, he advised.[76] While it may seem to have been premature for commentators to speculate on a postwar era as early as January 1944, corporate America was angling to create a certain kind of marketplace for women and their faces.

Editors, artists, social scientists, government bureaucrats, and the women they spoke to all inhabited a wartime society where faces mattered—a home front where make-up could create dreams, ruin reputations, and expose one's desires. The impact of Pond's wartime advertising may never be measured, but what is certain is that millions of women who saw millions of glossy magazine pages shouting "She's Engaged! She's Lovely! She Uses Pond's!" made the connections. Beyond the obvious, however, were messages linking whiteness, delicacy, and desirability, as well as subtle prescriptions for setting aside one's selfish wishes if they conflicted with the nation's goals. Cosmetics advertising, U.S. government propaganda, and other print media featuring women's faces inextricably bound together intimate lives, patriotic gestures, and gendered boundaries, all the while leading their female readers and viewers through a maze of changing expectations that never veered too far from traditional notions of home, hearth, and heterosexuality. What would complicate the image of traditional womanhood on the home front was the attention that mass media gave to particular extremities. The fetishization of hands and legs would encourage the sexualization of American women on a scale not seen before.

TWO

Tender Hands and Average Legs

Shaping Disparate Extremities

As the U.S. War Manpower Commission (WMC) intensified its massive campaign to recruit women for industrial jobs in 1943, mobilization efforts took their toll on female bodies. Daily exposure to metal filings, soot, and extreme heat, in addition to the physical demands of some assignments, such as holding a twelve-ounce rivet gun steady for several hours, yielded unsightly consequences that shocked many industrial neophytes, as well as their friends and family members. *True Confessions* magazine, a Fawcett Group publication, sponsored a war worker makeover to help a young woman who had "neglected" her health in the interest of carrying out her patriotic duty. Her weight loss, irritated skin, and rough hands prompted *True Confessions* representatives to spend four weeks restoring her health and teaching her how to maintain it. They claimed to have "performed miracles with her morale" by helping her to stabilize her body weight and teaching her how to keep her hands soft. Such concentrated attention to her physical body's decline, with progress toward the standards of American female beauty, had presumably made her a better worker, a more reliable contributor to the war effort, and ultimately, the kind of patriotic woman that the nation needed in early 1943. She was anointed "Fawcett's Winning War Girl."[1]

Female bodies would require extra care in order to maintain the high spirits demanded of them in the sociopolitical culture of the early war years. Declining morale suggested the possibility of home front problems that could rapidly transcend one individual or family to affect the nation as a whole. Would the production schedule proceed apace if female war workers neglected their hands, their legs, and the rest of their bodies? Would a dispirited workforce diminish the WMC's recruitment of women, in turn crippling the home front war effort? More broadly, would American support for the war wane if the physical sacrifices of its women—not just working women—seemed too severe? Which bodily sacrifices were worth it, and which compromised standards of femininity too much? And finally, how could images of female bodies be used to promote the American war effort?

This chapter attempts to answer these questions through an analysis of messages featuring women's hands and legs during the war years. Popular magazine advertisements merged with an assortment of war agency prescriptives to inform American women that their patriotic fervor could, in fact, be measured by their attempts to shape and maintain "ideal" parts from the neck down. In particular, time spent softening their hands, caring for their nails, and shaping their legs to desired formulas would enhance their overall value. They could ensure their political status as objects worth fighting for, thus providing the personal edge they needed to maintain satisfying intimate lives "for the duration" and into the postwar years. Military service personnel, blue-collar wage earners, pink-collar workers, and homemakers saw their hands and legs inextricably linked with both public and private victory.

Corporate America's print advertising campaigns moved in step with and often precipitated the messages emanating from federal government offices and their various ancillaries, such as the Office of War Information's (OWI) Bureau of Motion Pictures in Hollywood. That the War Department would purchase and distribute to military personnel nearly five million copies of a Twentieth-Century Fox movie poster featuring a swimsuit-clad Betty Grable reveals its desire to influence social standards and define gender boundaries. While perhaps an extreme example, this official action nevertheless denotes the political efficacy of using women's bodies to shape cultural thinking during the war. Such circumscription put forth ideal female bodies marked by heterosexuality, whiteness, youth or innocence, and middle-class values. These idealized bodies served to check notions women might have entertained about their civic sacrifice (especially if it came with a nice paycheck) rewarding them complete autonomy. If keeping morale high seemed the ultimate priority on the American home front, then women's bodies would be put into service of the goal. And women everywhere would confront messages exhorting them to expend personal energy on their physical appearance for the nation's sake and their own.

While some messages to women indicated their hands would mark their level of respectability, other messages challenged them to use their legs to test their patriotic fervor. Hands worked, yes, but they also functioned as time fillers, body parts to be kept occupied in worthy pursuits while men were away in training camps or overseas on the battlefronts. A Eureka Vacuum Cleaner advertisement featured a woman who claimed, "My Heart's Overseas but My Hands Are on the Job," echoing the mythic trope of busy hands keeping temptation at bay.[2] And whether to use nail polish was tricky. Depending on a woman's station, she could get or lose a job if her nails had too little or too much color. Contradictory messages set hands against legs as well. The sexualization of middle-class American women through pin-ups that focused overwhelmingly on their legs laid the foundation for postwar transmogrification of cheesecake into soft-core pornography.

Women's hands underwent close scrutiny during the war years, especially as millions took jobs outside their homes. The price exacted by hours of welding, riveting, bucking, or pressing seemed much higher to more socially conservative Americans than the toll taken by dishwashing and laundry. What high-paying wage labor did to women's hands appeared to challenge mainstream standards of femininity much more dangerously than did the detrimental effects of housework, which functioned safely within gendered boundaries. In some ways, Fawcett's Winning War Girl had her own war story. *True Confessions* readers could embrace the narrative of success, regardless of the kinds of work or leisure in which they themselves engaged, because the tale mirrored so many of the chronicles they read each month in the magazine. *True Confessions* and other magazines in the confessional genre, such as *True Story* and *True Romances*, featured autobiographical tales of women who had faced adversity with verve, cleverness, and usually a bit of luck. Readers were accustomed to sensationalized short stories featuring risk-taking heroines and their romantic liaisons. The magazines' readership—a largely young, unmarried cohort from lower-middle or working-class families—had kept their circulation figures in the millions since the 1920s. Editors at *True Confessions* and its all-fiction "pulp" counterparts had ardently embraced war-related subject matter, with a focus on recruitment of women for industrial or nurse training and other kinds of civilian sacrifice. Their early and enthusiastic contributions had impressed Washington war agency administrators. Many young wage laborers among confessional magazine readers took advantage of work opportunities in "war boom" areas, some far away from their neighborhoods and hometowns. Fawcett's Winning War Girl no doubt struck a familiar chord with thousands of young women like her who had seized on industrial employment opportunities but had found the labor, the work schedules, and the commutes physically debilitating. Their hands, in particular, revealed the telltale signs of manual labor, compromising their quest to accomplish what their role models in popular magazines had accomplished—elements of ideal femininity. If readers had not yet managed to enjoy a satisfying romantic encounter, they at least could buy and use the same products as those who did. And hope.[3]

Market-conscious manufacturers were encouraged to devise "health or beauty 'package[s]'" for women in factories, as well as to provide "convenient dispensers" in restrooms so that employees would see the product name frequently and perhaps decide to buy it on their own.[4] Pitched as small measures to placate the female worker, these marketing moves also attempted to secure the proper womanhood of those who had stepped into jobs previously held by men. Not unlike so many hundreds of wartime ad campaigns, the factory "packages" revealed the importance of cultivating habits in female consumers that would continue in the postwar years after they left the workforce, a well-publicized forecast. Hand hygiene, which was to include thoughtful decisions about soaps, lotions, nail enamel, and protective gloves, among other things, would lead a conscientious woman to realize that her work-worn hands would be only temporary. Likewise, the solace offered to the American public by campaigns admonishing women to keep their hands and nails beautiful meant that the challenges to femininity posed by "men's work" would be resolutely confronted and defeated. Mainstream media promoted the idea that women had rarely performed jobs outside the home that could compromise their hands, even though hundreds of thousands had previously worked in agriculture, textile mills, and other places where their hands were soiled regularly or damaged permanently. Soft skin on tender hands belonged to women of a certain socioeconomic class, or so the dominant culture assumed.

Women who held pink-collar positions—as office clerks, secretaries, and bank tellers—constantly had their ungloved hands on display to customers, colleagues, and supervisors. In many ways their hands endorsed the extent of their femininity, as they moved gracefully or awkwardly along typewriter keys and other office machinery. Although women had filled clerical positions for nearly half a century, the war accelerated the trend. They took certain places as men vacated them, with the U.S. government offering hundreds of thousands of desk jobs to those who could file, type, and take dictation. Gulielma Fell Alsop and Mary F. McBride described them in their 1943 handbook, *Arms and the Girl: A Guide to Personal Adjustment in War Work and War Marriage*: "Women have made office work their own, as they have made telephone work their own, by the qualities that are peculiarly women's: their quickness, their capacity for detail, their deftness, their alertness. Even in the Army and Navy the new women of the war are finding their secretarial positions."[5] In this atmosphere of political import and global implications, women's hands mattered more than ever before.

In addition to expanding the bureaucratic structure of war, American business was also forced to open its doors and offices to female employees. With the military draft taking its share of middle-class male clerks and salesmen, openings for women abounded in the consumer economy. Radio stations, insurance firms, and advertising agencies took on more women, but no business field became as "feminized" as banking. In 1932, 36,000 women had been in banking; by 1942, the figure had risen to 65,000, owing in part to the stabilization and growth of banks after New Deal policies such as the Federal Deposit Insurance Corporation (FDIC) were established. But the greatest growth in female employment took place at the height of the war, so that by the end of 1944 approximately 130,000 women were bank employees, constituting nearly half the nation's total bank personnel. An all-woman bank in Oklahoma got special attention in 1942, mainly for the employees' appearance. One reporter observed, "[I]nside the caged windows designated as teller, receiving, and the usual bank offices are bright feminine blouses, Victory bobs, red lacquered nails—women every one. The only men in range of vision are in the bank lobby waiting in line to transact business." Newly independent women—those employed in wage work for the first time or those who had to assume family financial responsibilities with husbands and fathers away—found themselves on the other side of caged windows as well. They wrote and deposited checks as never before. Advertisements revealed the realities of women's greater financial independence during the war years. JWT produced a series of advertisements for Irving Trust Company highlighting young women alone with their checkbooks. Another series that featured the growing connection between women and banking touted Eastman Kodak's Recordak photographic system, designed to produce facsimiles of records. Pitched as an especially helpful tool in an industry where much of workforce was "new to banking" and had been "hurriedly trained," Recordak would help businesses find the beginners' mistakes.[6]

Advertising companies dealt with women's entrance into business by recognizing the public's potential apprehension over it, then integrating these doubts into their clients' endorsements. The popular Fuller Brush Company selected its door-to-door saleswomen not solely on "intelligence" but equally on "poise and grooming." These last attributes must have mattered to their customers, since early reports noted not only their impressive sales, but the fact that customers often insisted the women "stay for tea." How a saleswoman or clerk kept her hands was conflated with her efficiency. In 1943 the fear that women would make mistakes was unabashed; by 1945, after they had become so firmly entrenched in the banking world as clerks and tellers, advertisements intimated less about female error and more about the burgeoning workloads their hands could not handle. Employers had to help women keep their hands beautiful by investing in technology to assist them. As female bank employees found themselves "swamped with paper work" and anticipated a postwar increase in transactions, Eastman Kodak promoted its photoduplicating machines as necessary since a woman had "only one pair of hands." The ads legitimated the presence of women in the banking industry while also characterizing their work as more manual than intellectual in nature.[7]

Housewives and mothers, whether or not they worked outside their homes, were pressured to maintain corporeal marks of the feminine ideal. Frequently pitched as advice on how to please children and husbands, the messages combined the domestic expectations with the nation's needs, namely that middle-class women created exteriors and attitudes to uplift everyone around them in the midst of war.

If looked at cynically, these entreaties could be seen as the emotion-filled propaganda of a nation not suffering on its home territory as its allies were; in other words, a "country virtually compelled to fight the war 'on imagination alone.'" Wide-circulation periodicals directed primarily at married middle-class women, such as *McCall's* and *LHJ*, ran many advertising messages to play on women's fears of displeasing their husbands or misdirecting their children. From January 1942 through the end of 1945, advertising's predilection to encourage faithfulness in marriage and attentiveness in motherhood was augmented by the quite public element of devotion to "the American Way of Life." Feature articles augmented the ads by encouraging mothers to devote their energy to their "primary" responsibilities and forego war work, lest they be responsible for exacerbating the growing problem of juvenile delinquency. Since the late nineteenth century, women's magazines had shaped and reflected middle-class attitudes about domestic roles, personal habits, and consumer behavior.[8]

During the war years the middle-class married woman's hands were sites of judgment about cultural standards and expectations. As extremities visible to the public, hands could reveal a great deal about a woman and serve to instruct other women. In the fall of 1942, Mrs. Leroy Washburn's testimonial about her "rough, red-horrid" hands warned *McCall's* readers about the unsightly effects of harsh dishwashing soaps. Washburn had managed to transform her "dishpan hands" in just a few days by using "gentle" LUX soap in her daily kitchen routine. The stunning results in "unretouched" photographs dominated Washburn's narrative of success, showing viewers that a dry, scabrous hand, even if well manicured, would find its place narrowly relegated. The "soft, smooth" improved hand, however, could make its way onto the chest lapel of a finely suited man (presumably that of Mr. Washburn, given the prominence of a wedding band in both images). The right product enabled this American wife to reconnect physically with her partner, restoring the idealized heterosexual relationship and its promises of intimacy.[9]

By mid-1943 military officers' wives starred in LUX ads, raising the stakes. *McCall's* readers learned that after an Army Air Corps lieutenant complained about his wife's "red hands," her rapid response with LUX visibly improved them in under a week (fig. 19). More importantly, the lieutenant's wife had restored her desirability as a companion. When coarse, her hands had been exiled to a game of solitaire; but softer, they appeared on a backgammon board. If forced to entertain herself or play "alone" due to unsightly hands, a solitary figure might arouse suspicion, leading neighbors to wonder about her peculiarity or, worse, her disinterest in home front activities. By softening her hands at a military officer's behest, this LUX user could strengthen her marriage and simultaneously guard what he and other men said they were fighting for—home and family. She

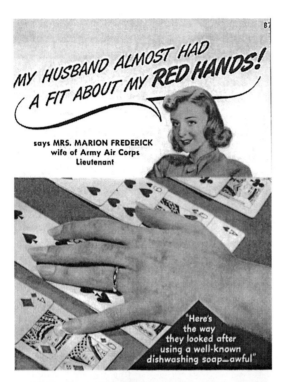

MY HUSBAND ALMOST HAD A FIT ABOUT MY RED HANDS!

says MRS. MARION FREDERICK
wife of Army Air Corps
Lieutenant

"Here's the way they looked after using a well-known dishwashing soap—awful"

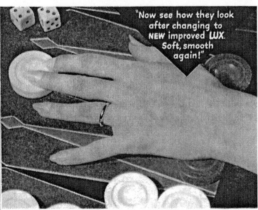

"Now see how they look after changing to NEW improved LUX. Soft, smooth again!"

Hands began to grow lovelier in 2 to 7 days

NEW IMPROVED

In the same familiar box— your dealer has it NOW!

● Scores of women proved in actual tests how easy it is to get rid of dishpan redness... simply changing from strong soaps to new, improved Lux does it, as these unretouched photographs show. Hands began to improve in from 2 to 7 days.

New, improved Lux is the *mildest ever made*—kinder than ever to hands. *Richer, longer-lasting suds! Thrifty!*

Figure 19. LUX advertisement for *McCall's*, April 1943. JWT Archives, Hartman Center, Duke University.

represented these social pillars. If she failed to uphold them, she weakened the larger war effort.[10]

What the LUX ad allowed, however, was the possibility of a backgammon competitor other than the woman's husband. Viewers saw only close-up images of the left hand, the discrete body part, first on the solitaire cards (the "before" image) and then on a backgammon board (the "after" photo). Who, in fact, could play the game with her after she achieved a "soft, smooth" look again? Viewers were left to speculate about the actual winner in this story—was it the disgruntled husband, the restored wife, or an unidentified backgammon partner? Given the rising incidence of extramarital affairs during the war years, the message could have been interpreted both literally and figuratively. That wives might enjoy some latitude while their spouses were away—and many did—remained a worrisome social issue.[11] But it coexisted with and was buoyed by thousands of seduction narratives in wide-circulation print advertising. These kept sexual allure and the prospect of sexual activity ever present, reinforcing the need for soldiers to see bodies and their disparate elements as worthy of their sacrifices.

The fragmentation of body parts during the war years may be attributed to the modernist aesthetic introduced a generation earlier and explored in several visual art forms. Revered art photographers Alfred Stieglitz and Edward Weston had disembodied their female subjects in hundreds of prints, most famously with their respective muses, Georgia O'Keeffe and Bertha Wardell. The highest paid advertising photographer in the 1930s, Margaret Bourke-White, had isolated the components of industrial machinery with intense lighting and close focus, imbuing them with a sensuality that evoked human figures. As a method of visual communication, fragmentation flourished in the American marketplace during the war years. Women's magazines featured isolated female body parts—like the hand in LUX advertisements—that as discrete elements could be sexualized. A number of cultural theorists have discussed the link between fragmentation and sexualization, but what remains the most compelling theme for this argument is feminist cultural critic Rosalind Coward's contention that once fragmented, a separate body part can then "come under the scrutiny of the ideal." Coward identifies these fragments as "new areas constructed as sensitive and sexual, capable of stimulation and excitement, capable of attracting attention" and therefore demanding "*work* and *products*."[12]

The "work" in the LUX advertisements seems to be relatively easy, a simple choice of one dishwashing product over another, used for a few days to elicit the preferred result. The ad text leaves unsaid the necessity of *continual* use of LUX in order to avoid grotesque, loathsome hands. Maintaining a particular level of desirability required not only consumer savvy but constancy, the development of habit.[13] Throughout the war, LUX advertisements featuring married women with "dishpan" hands appeared regularly in newspapers and popular women's magazines such as *LHJ* and *McCall's*. The presumption that loyal wives and faithful fiancées would reap great personal benefits from constant self-care applied to unattached women as well. If unpartnered through the war years, women could change their status to "married" by attaining the ideal presumed to be at the forefront of the male imagination. Moreover, faithfulness to their hands signified allegiance to a cultural model entwining femininity with political obligation. If they worked to reach the ideal by recognizing their shortcomings first then responding with corrective products, their spouses, sweethearts, and other American men would return home satisfied, as Madison Avenue advertisers promised.

A third tier of lifestyle magazines appealed primarily to upper- and upper-middle-class American women, or those who aspired to or dreamt of reaching such heights. Publications like *Cosmopolitan, Harper's Bazaar, Town & Country*, and *Vogue* wrapped their content primarily in the attribute of *elegance*, with pages revealing the signs of prestige, financial comfort, and leisure time. Images of sparkling jewels, fur coats, couture clothing, and fine furniture were designed to capture viewers' attention. The monthlies with higher-echelon audiences had to publish appeals to the urbane and sophisticated that went beyond the effects of dishwashing and other household chores that many upper-class women simply did not do. A *Harper's Bazaar* article on fashion for the 1944 fall season noted, "You'll pull on longer gloves of plaid or striped or plain wool jersey . . . or bold fur gauntlets to balance your fur hat . . . and, in the evening, real creations—long taupe satin gloves, tufted and ballooning over the elbow." Underneath those gloves would be exquisite hands such as those in a 1944 anti-inflation campaign message published in *Vogue* (fig. 20). In an image that likely appealed to a broad audience of American women due to its subtle suggestion of sacrifice, a delicate hand with slim fingers and carefully manicured nails lifts a chipped cup. The caption informs the viewer that this hand belongs to Mrs. Jones, a responsible household manager who resists wasting her family's resources during a time of national crisis. She "brings out" old dishes with "a thrill of pride," eschewing conspicuous consumption. The words aside, however, the image says to its viewers that Mrs. Jones devotes time and attention to maintaining her femininity by keeping her hands soft, her nails manicured, and her gestures elegant. Wartime shortages and hardships have not undermined Mrs. Jones's decorum, her pride in personal appearance, and consequently her American womanhood, which remains intact. The cup may be chipped but her hands and nails are in perfect condition.[14]

Mrs. Jones's younger counterpart in the comfortable middle class was an enthusiastic woman who appeared in Gerber Baby Foods advertisements. Pointing to herself with a brightly colored nail, she claimed to have meant a lot to the company

The chipped teacup of the PATRIOTIC Mrs. Jones

No matter who the guest—Mrs. Jones brings out her chipped teacup with no embarrassment. On the contrary, with a thrill of pride.

Not very pretty, that chip. But it bears witness to the fact that Mrs. Jones has her nation's welfare at heart.

Mrs. Jones has given up all unnecessary spending for the duration. By doing *without* —she is helping to fight inflation.

Maybe she doesn't know all the complicated theories about inflation. But she does know that her government has asked her *not to spend.*

So Mrs. Jones is making all the old things do . . . not only that teacup. She's wearing her clothes for another year—and another. She's not competing with her neighbors for merchandise of any sort.

And the dollars she's not spending now are safely put away (and earning interest) for the peacetime years ahead. *Then* those dollars will buy things that can't be had for any price today.

If we all are like Mrs. Jones, there will be no inflation with skyrocket prices. If we all are like her, dangerous Black Markets cannot exist.

A chipped teacup stands for all that . . . for a *sound, secure* U. S. A.

---

7 RULES FOR PATRIOTIC AMERICANS TO REMEMBER EVERY DAY

1. Buy only what you *absolutely need.* Make the article you have last longer by proper care. Avoid waste.

2. Pay no more than ceiling prices. Buy rationed goods only by exchanging stamps. (Rationing and ceiling prices are for *your* protection.)

3. Pay willingly any taxes that your country needs. (They are the cheapest way of paying for the war.)

4. Pay off your old debts—avoid making new ones.

5. Don't ask more money for the goods you sell or for the work you do. Higher prices come out of everybody's pocket—including *yours.*

6. Establish and maintain a savings account; maintain adequate life insurance.

7. Buy all the War Bonds you can—and hold 'em!

HELP US KEEP PRICES DOWN

Use it up . . . Wear it out . . . Make it do . . . Or do without

A United States War message prepared by the War Advertising Council; approved by the Office of War

Figure 20. Ad Council design for the Magazine Publishers of America. *Vogue*, August 1944. Ad*Access On-Line Project—Ad #w0004, Hartman Center, Duke University, http://library .duke.edu/digitalcollections/adaccess/.

because she had "much more money than the average to spend." Her adventurous spirit as a savvy consumer was matched by her purse, mirroring that of well-heeled Americans whose disposable incomes rose due to durable product shortages. New big-ticket items for domestic use were not on factory assembly lines, since heavy industry had successfully completed its conversion to a war production economy. Advertisements such as this revealed one of the undisputable trends in the American economy during World War II: with unemployment at an all-time low, the standard of living rose for women situated at several socioeconomic levels. Whether they spent their extra coins and dollars on movie tickets, salon services, or war bonds, they were vigorously appealed to in magazine advertising as consumers. But the Ad Council directed them to spend money on the right things. Whereas Mrs. Jones would have been viewed as frivolous albeit unpatriotic for splurging on a new set of china, the young mother who purchased Gerber Baby Food designated her dollars wisely, fulfilling the most sacred of her responsibilities—feeding her children. Both messages went beyond household expenditures, though, to herald American women physically defined by their elegant hands and expertly manicured nails.[15]

Just as industrial workers, wives, and mothers were to care about their hands and nails, so too were women in uniform. WASP flyer Marion Stegeman tried to keep hers "as well groomed as possible." WAC director Oveta Culp Hobby asked a subordinate to give her a quick manicure in the office after learning late one morning that she was to have lunch with General George C. Marshall and his wife. Even H. I. Phillips's fictional Wac, Arlene Applegate, complained, "What an all-out war does to a girl's hands!" The U.S. Marine Corps Women's Reserve (USMCWR) encouraged its female members to take advantage of nail polish, recommending they choose a shade to "match or blend with the scarlet hat cord." One recruitment pamphlet opened with the exclamation, "A touch of red makes a woman Marine's life different!" And from there, the enticements to join centered overwhelmingly on appearance. To root the solicitation in reality, a "sprightly young marine sergeant" offered a testimonial to the color's impact: "You have no idea how that touch of red peps us up and what it does for our morale. . . . Every girl spends lots of time on her make-up, her manicure and her hair dressing." Driven by the elements and language of fashion, the narrative reminded prospective recruits that they could become part of "a military organization with a long and glamorous record of achievement behind it." The USMCWR's willingness to disseminate such a message—one that fostered a time-consuming construction process of idealized womanhood—reveals the extent to which the wartime women's military organizations yearned to placate an American public wary of gender boundary erasure. Yet the Ad Council forthrightly warned advertisers "to avoid copy angles or pictures" that glamorized women in the WAC. Popular women's magazines sought to bridge the gap between women and military uniforms. In *Good Housekeeping*'s suggestions for women in the service, a specific entreaty on nails suggested they be "rounded to a moderate length." Without equivocation the editors warned, "Don't paint them luridly." To be taken seriously by her superiors and the public at large, the servicewoman was to adorn her hands with nothing more than a wedding ring, if she had one.[16]

What allowed the USMCWR promotions to encourage red nail polish while *Good Housekeeping* advised military women against it? A closer look at the composition of the respective military services for women provides some clues. The marines enlisted women who had at a minimum two years of college credit. WAVES required a high school diploma with college "strongly recommended," and banned all women of color for nearly two years. The WAC, on the other hand, was open to women, black and white, who had completed only two years of high school. As a result of the minimum standards for enlistment in these services, the WAC became home to a more ethnically and racially diverse population. It also enlisted women from a wider range of socioeconomic backgrounds, including those whose families could not afford to send them to college. Initially, WAVES training took place at Smith College in Massachusetts, while the WAC units went through basic training at U.S. Army camps. Would not then the stereotypes working against these women encourage more circumspection about nail paint? *Good Housekeeping* directed its instructions to women for whom flashy nails might be seen as "lurid" and perhaps even dangerous. Readers knew that in the past certain women had painted their nails with bright colors in order to attract paying customers. Despite the image lingering in the popular imagination, the U.S. military organizations had no standard policy on which all agreed. Individual officers could call out troops for violations, however, if they deemed their nail polish too unseemly for the unit.[17]

Another group of women crossing into previously all-male territory—players in the All-American Girls Professional Baseball League (AAGPBL)—learned how important their hands were in maintaining a certain image of femininity. The players were instructed to tend their nails daily, maintaining their length according to "the requirements of [their] play." They were to use "protective cream" to "keep hands soft and pliable."[18] With their hands on display in their numerous public appearances both on the field and off, these athletes were to reinforce the notion of all-American womanhood marked by youth, vigor, desirability, and respectability. The organization required "a high standard" of conduct as well as appearance because, as the members' charm school guide reminded them, they were "in the limelight." And although the limelight was national if measured by the media coverage they received, the league had its true center in the Midwest, where the teams played their games. League organizer Philip K. Wrigley, owner of the

Chicago Cubs, had not been able to interest professional baseball team owners outside the region to embrace a women's game. The league's "Victory Song" spoke to the overwhelmingly white, even "Nordic," character of its players. Cowritten by players Lavone "Pepper" Paire Davis and Nalda "Bird" Phillips, the verse emphasizing team members' diverse backgrounds reveals in fact their racial and ethnic limits: "We come from cities near and far, We've got Canadians, Irishmen and Swedes."[19] The references reinforced a mainstream identity for an organization testing the limits of femininity inside a traditionally male arena. If AAGPBL players could convince their fans and the public of their unsullied collective reputation, the new wartime entertainment might succeed.

Nail enamel had been on the American market since the early 1920s, but as Kathy Peiss points out, it "won acceptance slowly" among middle-class women who considered themselves "respectable." One professional who worked in advertising in the 1930s remembered that she considered nail varnish "extremely vulgar" at the time. And for girls and young women it remained even more so. One telling lesson, recorded by a high school senior in her diary, was a "nail polish removal" activity in her school's morning assembly on January 13, 1939. That one of her teachers reveled in such events struck the diarist strongly enough to describe the woman's gleeful response to the collective disciplinary action. These lessons in propriety distinguished good grooming and nail hygiene from garish displays of color. But by the 1940s, color for nails had become an acceptable and even desirable accessory to fashion, changing seasonally with clothing styles. As early as 1941, advertisements in *LIFE* magazine for everything from eyeglasses to automobiles showed women with brightly polished nails. And the women who wore them were not just society debutantes or showgirls. A young mother at her stove preparing Campbell's Vegetable Soup for her family and a housewife urging readers to buy coffee in glass jars wore red nails. As did the women on *LIFE*'s covers—a "government girl" at the U.S. Navy's Bureau of Supplies and Accounts, a woman modeling a spring hat, and college student Peggy Tippett, who learned how to knit sweaters in answer to an appeal made by the Citizens Committee for the Army and Navy. By the time the United States declared war, many American women had added nail polish to their beauty routines.[20]

In June 1942 the *Philadelphia Evening Bulletin* projected the kinds of questions American women would likely ponder while their nation fought a world war. They would ask about practical issues, such as the availability of canned baby food and kitchen ware, but they might also dwell on ethical questions with political overtones, including "How does nail polish help morale?" The queries appeared at the same time the War Production Board (WPB) sought to determine the "essentiality" of personal items. As cosmetics came under close scrutiny, all types of nail products were reviewed. In an April survey of women employees in the Office of Price Administration's Consumer Division in Baltimore, respondents were asked to identify their "primary" and "secondary" cosmetic needs. Of the 201 respondents who answered a questionnaire, 137 claimed nail polish a primary or secondary need. Those between the ages of twenty-five and forty considered it overwhelmingly more "primary" than those younger than twenty-five or over forty. Similarly, the nail polish wearers in their late twenties and thirties ranked nail polish remover as "primary." Another element in the survey asked women if they would be willing to purchase products in larger containers. Given the WPB's efforts to regulate and restrict the use of crucial materials on the home front, the production of bigger boxes and bottles would be more efficient and conceivably conserve a critical mass of plastics and metals. The WPB insisted that small sizes of particular cosmetics be eliminated altogether, recommending production and circulation of "half as many bottles and jars." Nail polish, however, was saved from this fate after being identified as "perishable." Nevertheless, all nail products containing tin oxide (enamels, pastes, and powders) were placed on a restricted list alongside other "essentially less needed cosmetics" or those requiring raw materials to an extent that they would "constitute a diversion from the war effort." To counter the potential fallout from these restrictions, the WPB estimated in mid-1943 that product reduction would not move below 64 percent of the current rates. Women who had come to enjoy the latest culturally sanctioned mark of feminine distinction—colorful nails—would benefit from the WPB's policy to allow some nail products to remain in full production for the duration of the war.[21]

Whether the WPB had depended significantly on women's opinions or not, the government scheme helped to ensure that the feminine ideal would include colorful nails. A 1944 anti-inflation campaign further sanctioned the notion with an illustration of a home front conservationist patching her charge's trousers with needle and thread in carefully manicured hands. Not superfluous, her polished nails could coexist with the patriotic sentiment urging viewers to *use it up, wear it out, make it do, or do without.* Corporate designers also used women's manicures to highlight various kitchen products and foods. After MacFadden Women's Group conducted a spring 1945 survey asking women what they wanted in the postwar market, one of the five featured responses was "After I get all the household things I need, I'd like to see improvements in cosmetics . . . especially nail polish and hand cream that will really stand dishwashing." By war's end, the American public would assume decorative nails to be standard in a woman's hand care regime.[22]

Cosmetics manufacturers, home appliance makers, and the OWI's graphic arts division all helped to popularize nail polish, but the examples set by Hollywood stars reigned supreme. Among the many body parts inviting viewers' scrutiny in

LIFE magazine's August 1941 boudoir portrait of Rita Hayworth were her hands (fig. 21). The slender, graceful fingers, resting on a white satin-draped thigh, show off long, darkly enameled nails. And although more has been written about the other elements of Hayworth's seductive pose, her sleek hands emphasize the cachet of nail color. Poised as a siren in this LIFE image, Hayworth was known to viewers for her roles as a call girl, an ex-girlfriend, and an accused murderer in films the previous year. But her career trajectory had already begun to change. While she could not shed entirely her on-screen reputation as seductress, Hayworth took different kinds of roles in the succeeding months that allowed her to be taken more seriously during the war years. When she appeared on LIFE magazine's January 1943 cover, she was more conservatively dressed than in 1941, but her dark fingernails remained, anchoring the photograph at its center.[23]

Hayworth's career, like those of many Hollywood actresses, took shape according to the owi's Bureau of Motion Pictures, a wartime creation determined to bring more respectable female characters to the screen, lionizing those who had risen to meet home front challenges. Since movies were "the nation's leading entertainment outlet" during World War II, with eighty to ninety million tickets sold each week, their messages reached deeply into the American population. In some industrial cities, where round-the-clock shifts kept workers coming and going at all hours, the movie theaters never closed. And most of their patrons were women. That Hollywood appealed to their dreams of romance, independence, and upward mobility, while warning them of illicitly gained prizes, revealed its complicity in shaping ideal womanhood on the home front. Film historians Clayton Koppes and Gregory Black maintain that during the war the owi "exerted an influence over an American mass medium never equaled before or since by a government agency."[24]

From 1942 on, even as the Bureau of Motion Pictures scrutinized every Hollywood film for morally suspect content, dark enamel appeared with increasing frequency on the nails of admirable female characters. In their varied roles, from loyal homemaker to inspirational patriot, these women wore painted nails. Posters and photographs advertising their films captured them in postures alluding to their characters' strengths, weaknesses, and allure.[25] These hearty, devoted characters joined the ranks of song-and-dance performers and morally ambiguous women whose dark nails had helped to denote their lightweight or wanton status in 1930s films. And although the latter types did not disappear from movies during the war, they were challenged by a new kind of antiheroine who enjoyed a heyday in the 1940s—the femme fatale. Characters in this vein dominated an increasingly popular wartime genre later dubbed film noir by French critics. Marked by psychological tension and confusion regarding guilt and innocence or good and evil, these stories introduced mysterious and often alluring women who engaged

Figure 21. Rita Hayworth. Photograph by Bob Landry. *LIFE*, August 11, 1941.

audience members' sympathies. They also provided female moviegoers with additional models to consider, those with sleek hands and darkly colored (and often sharp) nails. Shepherded by British director Alfred Hitchcock as well as his expatriate counterparts Billy Wilder, Otto Preminger, and Fritz Lang, these femmes fatales harbored secrets, lied convincingly, and suffered inner conflict and terror.[26] The actresses who portrayed them got wide coverage in fan magazines such as

Photoplay and *Modern Screen*, endorsing everything from bath soap to hand cream, parceling out advice to millions of young female readers.

As workplace and leisure time boundaries loosened for American women, messages swirled everywhere exhorting them to use their hands and nails to mark their femininity in the war effort. Some women employed in heavy industry were expected to meet a high standard given the nature of their work. When *LIFE* magazine ran a feature story on Boeing Aircraft employee Marguerite Kershner, it emphasized that she might return home from work with bruised hands and greasy nails, but by 6:30 the next morning, the author assured readers, "her hands will be smooth, her nails polished, her makeup and curls in order, for Marguerite is neither drudge nor slave but the heroine of a new order." Few workers followed the advice in *Independent Woman* that suggested, "If your long fingernails break, cut them off." In war boomtowns such as Evansville, Indiana, the expanding female population demanded manicures. One beauty shop operator noted that higher prices for manicures had not deterred Evansville's female population. In fact, she attributed the flood of calls for appointments to high wartime wages, admitting that women were willingly spending more on themselves.[27]

While *LIFE*'s heroine and others who looked like her could indulge themselves in painted nails, other women had to be more circumspect. Among those forced to negotiate the standard were African Americans who wished to advance in war work. The National Urban League touted the opportunities in heavy industry but warned prospective employees about tough personnel screeners who would look for reasons to turn them away. If lucky enough to reach the interview stage, having impressed screeners with their "neatness and cleanliness," black women were advised to follow a list of prescribed "don'ts" before meeting a personnel manager. Wearing "deep-red nail polish" and sporting "excessively long fingernails" came right behind chewing gum and leaning on the interviewer's desk as the worst offenses. These held a higher place on the "don'ts" list than outlandish jewelry and "lacy" clothes. The author concluded that employers would see a "chippy" and immediately link her to "laxity and inefficiency at the work bench." Such a "glamour girl" would lose out to her more sensibly presented counterparts 90 percent of the time, the advisor warned. The *Brown American* featured an ideal war worker named Georgia whose letter to her friend Bill focused on how much she had changed since joining the industrial workforce. More independent, self-sufficient, and time conscious, Georgia listed among her personal improvements her decision to "wear no nail polish." For black civilian women, brightly colored nails indicated a lack of seriousness and a threatening sexual expressiveness that could prevent them from the chance at upward mobility that factory work could provide. Although female office workers were not subject to the same scrutiny, all African

American working women were forced to be more cautious than white women about their appearance.[28]

Upper-middle-class women of color, however, enjoyed a wider berth with paint and polish, since financial success, respectability, and "society" networks secured their already-established reputations. Seen frequently on the covers of *Crisis*, such women could show off bright nails more acceptably than their working-class counterparts. *Crisis* featured highly stylized formal portraits of "A New York Secretary" and "Sarah Lawrence Student" on its covers in 1944 (see fig. 6). Photographed at M. Smith Studios in Harlem, these women and many like them had made countless preparations before sitting in front of Morgan and Marvin Smith's cameras.[29] Among their preliminaries were manicures with new, noticeably darker nail polish colors. Women whose pedigrees and college educations granted them status in the black community could get away with it. A college degree, a white-collar position, or a cover portrait on *Crisis* could determine or secure a woman's respectability.

By mid-war, as sacrifice became the predominant theme in American home front culture, the limits to which a woman's hands could show want had been set. Whether working or not, women were to keep their hands soft to the eye or touch. Volunteers in the U.S. military were to eschew flashiness, unless they were Marines, who could be expected to match nail polish to their uniform's red accents. Working-class women of color were to avoid bright nail polish, while middle-class homemakers were to keep their nails unchipped amid a variety of domestic tasks. Signing mortgages for clients, welding airplane parts, wielding a bat and glove, or preparing orders for fellow soldiers, women's hands were on public display as never before, and women were to pay close attention to them. From New York to Washington to Chicago to Hollywood, Americans fetishized women's hands during the war; yet the effects seem tame compared to the obsession with female legs.

By 1941 American women's legs had been exposed publicly for just a generation. Long skirts had covered them in the nineteenth century and before, whether the women spent their days enjoying long lunches and afternoon visits or working in fields and factories. The acceptance of visible ankles had moved slowly into mainstream culture in the early twentieth century. Female athletes who bicycled and played lawn tennis, feminists who marched for peace and suffrage, and women who fought against child labor and lynching and urban squalor found their active, purposeful lives aided by slightly shorter skirts, thus sanctioning the right to show a bit of lower leg. But another group of women exerted staggering influence on the wider exposure of female limbs and their subsequent sexualization—young, urban, working-class wage earners who became models of rebellion and independence.[30] Shorter skirts made their work less difficult and their leisure more exciting.

Many of these women labored in the garment industry, while others found one of an increasing number of places in clerical or service work. Saleswomen or "shop girls," maligned as "shoppies," stood behind department store counters for many hours daily with few breaks to rest their feet and legs. If unable or unwilling to pay streetcar fare, they walked to work. Extreme weather conditions in addition to the desire for an easier stride led them to raise their hems a few inches. Some allowed men to "treat" them to meals and entertainment in return for companionship or sexual favors. Middle-class guardians of morals and other critics viewed such expressions of independence and other behaviors as dangerous. This new generation of young, single women sought pleasure *in public* during their leisure hours, rather than spending time at home in domestic arts as their mothers and some of their middle-class sisters continued to do. Their activities helped to promote a model of heterosocial activity that blurred lines between male and female worlds, as well as work and leisure time.[31]

As their work lives influenced their free time, women's choices in entertainment informed their sexuality. The "cheap amusements" they sought put their legs on display. Coney Island, a wildly popular working-class destination in Brooklyn, featured rides and other entertainment "contrived to lift women's skirts and reveal their legs and underclothing." Romance, nudity, and sexual expression were the hallmarks of these attractions, further encouraging the development of a heterosocial culture in modern America. The sexually charged energy generated at amusement parks had its match in the single most important leisure activity for working women—dancing. In addition to their own enthusiastic participation at balls and social club dances, young women reveled in the performances they witnessed at musical revues and shows. Whether revealing their own legs or gazing at others on display, they yearned for entertainments in a culture that had gone "dance mad." In particular, the Ziegfeld Follies excited viewers with choreographed female flesh. Although Florenz Ziegfeld claimed to have "invented the American Girl," the scantily clad siren who paraded on stage in his lavish productions, he built on images already in circulation: postcards showing women both in and out of their lingerie, photographs of chorus girls posing as temptresses in their bath tubs, and "peep shows" with evocative titles such as "A Busy Day for the Corset Models."[32] In all of these mass culture media, the fine line between physical exposure and sexual awareness stimulated the American imagination.

In the 1920s and 1930s mass culture trends touched young women everywhere. Clara Bow, Joan Crawford, and other movie stars bared their legs on large screens scattered all over urban and rural America. Advertising enlarged its influence by developing methods that appealed increasingly to consumers' personal desires and sexual allure. One could find a world of luxury and places of mental escape in advertisements for tooth powder, face cream, and dinnerware, where women lounged in elegant gowns. These images of fantasy worlds were augmented by thousands of others as documentary photography came into vogue, as wire-transfer technology of images was perfected, and as a swelling number of glossy picture magazines exploded onto the American scene. *LIFE, Look,* and *Survey Graphic* showed ordinary American women going about their daily lives in much shorter skirts than their mothers had worn. Even U.S. government–sponsored documentary photographs—of women at a funeral in Appalachia, of a young wife stripping tobacco in Orange County, North Carolina, of elderly matrons cheering on the horses at Miami's Hialeah Race Track, and of teenaged fans at a Montana rodeo— proved that female legs had been unveiled for good.[33] With all of these forces at work, what had once been relegated to specific and limited spaces such as Coney Island had moved irreversibly into mainstream culture. What had seemed edgy or morally questionable in the early years of the century seemed tame by 1940. Nearly everyone could glimpse women's legs in some public venue.

Mere exposure did not presume automatic sexualization. But in the 1940s, deliberate efforts to eroticize and circulate the ideal female legs for common consumption and middle-class audiences escalated. Animators, advertisers, and other purveyors of popular culture remained the principal creators of this cultural phenomenon, with the U.S. government aiding the effort after the nation's declaration of war. Even a razor ad could admonish its female readers: "Let's Look at Your Legs—Everyone Else Does." One venue where women's limbs got tremendous exposure was *LIFE* magazine, a publication boasting circulation of several million each week. Its presentation of female legs in several photo-essays in 1941 established mainstream media's willingness to use women's bodies in increasingly more provocative ways to stimulate a range of appetites. As a measure, these narratives illuminated firmly circumscribed gender expectations, all of which promoted the importance of using women's bare legs publicly for sexual allure.[34]

In a January 1941 story entitled "Utah Sorority Regulates Leg Competition of Campus Flirts," readers learned that Chi Omega members at the state university reported women who used their legs to attract male attention. Aware of their success and attendant notoriety in the competition, offenders proudly posed for *LIFE's* photographer to document their "crimes"—sitting carelessly in a knee-length skirt, wearing a gym suit *outside* the college gymnasium, and lifting a dress to straighten a stocking. According to *LIFE's* reporter, such blatant activities stemmed from the fact that women outnumbered men on campus. Female legs served as the conduit for competition in a place where a skewed male–female ratio had attuned women to the role of sexual expression and its rewards. With its story, *LIFE* illuminated but did not directly acknowledge the national trend of declining male populations at coeducational institutions. The drain had begun after the 1940 Selective Service Act initiated a draft for men ages twenty-one to thirty-six, and patriotic fervor led others to join the U.S. military before being summoned. The lack of available men to date or marry would contribute to a frustrating social atmosphere for many young women. They no doubt became more acutely aware of honing their sexual attractions, but a popular media outlet such as *LIFE* could make the competition seem terribly stiff, if at the same time a source of humor. The magazine's promotion of heterosexuality shored up its role as a mainstream voice throughout the war.[35]

LIFE's tracking and promotion of female legs continued in the months leading up to U.S. entry into the war. In April viewers were treated to a tougher kind of female competition than the University of Utah surveillance. A photo-essay about a Los Angeles high school's ice hockey team featured an on-ice collision scene, with short-skirted athletes' legs and skates entangled. A postgame photo revealed a battered but smiling player happy to expose the bruises and scrapes on her thighs. Despite hockey's physical hazards, female players wore short skirts on the ice. Much like female baseball players' uniforms during the war, which were designed to mimic figure skaters' costumes, skirts marked gender boundaries even though they were impractical. Players' sacrifices for the sake of wholesome wartime entertainment meant lots of lacerations and similar injuries. Women could compete in the 1940s, but their sports had to provide spectators some titillating entertainment as well. *LIFE* magazine not only took full advantage of these gender-defined expectations; it promoted them.[36]

As objects of desire, women's legs were scrutinized carefully in other competitions as well. The New York Art Directors Club "Most Beautiful Legs" contest allowed *LIFE*'s designers to fragment female bodies in order to fetishize legs. In large black and white photographs, the six pairs of winning legs appeared side by side, the women having lifted their skirts to exhibit all from thigh to foot. These pictures allowed *LIFE* viewers to compare and judge for themselves. Would ordinary readers agree with the experts, those trained to recognize beauty and aesthetic form? Although photographs dominated the feature story, the text situated the place of women's legs in the cultural imagination. In a curious blend of nationalism and female objectification, the story highlighted America's responsibility for bringing "the lower limb to full recognition" due to the "unsurpassed excellence of U.S. legs." The reporter noted that the ancient Greeks had draped women's legs, that Renaissance painters had given them only "scant attention," and that nineteenth-century artists had "almost ignored" them. "It remained for America's athletic life to strengthen, lengthen and expose the limbs of its women, thus bringing to its full height the art of the leg." Here *LIFE* perpetuated the myth of the New World's demands for physical strength and the love of a strenuous life that had kept

Americans hearty and youthful. That these qualities allowed them to maintain a kind of innocence made the myth even more palatable. Female legs displayed under these pretenses could remain untainted, perhaps even noble, not like those exposed by penny arcade peep shows, vaudeville acts, and amusement park thrills. Whether any of the "Most Beautiful Legs" winners had personally experienced the strenuous life mattered little; they could expose their legs safely under the guise of American myth, which remained large enough to cover middle America's growing desire for "cheesecake" images.[37]

On campuses and at models' competitions, women's legs were revered for their sexual power and aesthetic qualities; yet the venue considered by many to be the final arbiter of national feminine beauty, determining what constituted "the ideal woman," was the Miss America pageant. Established in 1921 as means to attract tourists to Atlantic City, the spectacle had grown by 1941 to include contestants from all states. That year the Miss America pageant, a nonprofit corporate organization, gave participants what they desired more than prizes, a crown, or a robe: the chance "to publicize themselves in the hope of launching stage or movie careers." Given their aspirations, exposure at the pageant could open important doors for them. In September, LIFE photographer Joseph Smith accomplished "something of a feat" at the Miss America pre-pageant photo shoot. All previous official group portraits in Atlantic City had featured the competitors standing shoulder-to-shoulder in swimsuits, showing off their smiles, their state sashes, and other notable attributes. While Smith did demand the traditional group pose, he also asked contestants to do an about-face in their heels in order to give LIFE readers another view of the nation's collected beauty. A witty caption writer posited that the women were "presented here for the gratification of people who like to know what is going on behind the scenes."[38] This particular angle on the contestants, with its emphasis on their derrieres and what followed below, would portend one of the most instantly recognizable wartime images: Twentieth-Century Fox Studio star Betty Grable's full-length rear view pose (see fig. 25). But months before Grable's picture was widely known, Americans could view each state's ideal woman from behind.

Standing on its own without caption or text, Smith's photograph could have re-iterated the growing focus on women's legs as vehicles for scrutiny and sources of titillation. But the narrative accompanying the "rearview" angle worked to keep the American imagination within bounds. LIFE's Miss America story juxtaposed imagery of the swimsuit-clad contestants with an essay highlighting their solid, respectable family backgrounds. These women, it implied, were not chorus girls or shoppies or Atlantic City bathing beauties out on holiday as their predecessors had been. Rather, the new Miss Americas hailed from important families who had shaped the nation's political history. The captions announced: "Both Miss Iowa and Miss Delaware claim Thomas Jefferson as an ancestor, and Miss Mississippi claims both John Marshall and Robert E. Lee." The ancestors of other contestants had contributed to America's mythic frontier past. Miss California had "Indian" fighters in her lineage, and Miss Florida was a descendant of Davy Crockett, the iconic backwoodsman who died at the Alamo. Their direct connections to the nineteenth-century quest to "civilize" the continent fortified their own "whiteness," thus securing their rightful place in the 1941 Miss America pageant.[39] LIFE's narrative further solidified the pageant's racial and ethnic composition by emphasizing a third element in the contestants' backgrounds. Beyond the descendants of American political giants and Manifest Destiny's heroes were a few women singled out for their precolonial pasts. That Miss Colorado could "trace her ancestry back to 1600" and Miss Wisconsin descended from "the Lloyds of London" took them back generations before a United States existed, to the kind of Anglo-European heritage that many Americans preferred to have represent them. As the United States moved closer to war, the Miss America competition moved the culture a step closer to the idea that exposed female legs could be wholesome if attached to proper women. The path blazed at Coney Island forty years earlier had continued on the Atlantic City boardwalk, but now it meandered in a more respectable direction, LIFE suggested, where young women from middle- and upper-class families could safely pose almost nude for millions to consider and still keep their reputations intact.

Mainstream media had helped to expand the range of *whose* legs could be safely eroticized. The limbs no longer belonged only to show girls, bawdy women, or working-class sunbathers. On the eve of war, young white middle-class women could expose their legs and not suffer criticism. In fact, they would be praised, even more so if their competitive spirit yielded a victory, a crown, a scholarship, or male attention. After the United States declared war, women's legs were coopted by corporate America to meet a variety of goals, from raising awareness about rationed materials to keeping male soldiers' "morale" up. The U.S. government secured the cultural moment for bare legs after silk and nylon supplies were officially commandeered for the military. The War Production Board continued to limit domestic access to silk throughout the course of the war. As early as August 1941, LIFE had forecast "a drastic change in appearance" for the "female American leg" after all raw silk was diverted for parachute construction. The magazine eventually showed women how to create stylish legs without silk or nylon, including a "bare" option. For those who wished to trick an onlooker with the illusion of stockings, a penciled seam running the length of each leg could provoke curiosity. Their artistry might also invite closer scrutiny, enhancing or intensifying gazes upon their limbs. The combination of home front sacrifice and erotic appeal persisted throughout the war. Even professional women embraced the opportunity. When *Washington Times Herald* reporter Eileen Knapp donated her silk stockings to a Takoma Park Girl Scout troop's salvage campaign, the newspaper headline shouted, "Reporter Strips for Victory." A photographer captured Knapp in the act of peeling off a stocking, while a local campaign leader watched. With deeds such as this eroticized and sensationalized, behavior previously considered risqué could be deemed patriotic and therefore honorable.[40]

Government agencies and corporate advertising worked in conjunction to exploit female legs for the war effort. Together these entities gave full sanction to prurient scenarios. With social and sexual opportunities opening wider for women during the war, advertisers nudged along the new mores with suggestive themes using women's legs provocatively. As might be expected, wartime advertising depicted female legs in promotions for lingerie, foundation garments, stockings, and various laundry soaps for these delicate items. And whether subliminal or overt, the messages in these ads suggested and condoned exhibitionism, voyeurism, and desire. A 1942 newspaper ad for LUX demonstrates how these themes functioned. In a vertical layout a topsy-turvy woman pulls her skirt much higher than necessary in order to reveal a damaged stocking on her lower leg (fig. 22). At first glance she appears to be suspended in space, her head at the "foot" of the graphic and her feet in the air; but her body's angles, in particular her bent hips, show her to be reclining, although no bed, sofa, or floor visibly supports her. The seductive pose, with skirt gathered up to emphasize the legs, puts the figure in a vulnerable position; gravity could take her skirt further in the wrong direction if her hands fail to secure it. But could she in fact be trying to reveal even more? Crossed ankles and knees prevent morally objectionable exposure, but those gazing at the pose could envisage a sexual position, with the woman's legs and feet precariously suspended in midair. That the text bubble is attached to her legs instead of her mouth implies the absence of her natural voice; the animated legs/stockings wield control through their ability to speak. With a slight smile on her lips, the figure appears content. Eyes nearly closed, she confronts no one; nor would she be able to, since her position inhibits her awareness of being spied on. The hints of exhibitionism, the subject's muteness, and her inability to see her observer have rendered her almost powerless, making her a model object of desire. Although these qualities cast the image as erotic, the ad's didactic text and its context prevented it from being classified as pornography in 1942. After all, viewers read about proper laundering techniques for stockings. Moreover, the ad appeared in newspapers, not a venue that tended to test legal definitions of pornography. With the outpouring of glossy picture magazines in the 1930s, newspapers had to hold their own in the competition for

TIPS *on the new* RAYONS

RAYONS NEED GENTLE CARE! CUT DOWN RUNS THE LUX WAY!

The lovely new rayon stockings need *gentle* care—they're temporarily weak when wet. Lux them just as you do silks and nylons . . . gentle new, quick Lux saves stocking elasticity, cuts down costly runs.

1. **Lux in lukewarm suds** after *each* wearing to remove injurious perspiration. Avoid harsh soaps, cake-soap rubbing.

2. **Roll in a Turkish towel** to remove moisture . . . don't wring. Hang away from direct heat.

3. **Dry *thoroughly*** before wearing (24 to 48 hours).

New Quick LUX is thrifty . . . see how much one box will do!

Over 90% of all makers of stockings *(silk, nylon, rayon, cotton, wool)* **recommend LUX**

4679 (1942)

This advertisement appears in Newspapers—April

Figure 22. LUX advertisement for newspapers. April 1942. JWT Archives, Hartman Center, Duke University.

advertising dollars. By coopting the kind of imagery that magazines began running regularly in the early 1940s, newspapers could successfully compete for readership. During the war, both venues came to embrace the popular art of the "pin-up," contributing to the genre's seemingly innocuous nature.[41]

The colloquialism "pin-up" first appeared in *Webster's* in 1941. And although convincing arguments have shown the representational genre to have existed decades, even centuries, earlier, during the Second World War it reached new heights as millions of pin-up images circulated. In her history of the pin-up genre, Maria Elena Buszek points out its association "with mass reproduction, distribution, and consumption." Not surprisingly these were the principal home front issues that the U.S. government grappled with during the war years—mass (re)production of war materials, steady if rationed distribution of goods, and constant consumption of everything from lipstick to movies. The phrase "The American Way of Life," frequently invoked by moviemakers, official propagandists, corporate spokespersons, and ordinary citizens as something worth fighting for, usually translated to mean ready availability of goods and services for consumption. "Freedom from Want," one of the Four Freedoms announced by President Roosevelt at the 1943 Atlantic Conference and popularized by illustrator Norman Rockwell, meant for many Americans the freedom to consume.[42] The ubiquitous pin-up image, passed around and posted in windows, workrooms, bedrooms, barracks, and foot lockers, allowed the featured woman to be studied and consumed over and over again. The military bunk space surrounded by pin-up images became a cliché during the war, reinforced by photographs in *LIFE, Crisis,* and many other magazines.

Due to their public nature, pin-ups generally were not considered pornographic material during the war, despite some racy content. Cultural historian Casey Finch has placed these images outside the realm of pornography because they do not demonstrate a sexual act or present a sexual partner. Instead, they "negotiate a space that oscillates between portraiture and pornography." The "Tips on the New Rayons" ad did not meet the legal criteria for pornography since the featured woman was not engaged in a sexual act. Yet the power dynamic situated her in a vulnerable position, ripe for viewers' various uses. Historian Joanne Meyerowitz has shown that audiences in the early 1940s would have distinguished cheesecake representations from "borderline material," the more risqué imagery that employed partial or full nudity. In a celebrated case pitting Postmaster General Frank C. Walker against *Esquire* magazine for what he considered "obscene, lewd, and lascivious" images, female witnesses defended the magazine, suggesting that the titillating sketches would have no adverse effects on "normal" viewers. Such pictures "only corrupted the abnormal mind."[43] These case testimonies reveal the vital role of the audience in categorizing such illustrations. In the end, a person's psychological profile and motivation determined whether an image was pornographic or not.

A female character's inability to see, acknowledge, or confront those who might be stealing glances at her was a pervasive theme in print advertising during the war. In the male-dominated world of sales and marketing, the ogled woman came to be seen as a source of influence on both men and women. Dwight Koppes, an *LHJ* promotion manager, explained how this developed at his publication. In an essay for the October 1944 issue of the trade publication *Advertising & Selling*, Koppes described the evolution of an *LHJ* ad campaign dubbed "Never Underestimate the Power of a Woman." Early in the war the campaign almost died because it depicted women as brutish and physically coercive when negotiating with men, particularly their husbands. Then, as Koppes reported, a couple of smart editors, one of them a woman, pointed out that the real power of women failed to surface in the ads. After rethinking the campaign and devising ways to show "Feminine Influence," they created a "formula" to make situations both "familiar" and "amusing." In each new script, an "attractive" woman exerted "characteristically feminine" influence over a man, whose "masculine resistance" would "dissolve" because he enjoyed the effect.[44]

LHJ's "Never Underestimate the Power of a Woman" campaign reflected current events as well. A typical example portrayed an election-day scene at a voting booth, where several polling place officials—all men—stared goggle-eyed at the booth. Their attention was focused on the legs and high heels of a female voter, visible below the privacy curtain. That the officials had abandoned their administrative duties to stare drove home the message of this particular woman's power. The image met the *LHJ* requirement for humor while suggesting the influence of female legs to captivate. The ad's place in the principal publication for American marketing, *Advertising & Selling*, moved it beyond sexy legs and cheesecake imagery; it instructed advertisers to recognize the power of middle-class female consumers, millions of whom read the popular *LHJ*. If a viewer of the ad delighted only in its titillation factor, then the promotion accomplished its primary goal: to encourage popular culture's use of female bodies, especially women's legs, as forces of persuasion. But another significant if less obvious message in the ad said something about a woman's influence as a voter. An *LHJ* reader might have taken this message seriously enough to get herself to the polls on November 7, and if Koppes's team accomplished its objective to generate more "subtle" communications, she would take her duty seriously enough to dress up and show off her legs for the occasion. Those who bought advertising space in *LHJ* and those who read the magazine learned that "feminine influence," first and foremost, meant fashioning the ideal female body for the enjoyment of onlookers.[45]

Advertising giants who wrote copy for their clients to sell products and simultaneously promote the war effort continued throughout the war to create scenarios where women's legs could be the focus of cultural attention. This meant that the U.S. government not only benefited from but indirectly encouraged the public's voyeuristic tendencies. Although the JWT campaign promoting LUX soap powder for care of stockings often used testimonials from Broadway costume mistresses, stage actresses, and film stars, images of anonymous women circulated just as widely as those with famous names. One of these "unknown" women appeared in a sketch for a May 1944 newspaper promotion (fig. 23). The image featured a pair of long legs crossed at the knees, emerging from a woman's skirt and lace undergarments. The woman seems unaware of her exposure, but the viewer could not know since the model's entire upper body, save her manicured nails, is covered by an open newspaper. Identified by legs only, fragmented, the figure has been sexualized. As in *LHJ*'s November voting booth scene, the woman's legs became a site for potential voyeurs. The bold "headline" of the paper she reads—"Stocking News"— offers alternative messages: one, that women would be enthralled by any available information on stockings, given their scarcity on the home front, and two, that the same women might conflate "stocking" news with stock quotes. Beyond the narrative's possible meanings stands the ad's primary attraction: viewers' pleasure in their stolen peek at the preoccupied figure. The same principle that functioned in the turn-of-the-century peep shows worked here, yet the newspaper reader in 1944 could gaze on the woman's legs at a bus stop, a barbershop, or the breakfast table. Clandestine getaways to darkened arcades were unnecessary; anyone within view of a newspaper could participate. And if readers looked closely enough at the fine print, they might even feel compelled to "Fight Waste!" The government got its due—a public service message about water conservation—while larger appetites were heartily fed.[46]

No fantasy images drawn by human hands illuminated the shifting expectations for American women like the Varga Girls. Named for their creator, Alberto Vargas, a Peruvian-born artist who lived in New York, these images first appeared in *Esquire* magazine in late 1940. Vargas had begun "drawing" sultry Ziegfeld Follies girls in the 1920s and 1930s, then moved on to depict Hollywood stars. His first centerfold for *Esquire*, published in the October 1940 issue, transcended the more innocent, doe-eyed female caricatures in the "girlie cartoons" drawn by the magazine's popular artist George Petty. As Buszek has written, this appalled some *Esquire* devotees "for whom the Varga Girl reflected a decadence and sexual self-awareness absent in the Petty Girl." Vargas's centerfold image for *Esquire*, featuring a long-legged blonde in body-hugging lingerie, would foretell how the female body would be idealized during the war. Dubbed "faultless in limb and shaping"

STOCKING NEWS

Tests prove **LUX**ing makes
one pair of stockings equal **2 pair!**

Now you can help *one* pair of
stockings give the wear of *two*
—that's like getting an *extra*
pair every time you buy one!
Just Lux stockings after every
wearing. Luxing saves elasticity—cuts down runs.

Strain tests *proved* Luxed
stockings last twice as long!
They didn't go into runs nearly
so quickly as those rubbed with
cake soap or washed with a
strong soap. Rayon, nylon, silk
and cotton stockings all showed
similar results.

Give *your* stockings gentle
Lux care. Always dry rayons
24 to 48 hours.

FIGHT WASTE!

Use all the Lux you need to get rich suds,
but no more than you need. Don't use
more water than necessary. Wash stockings after undies in the same suds, to
make Lux go even further.

Over 90% of the makers of stockings recommend LUX

3813 (1944)
Newspapers—May

Figure 23. LUX advertisement for newspapers. May 1944. JWT Archives, Hartman Center,
Duke University.

by *The New Yorker* the next year, the Varga Girls exuded a sensuality that bespoke
sexual independence and maturity (fig. 24). And the circulation of these ideal if
sometimes frightening female forms increased exponentially after *Esquire* began
publishing a Varga Girl pin-up calendar and sending free magazines to American military personnel. When USO entertainer and comedian Bob Hope quipped,

Figure 24. "Varga Girl." Illustration by Alberto Vargas. *Esquire*, Military Edition, April 1944.

"Our American troops are ready to fight at the drop of an *Esquire*," audiences understood the substance behind the humor. The Varga Girl images stood as the driving force behind the Postmaster General's wartime pornography case against the magazine.[47]

Since *Esquire* magazine had a large female readership, and according to a 1940 reader poll the illustrations were the main attraction for them, women could use the magazine's images to help them determine where they might fit into a wartime culture with rapidly changing gender roles. Women were known to mimic and even parody the pin-up styles for other female audiences, so the Varga Girls' postures and styles offered various sources of inspiration. Beyond their physical attributes, the Varga Girls blended allure with patriotic spirit, often donning military attire or invoking war-related messages. The figures encouraged membership in the WAC and WAVES, and from their lips came expressions of home front support and sacrifice for the war effort. The combination of these traits led Buszek to label the Varga Girl "the modern war goddess" who became "an icon for the new, wartime ideals of women's sexuality."[48] If viewed as routes to empowerment, the women created by Vargas provide a vital chapter in the development of American women's sexuality. That women claimed these imaginary figures in order to shape more complex identities makes the magazine pin-up an important force in reconfiguration of political and social culture during the war years.

Advertising and pin-up art successfully employed women's bodies to bind together the federal government's needs and corporate America's goals. While urging readers to fight inflation or buy bonds, mainstream publications reinforced the role of eroticized female legs in a patriotic setting. Among these graphic clues were diagonals emphasizing the length of women's legs, as well as a variety of sensual postures in which the characters remained either unaware or slightly suspicious of their exposure. Varga Girls, LUX users, or many other created women served as icons that some could yearn for, others could attempt to model, and still others reject as too risqué in a decent society.

The idealized wartime woman conjured in the artist's imagination and drawn with ink or painted with watercolor was surpassed in popularity and influence by the pin-up photograph. The power of the photographic image to inform or persuade stemmed from its suggestion of reality. Unlike Vargas and other artists who used pen and brush to create human bodies, photographers employed bodies that existed in front of their camera lenses. They may have enhanced, exaggerated, or omitted some aspect of their subjects with bright lights, sharp angles, or tight frames, but the bodies remained. Even if Vargas had used his wife as a model for the Varga Girl, as he claimed to have done, his work stands apart from the photographer, who required that a woman appear before the lens with each exposure. Distinguished by its referent, a photograph induces us to think differently about an image because, as Roland Barthes reminds us, "*the thing has been there*." The wartime generation's belief in photography to capture real life, exhibit the truth, and inform meant that professional photographers wielded tremendous influence. The growth of the documentary genre in the 1920s and 1930s had enhanced their status. The photographers who posed women as potential pin-up photos emphasized the elements of corporeal appeal likely to motivate viewers on many levels. Betty Grable, the woman in the most famous wartime pin-up photograph, articulated her generation's use of such pictures when she said, "A lot of guys don't have any girl friends to fight for. I guess you could call us pin-up girls kind of an inspiration."[49]

No wartime photograph established a more indelible standard for women than Frank Powolny's 1943 studio publicity still of Grable (fig. 25).[50] The most widely circulated photographic image of an American woman during the war, the "pin-up" that helped to popularize the term, highlighted the former vaudeville dancer's legs. When later asked about her success in show business, Grable identified "two reasons" then quipped: "I'm standing on both of them." In 1943 *LIFE* magazine reported that her face appeared more often on screen than her legs "but the legs carried it there."[51] Her famous pose would help situate unveiled female legs as an acceptable site for mainstream America to use in its development of the wartime feminine ideal. As cultural historian Robert Westbrook has argued, Grable's physi-

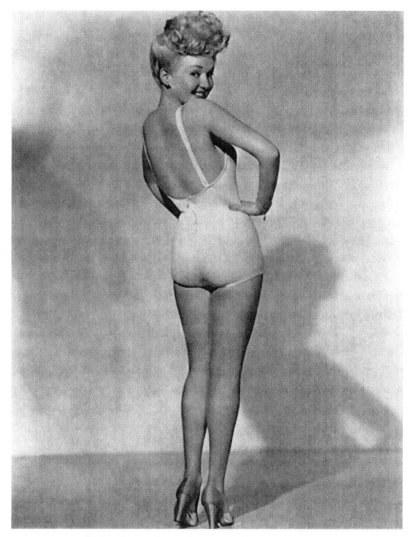

Figure 25. Betty Grable. Photograph by Frank Powolny for Twentieth-Century Fox, 1943.

cal appeal stemmed from two principal attributes: the "average" quality of her legs and her "whiteness."[52] Together these cast Grable as "the superior image of American womanhood" during the Second World War.

But Betty Grable's vulnerability in the famous pose also enhances her allure as the ideal woman. The rearview stance compromises Grable's balance, as she has shifted the upper half of her body slightly while turning her head more than 90 degrees in relation to her legs—all accomplished in shoes with three-and-a-half-inch heels, one of them off the floor. Even though viewers could intuit Grable's surroundings as the closed world of a studio, the nondescript backdrop fails to temper a pose casting her as physically defenseless. Feminist philosopher Carol Adams has linked modern "rear-entry" views of women with similarly designed images of animals, arguing that they urge consumers to identify women with animals and as a result, subject them to similar aggressive behavior.[53]

The gendered nature of Grable's posture can also be understood by examining an exercise that Adams conducts in her public lectures. After asking for a male volunteer to come to the stage and face the audience, Adams puts on the screen behind him an image of a female model in a position not unlike Grable's in its corporeal demands. The audience members must help the man (who cannot see the image) mimic the posture. They tell him where to put his hands, how to bend his knees and elbows, where to turn his head, how to cast his eyes and shift his hips, among a multitude of other instructions. How he maneuvers his legs is crucial, since they provide his balance. After a few minutes, the audience realizes it is prompting something akin to a contortionist's act. The young man teeters; in order to accomplish one facet of the pose, he wrecks another and grows frustrated with the medley of torturous mannerisms demanded of him. He is the only one in the room unaware that he is being asked to recreate a "normal" gendered body. The exercise highlights for him and the audience the range and extent of superficial postures required of modern women who attempt to meet society's requirements for corporeal femininity. In Grable's case, the lifelong dancer could balance herself easily, yet her posture made her easy prey, one who could stand temporarily but not walk or run too fast or far. A 1943 *LIFE* magazine story on Grable's legs iterated that "dancing [had] not made them muscular" nor did the star do any "special exercises" to keep "her figure shapely." Her wartime audience was to understand that Grable's appearance was natural, her body free from masculine characteristics and activities. If pin-up images like this one encouraged heterosexual fantasies among male military personnel, as historians John D'Emilio and Estelle Freedman have concluded, then women needed to add to their cadre of wartime postures a Grable-like style of vulnerability.[54]

Betty Grable's legs also provided a standard against which women could measure their own and determine how they wanted to use them. The 1943 *LIFE* magazine feature opened with two views, labeled bluntly "The legs, front" and "The legs, back." Captions offered factual information without commentary: "Betty Grable has an 18-in. thigh, 11-in. calf and 7-in. ankle; [legs] measure 15 in. from hip to knee, 14½ in. from knee to ankle." The close inspection and exacting measurements recall state fair competitions, where prize-winning cows and sheep win ribbons based on their appearance and model measurements; or thoroughbred horse sales, where the animals' dimensions and legs are closely scrutinized. American women who posed for their own pin-up style snapshots often unveiled or highlighted their legs, in keeping with Grable's prescription for stirring wartime imaginations. Faye Ross's photo gift to Ewart Shuler, who was stationed in Tokyo Bay in 1945, elicited a typical response: "That was the pin-up of all pin-ups. I really like that bathing suit that you're wearing." Whether a woman's intended audience was a spouse, a romantic interest, friends, or coworkers, the pin-up genre provided, in Buszek's opinion, "a model through which contemporary women on the home front could construct themselves: at once both conventionally feminine and subversively aware of her own power for sexual agency." LIFE magazine played up the former in its coverage of Grable.[55]

Betty Grable's "Great Average American Legs," as LIFE deemed them, assumed a life of their own in the magazine's photo-essay. Of the thirteen images that composed the "story," only two showed the actress's full body. The others, identified by Robert Westbrook as the "eleven decapitated photographs of Grable's legs," promoted the actress's daily life as ordinary—she steps into her shower, pulls on a stocking, sits at a soda fountain, climbs into her car, and poses for a photograph. To reiterate the "average" quality of Grable's legs, photo captions informed readers that they "walk, climb stairs, dance, and are generally flexed like other legs." Grable herself promoted her identity as a mixture of commonplace, disparate body parts, dismissing her hips as simply the place "where my legs hook on." The story's images and captions worked together to reinforce the seemingly unremarkable character of a high-paid Hollywood star's legs; that they were insured for one million dollars by Lloyd's of London was not mentioned. The popular conception of Grable as America's innocent "girl next door" set her apart from wartime goddesses such as the Varga Girls, whose overt sexuality and knowing gazes confronted and challenged viewers.[56]

Marriage and motherhood further raised Grable's modesty quotient in the public eye. The woman with the famous legs enhanced her power as a domestic model when she married trumpet player and big band leader Harry James in July 1943. Pregnant on her wedding day (like many wartime brides), she returned quickly from the Las Vegas nuptials to begin filming Pin Up Girl. The Grable-James union marked the convergence of two 1940s cultural phenomena—swing dance bands and patriotic Hollywood musicals. The chorus girl refashioned as the "girl next door" soon became a mother, foreshadowing the postwar feminine ideal: the innocent homemaker enthralled with her domestic world. LIFE's subsequent coverage of the Fox Studio star featured two large photographs on the same page, one of Grable and another of her seven-week-old daughter, Victoria Elizabeth James. Though not pictured together in either image, mother and baby struck similar poses—on their stomachs with legs stretched out full-length. The magazine layout, with its mirror images, suggested that the baby and the pin-up girl were inter-changeable—their suntanned bodies pure and innocent. Dark due to sun exposure only, *LIFE* emphasized, Grable's progeny possessed her mother's natural "white-ness." The captions further blurred the lines between adult and child, with Grable cast as a naïve young mother who liked "to dress the baby herself, as if playing with a doll." She enjoyed singing her current "favorite tune" to her infant, exclaim-ing "You're My Little Pin Up Girl." In *Our Mothers' War*, Emily Yellin notes that Grable "came the closest" to matching the three ideal wartime images of Ameri-can women in popular magazines—energetic career woman, desirable girlfriend and wife, and committed mother and homemaker—concluding, "Other women listened to Betty Grable and trusted her, and men loved her." *Photoplay* told its young largely working-class audience, "Girls who want to be brides should aim to be like Betty."[57] More than the "siren" images projected by Jane Russell, Rita Hayworth, Lana Turner, and the Varga Girls, Grable's sexual aura was carefully circumscribed to become a vital ingredient of ideal American womanhood. Mass media disseminated messages linking her "average" physical qualities with respect-ability, modesty, whiteness, and heterosexuality. All came together to produce an icon who would be described repeatedly, during the war years and later in memory, as "wholesome."

The descriptor became synonymous with Grable's wartime persona. In addition to Yellin's use and Westbrook's allusion, Grable biographer Doug Warren identi-fied a "magical wholesomeness" about his subject. In informal conversations I had with family members who fought in and lived through the Second World War, all used the term "wholesome" as their *first* adjective to describe Grable's appeal. My mother celebrated her tenth birthday the week that *LIFE* published its thirteen photographic angles of Betty Grable's legs. She lived in a world of adult conver-sation about the war, with two older brothers fighting in Europe and her only brother-in-law stationed in the Pacific. When we talked, she quickly followed up "wholesome" with "all-American" to describe Grable. In a separate conversation with my husband's parents, my father-in-law's first response to my query was that Grable was "wholesome," to which his wife replied in an amused tone, "I haven't heard you use that word in such a long time!" When I inquired about why Grable seemed to be more popular than other "pin-up girls," my father-in-law, a World War II Army Air Corps pilot, said he thought it was because she was a dancer when "song and dance" movies were at their peak. When I asked my mother about Grable's physical appearance, she described Grable as "not *too* curvaceous" but "not too thin either." Then voluntarily she returned to the notion of Grable's wholesomeness; comparing her to other pin-ups she exclaimed, "You didn't get the sense that she was ready to take her clothes off at any moment." That she admired

Grable's limited sexual expressiveness as appropriate for an "all-American" wartime woman hints at the actress's appeal as a patriotic role model, an image persisting in memory decades after the war. Those who knew Grable as a popular icon during the war years discussed her with a wistfulness, implying that whatever appealed to Americans then has since been lost. Grable's symbolic role in the 1940s served to stimulate desire but within limits.[58]

While their legs were more exposed than ever before, American women also covered their legs as never before. Pants became both stylish street wear and protective work attire for women during the Second World War. As the U.S. government recruited women to fill industrial jobs, information campaigns depicted current and prospective workers in trousers or coveralls (fig. 26). A nationally distributed War Manpower Commission recruitment poster featured women measuring, hammering, welding, and inspecting, among other home front tasks (fig. 27). All conduct their work in trousers except the food server, whose aproned uniform represents a field that became increasingly feminized during the war and would become even more so in the postwar years. Might this widespread de-gendering of female legs with traditional men's clothing have intensified the drive to feminize or sexualize them? Could the popularity of leggy pin-up images be attributed to their function as an antidote to the many trouser-covered limbs?

Urging real women to assume their patriotic duty by taking up war work, official images augmented popular privately commissioned drawings such as illustrator Norman Rockwell's "Rosie the Riveter" (fig. 28). On the cover of the May 29, 1943, issue of the *Saturday Evening Post*, Rockwell's Rosie appeared unfazed by her responsibilities. Her facial expression and head toss indicated confidence in her ability to help crush the Axis Powers, with a copy of *Mein Kampf* under her shoe. All of the war workers she represented would be celebrated the next year in a government-sponsored expression of gratitude: Cy Hungerford's sketch of a sailor, a soldier, and a pilot pointing to an image of a female war worker entitled simply "Their Real Pin-Up Girl" (fig. 29). Hungerford drew her in a three-quarter turn similar to Betty Grable's famous pose, head tilted, eyes cast down coyly on her admirers. The message suggested to women that underneath the masculine attire, the garb necessary for physically demanding and dangerous work, were the spirit and body of an American archetype. If the ubiquitous wartime phrase "for the duration" meant an expected return to life as it had been before the war, then the "*real pin-up girl*" wore the trappings of temporary rather than permanent change. A worker's trousers could be removed after her shift ended and replaced for good after the war ended, official propaganda insinuated. Buszek writes that "mixed messages" like these "represent an ominous shadow that followed all women's gains in the public sphere during this era." Real riveters might exude the same confidence in

Figure 26. "One of the many women employed at the giant Willow Run bomber plant operates a drill to bore holes in the 'Y' section of a supercharger bracket. Ford plant, Willow Run [Michigan]." Ann Rosener, July 1942. FSA-OWI Collection, Library of Congress (LC-USE6-D-005683), digital ID: fsa 8311136.

Figure 27. War Manpower Commission recruitment poster. Design by
Vernon Grant for OWI, 1944. RG 211, Records of the Bureau of Placement,
National Archives.

their work as Rockwell's Rosie, but the ideal woman would aspire to be a different
and softer kind of poster girl.[59]

The relative exposure or coverage of working women's legs invited media attention. As early as January 1942, a few weeks after the United States declared war,
workers in Southern California's defense and service industries revealed their
quick change from work togs to leisure clothes. *LIFE* magazine surveyed the Los
Angeles area for what it deemed "kids of the swing shift," the youngest of the 55,000
workers who "pour[ed] out of half a dozen huge plants" just after midnight. In-

Figure 28. Norman Rockwell's "Rosie" on *The Saturday Evening Post* cover, May 29, 1943. Reprinted by permission of the Norman Rockwell Family Agency, Copyright 1943, The Norman Rockwell Family Entities.

stead of going home to relax, they headed for the dance floors that remained open until five o'clock in the morning. Stockings rolled at midthigh, the young women demonstrated their swing moves, showing lots of leg in the euphoric atmosphere created by big band sounds.[60] Scenes like these circulated nationwide as the U.S. defense industry continued to grow and millions more women entered the world

Figure 29. Poster by Cy Hungerford, 1944. Prints and Photographs Division, Library of Congress (LC-USZC4–5601), digital ID: cph 3g05601.

of paid employment. Working-class women had long been viewed in America as more sexually available than their middle- and upper-class sisters, as had women of color. These pervasive stereotypes led to their widespread exploitation and abuse by employers as well as strangers. The fast-paced change in the wartime workforce, especially with the sudden employment of many more women, led to confusion about what distinguished "working-class" from "working." Would industrial plant employees whose fatter paychecks put them financially beyond their pink-collar counterparts still be considered working class and treated as such? And how were women whose desk jobs may have commanded more respect but not comparable remuneration now viewed? To temper social and economic changes, the nation's biggest home front club run by women for the benefit of men—the USO—instructed its hostesses to dress the part of respectable, middle-class women. The role required showing their legs in dresses, not too short and not too revealing, but just enticing enough to promote "wholesome" heterosocial activity.[61] Women's legs—as sights and sites—contributed to the overall confusion as thousands more women entered the world of paid employment and were in the public eye.

As hemlines edged upward and stockings disappeared, leg maintenance standards increased. Women who had tolerated their leg hair were urged to get rid of it. Razor use by upper-class women had escalated after World War I and become more popular in the 1920s and 1930s. In 1939 *Harper's Bazaar* beauty editor Elinor Guthrie Neff had instructed college women who wore ankle socks to use "some safe, dependable depilatory" and to do so "regularly—not just once in a blue moon as a kind of isolated experiment." She continued to encourage the hairless trend in the 1940s. The All-American Girls Professional Baseball League charm guide advised players to eliminate leg hair with "an odorless liquid cream" that could be showered off. And the American woman who donned another kind of uniform would incur similar scrutiny. Nearly all of the recruitment materials showed military women in skirts with knee-length hemlines revealing soldiers' and sailors' legs (fig. 30).[62]

Bare legs, trousered legs, the "Great Average American" legs—endless conversations, tensions, and worries about them denote the central place of women's legs in American home front culture during the Second World War. That legs could stimulate discussion and confer respectability, availability, and androgyny marks their power as both a reality and a discursive trope in the cultural landscape. Beyond the pin-ups, recruitment posters, magazine stories, and glossy advertisements were a few contemplative treatments of the subject. Novelist Zelda Popkin's exploration of the culture's fixation on legs appears early in *The Journey Home*. The protagonist, Air Force lieutenant Don Corbett, pursues his quest to find "beautiful girls," judging all of the women on the train by their legs. He is

Figure 30. WAVES recruitment poster. Design by John Falter, 1944. Collections of the Women's Memorial Foundation, Arlington, Virginia.

disappointed, for example, that "you couldn't see legs in the day coach. The tilt of the chairs, for visual purposes, sawed all the women in half." In another car, Corbett dismissed any woman in slacks, labeling her as either a "service wife" (if she wore a wedding band) or "kid sister" (if she wore no ring). An increasingly frustrated Corbett finally focuses his vision on an open Pullman car, where "X marked the spot. The X was a pair of superlative legs. They were slender with just enough of an arc at the calves, smooth at the ankles, without evident bones. They looked brown, nude, knee-dimpled and hairless, which meant that the stockings were sheer." Corbett stood "enjoying the legs, before the girl knew he was there." And after she looked up at him, he determined that "[h]er face matched the legs . . . perfect and lovely." Following some awkward initial remarks, Corbett asked "very seriously" if he could touch her legs: "He knew that he had to explain. 'It's been a long time since I've seen first-class American legs.' She studied his face for a moment and he saw her expression change, something like pity enter her eyes. She thrust her legs out." Corbett lightly caressed them, then the woman laughed, "Make you happy?" to which he replied "You bet." The flirtation continues in witty repartee until the two introduce themselves and shake hands. Immediately Corbett asks Nina Gilmore if he can touch her legs again. "She laughed. She raised her legs, held them straight out." Popkin's novel captured the "aesthetic truth" of this historical moment. Corbett's fantasy life, developed in a culture teeming with pin-ups and oozing with women's apparent sexual availability, transmogrified into reality. Like Corbett, many servicemen came to expect everyday life to match and fulfill such dreams.[63]

Between 1941 and 1945 female hands and legs were put on view in unprecedented ways. Blue-collar bodies came to mean a great deal more in the United States than they ever had before; to rescue women for their own sakes mattered somewhat, but to enhance their physical appearance by saving their extremities was politically efficacious, since high morale in the workplace meant more efficient war production. Young women on munitions assembly lines found their suffering limbs could be rescued by products. American women everywhere, including those whose mothers and grandmothers may have been protected from full-fledged corporeal commodification, witnessed the increasing sexualization of hands, nails, and legs during the war years. The trend took hold as these extremities were illustrated more commonly as discrete parts, confirming the central role of mass media and a modern aesthetic on this particular home front. Whether sketched in pen and ink or photographed with flashbulbs and film, the female subject was reproduced by the millions, generating contradictory messages about sexual expression and availability. Some women could afford to strike bolder poses than others; those safely ensconced in a bubble of middle-class respectability ironically came to enjoy a wider berth on this score.

Near the end of the war, a "readjustment" guide published by the U.S. government advised, "Let him know you are tired of living alone. . . . You want him to take charge. You want now to have your nails done."[64] Since wartime housing shortages had prevented most women from "living alone," the message actually encouraged a retreat from independence. That the official line linked a woman's surrender of power to a manicure foreshadowed where America's female citizenry might be headed. For many working women such a suggestion was preposterous, however, since a salon service was a luxury. Those who were forced to give up regular wages in industrial work would find disposable income elusive, the promise of postwar financial security compromised. Women would negotiate a postwar culture that determined its success on their appearance. Or perhaps just as important, cultural winds hinted, genuine victory would be measured by the extent to which women felt compelled to work on their hands, nails, and legs as construction projects for a cause more national than local, more collective than individual. These projects, part of a much larger framework of softening, sculpting, and cleaning, would yield worthy results if done right.

THREE

Pleasant Aromas and Good Scents

Cleansing the Body Politic

In April 1943 U.S. Labor Department field researcher Sara Buchanan completed a ten-page progress report on the state of housing for women war workers. Later published as Women's Bureau Special Bulletin Number 17, the document represented the final analysis of hundreds of interviews and surveys, as well as information that Buchanan and her staff at the Women's Bureau (WB) had gathered from newspapers and magazines the previous year. More groundwork had gone into this report than into any of the WB's sixteen previous special bulletins. What could justify such monumental expenditure of division members' time and energy? Was the subject of housing truly more crucial in the estimation of this U.S. Department of Labor agency than issues more clearly within its jurisdiction, such as workplace safety or job discrimination? Evidently so, as the report's opening statement pointed to "acute problems" and "grave" circumstances women faced when seeking places to live. Beyond typical overcrowding and substandard facilities, a more significant issue surfaced: boardinghouse keepers' general "aversion" to women—young industrial workers in particular—whom they considered the most undesirable of tenants.[1] What lay beneath this disdain for female boarders? Did the unfriendly, even combative, attitudes toward them reflect widespread sentiments in American culture, or was something else going on inside those home front households? This chapter addresses these questions by unveiling a web of connections linking employment, boardinghouse culture, and personal hygiene standards for women in wartime America.

Model womanhood depended on the extent to which real women managed to control what was considered naturally uncontrollable—the female body. Advertisements addressing personal cleanliness—of body and clothes—reveal the pressure on women to conform to a predetermined definition of femininity. The classed, raced, heterosexualized image of the ideal American woman gave some women opportunities to strive for it and perhaps secure safe places for themselves in the wartime and postwar culture; others would have to work much harder even to approach the ideal and had no guarantee of achieving it. Those willing to undertake "individual self-surveillance and self-correction" sustained an illusion of power while actually widening the purview of corporate America to instruct them on cleanliness.[2] Two widely disseminated magazine and newspaper advertising campaigns in the 1940s—one for Lux Toilet Soap and the other for LUX laundry soap—illuminate the relationship between controlling the female body and shaping ideal femininity.[3] Set against the broader context of American boardinghouse culture and U.S. government need in the early war years, these messages confirm an arresting home front incongruity: that individuals considered to be the nation's most *undesirable* housemates could at the same time be its most *desirable* women.

Before the United States entered the Second World War, Americans understood women's contributions to national security as tasks within the domestic realm. More than a year before the Pearl Harbor attack, National Defense Advisory Commission official Harriet Elliott articulated the appropriate role for women in the nation's "total defense" effort. With no mention of taking on paid work, her call centered on the responsibility "to build up a spiritual and physical reserve" for the future. This reserve could be constructed and maintained, Elliott argued, if each neighborhood child had a hot, nutritious meal every day and all community residents had sufficient recreational activities, thus relieving "the nervous tension and mental strain generated by daily front page[s]." She concluded that America could be made "impregnable" if its citizens were "sturdier in body, steadier in nerves, surer in living."[4] To meet these lofty goals, she enlisted the nation's women, especially its wives and mothers. But two years later, those same homemakers heard a different call from their government; national impregnability would require more than meal preparation and community theater. Women would have to step outside the realm of home, family, and neighborhood volunteer work in order to contribute more meaningfully to the defense effort.

"WOMEN WORKERS WILL WIN THE WAR" announced a War Manpower Commission (WMC) recruitment campaign late in 1942. Estimating that "the great majority" of some five million new workers in 1943 would have to be women, the WMC identified one hundred cities as "Critical War Areas." In order to avert a labor shortage disaster, the WMC hoped to bring what it identified as "widely dispersed" womanpower reserves into these "highly concentrated" industrial regions. The plan emphasized local recruitment in these areas, thus implying that fewer women would need to move from the homes *in which they already lived* in order to assume war jobs. In the previous months those reading popular magazines had been solicited to make civilian sacrifices, to join nurse-training programs, and to answer a "Girls for Washington jobs" appeal. These stories appeared after the Office of War Information (OWI) gently nudged magazine editors to rally women to the cause, igniting their sense of American "initiative." Thousands demonstrated such initiative by leaving their hometowns to join the war effort in numerous industrial areas. Of young women seeking chances, Mary R. Beard observed, "Girls literally in hordes decided that they could live the life of adventure, and by hook or by crook they flocked to war agencies asking for chances to enjoy a run around." Migration in 1942 was so staggering that the WMC decided to counter the great moving throng with a different kind of campaign, recruiting locals—"particularly housewives"—to take up paid work. Agency administrators considered it a possible solution to the chronic problems resulting from large-scale migration to industrial centers: overcrowded boardinghouses, makeshift accommodations, brimming sewers, limited water supplies, and hard-pressed local schools.[5]

From Baltimore to Seattle and numerous cities and towns in between, new workers' living conditions horrified long-time residents. In Portland, Oregon, community women "scorned" female shipyard workers who after a day's work came into town "dirty and tired." In Mobile, Alabama, migrants faced the derisive Depression-era moniker "Okies." One teacher berated them as "the lowest type of poor whites, these workers flocking in from the backwoods. They prefer to live in shacks and go barefoot. . . . Give them a good home and they wouldn't know what to do with it." In Detroit's notorious Willow Run community, perhaps the nation's worst "war boom" area, the employment rush at a nearby Ford Bomber Plant had resulted in "overcrowded and squalid living conditions" by late 1942. According to a county health department report, there were "3,000 workers housed in basements and garages and 13,000 in trailers, tents, and substandard rooms and houses." Sanitation facilities were either poor or nonexistent. By early 1943 a despondent Detroit housing official characterized the situation as one rapidly sliding from "desperate to hopeless." This contingent of American workers—willing to resettle anywhere that high wages and job security awaited them—included entire families, married men who had left their wives and children at home, and married women who had moved with their husbands but left their children behind with relatives.[6] But countless transients in the mobile population were unmarried women, attracted by promises of financial *and* personal independence.[7]

Perhaps no American city felt the overwhelming presence of young single women as acutely as Washington, D.C. In the nation's capital, burgeoning government agencies needed office workers, so propaganda efforts enticed prospective employees by connecting clerical and other service positions with "adventure, glamour, and romance." Thousands of women arrived in the spring of 1942, further pressing the area's already-limited housing space. Wartime writer Mercedes Rosebery said that "the spectacle in Washington" at this moment "staggered the imagination." Many Washington hotels limited stays to five nights; by the fall, it was down to three. Rumors about "impossible living conditions" were so fierce that several civil service veterans embarked on a summer recruiting tour to dispel the dismal reports and paint a cheerful picture for prospective female employees. In Atlanta the recruiters claimed that sensational stories about a housing shortage in the nation's capital were "just bosh," further pointing out that the Defense Housing Registry kept lists of available rooms and houses and could guarantee "to place all the girls in inspected living quarters." But it seemed that only astute advance planning could ensure a new arrival in the Capitol City of a government-approved bed. Traveling on her own put the newcomer at a disadvantage, as she might land in Washington with a suitcase in hand but no place to drop it. That she could find or keep a decent job was certain; perhaps her hometown U.S. Employment Service office had already placed her in a position. Whether she would find or keep a decent place to live was questionable, however. Washington newspapers caricatured such women in cartoons and essays, and the image of the bewildered newcomer so firmly ingrained itself in capital lore that tales of young women sleeping on park benches persisted throughout the war.[8]

What could women who had answered the nation's summons expect? When not sitting at desks, administering first aid, making office coffee, or sweeping floors, just where and in what conditions did they live? They could not depend on the promised "duration" housing. In the fall of 1942 the publicly funded construction of "girls' dormitories" in the Washington area was going slowly. Of the planned 15,000 "beds" for white women and 1,200 for black women, only a few were available. The huge Arlington Farms project in Northern Virginia, designed to accommodate 7,250 occupants, had been delayed due to shortages of materials and stood only 2–3 percent complete. The Stadium Armory project in East Potomac Park, as well as the one in Suitland, Maryland, reported a "small percentage" finished, while the Langston Stadium venue for African American women was a mere 5 percent complete. Six months later, a Women's Bureau special committee discovered that the few recently finished sections of "duration barracks" contained "non-descript, cheerless furnishings" that did more "to drive women away" than attract them.[9]

Women who traveled together to Washington, as some high school and college classmates did, could offer not only comfort and protection to one another but they also could pool their resources to rent an entire house for the group, if they could find a vacant one. The *Washington Post* featured such arrangements in a September 1942 story headlined, "No Housing Problem Here!" One "sextet of girls" shared a house at 5122 Nebraska Avenue, which they labeled "Club 5122," while eleven Texas women landed a five-bedroom home on Broad Branch Road for a manageable monthly rent of $175. The story emphasized the advantages of spacious quarters, recreation rooms, and hot meals. Both groups of women found these arrangements cheaper than boardinghouse rates, but perhaps more importantly, they enjoyed freedom from the watchful eye of a domineering matron or the unpleasant demeanor of a stingy in-house landlord. For many women in Washington, such overseers held powerful sway over their daily (and nightly) lives. But until sufficient public housing was constructed for them, most female workers had to contend with boardinghouses and the people who ran them.[10]

In residences operated by women for women only, rules were designed to uphold the occupants' respectability and moral character. At the Lodge for Girls on N Street NW, tenants enjoyed Sunday afternoon tea in a home appointed with antique cherry furniture, inviting fireplaces, and a grand piano. The lodge keeper, Miss Engle, who claimed to offer her renters "more than bread and meat," kept track of her renters' evening forays by requiring them to sign out on leaving and to sign in when they returned home. Tenants most comfortable with such strict oversight were college women, having experienced similar *in loco parentis* arrangements in their campus residence halls, and those who had lived previously in houses run by philanthropic institutions or religious charities. One renter who had found boardinghouses lacking in affection enjoyed Miss Engle's "personal interest" in her tenants. In nearby Baltimore the Margaret Bennett House quartered a similar clientele, primarily unmarried office workers in their twenties and early thirties. In addition to sleeping accommodations, each woman got three meals a day or two meals and a packed lunch—all for eight to ten dollars a week. No resident possessed a house key, since a supervisor was always on duty. If a tenant returned home after 1:00 a.m., she had to pay a fine for violating the house curfew. Operating under the principle that young women needed "strict codes of conduct" when entertaining, the house director required that all lights remain on and all parlor doors remain open when men were present. Private rooms were off-limits to male guests.[11]

The Lodge for Girls and the Margaret Bennett House operated in a tradition established in the late nineteenth century to protect the reputations and check the independence of young unmarried wage earners in urban America, who became known in the culture as "women adrift." Those who lived outside their family homes often chose lodgings with watchful matrons instead of commercial apartment buildings that offered single rooms and little oversight and, moreover, put tenants too near the paths of predatory men. The arrangements could prove beneficial if a landlady took a genuine interest in her tenants' health and welfare, becoming a sort of "surrogate family" for them. Some young women found it advantageous to build familial relationships in their lodgings in order to secure their reputations, for a woman alone signified moral laxity.[12]

Careful attention to tenants' nighttime and weekend activities may have flattered a few women, but many more found household scrutiny confining. The Washington Housing Association identified the "chief complaint against landladies" to be their unwillingness to "respect the privacy of the roomer, her mail, personal possessions, or her time." When the Women's Bureau determined that such conditions had become problematic, the agency printed a trifold brochure instructing the "the paid hostess" to maintain a "businesslike" relationship with her "paying guests." In addition to providing lists of charges and written receipts, the ideal householder would respect her tenants' "personal rights," and not interfere with telephone calls or mail. And she was to offer advice "only if requested." The suggestions were directed particularly at landladies who rented to female workers. Such heavy oversight had been a source of boarders' complaints for years by women feeling their "sense of self-respect" challenged by rule setters and enforcers.[13]

Although white women faced problems when seeking adequate and pleasant accommodations, their African American counterparts in Washington fared even worse. Kept out of most boardinghouses by segregation laws, they confronted a host of challenges in the city. They had "only 3 decent places to eat" in the nation's capital, reported Francis McPeek, who headed the social welfare department of the Washington Federation of Churches. John H. Johnson, who began publishing *Negro Digest* in 1942, noted that "the only public place a Black could get a meal" in Washington was the train station.[14] Virulent race baiters in the halls of Congress intensified the atmosphere with their rhetoric. U.S. Senator Theodore Bilbo from Mississippi railed against conditions in the nation's capital, where he identified "the most disgusting thing" as seeing "nice sweet girls from North Dakota being forced to use the same stool and toilets used by the Negroes who come from the slums of Washington, a large percentage of them affected by Negro diseases." Bilbo's comment reflected the feelings of many outspoken political leaders who sustained and disseminated stereotypes of the "the uncleanly black woman." But it also reveals his categorization of working women in the wartime capital: "white" women were pink-collar newcomers while black women constituted the city's resident underclass. He failed to recognize the influx of middle-class African Americans who had moved to Washington for war work. Moreover, he lionized a rural America he saw as "white." He could easily have invoked his own home state or any other largely rural southern state, but his message required a locus whose racial demographics were understood at the time. His own Mississippi would not have worked in his message, nor would South Carolina, Louisiana, New Mexico, or any state with substantial populations of African Americans, Native Americans, Asian Americans, or Hispanic Americans. Bilbo's "nice sweet girls" were raced as white, his rhetoric made clear. While his may have been a reactionary voice in racial politics, he openly stated what many Americans only whispered or assumed: that African Americans and racial "others" were inherently smellier and dirtier, lacking moral standards and therefore more likely to spread sexually transmitted diseases.

For traditional racial purists, segregationists, and others who were appalled by wartime social and economic mobility, the "[f]ear of bodily closeness was real."[15] Historian Eileen Boris has argued that African Americans' quest for social equality in home front employment intensified conflict in workplace restrooms, where employees inevitably saw one another. The increasing number of female bodies required to run a burgeoning wartime bureaucracy pressed the American imagination, which fomented discriminatory racialized structures on many fronts where real people lived.[16]

Although the number of black in-migrants to Washington, D.C., was considerably lower than that of whites in 1942, their room-and-board options were almost nonexistent. African American women workers desperate for lodging faced exclusion even by middle-class black families, who did not want to open their homes to them. Francis McPeek reported that due to the entrenched "caste system" in the black community, D.C.'s resident middle-class families refused even to "assist" female workers, let alone take them in. Class stratification in urban black communities was not unique to Washington, but it was indicative of strains in American urban areas where earlier in-migration of rural African Americans had frustrated longtime black residents who considered themselves more respectable and civilized, and who viewed less-sophisticated newcomers as threats to hard-fought gains toward social and political equality. In the 1940s their prejudices extended to college-educated professionals who took advantage of better-paying war work. Morehouse College sociologist Walter Chivers identified the critical "sermonizing" directed toward them, in the forms of "shame on you" for turning away from "opportunity for service" in the African American community. Many black schoolteachers who had left their teaching positions to fill clerical positions in federal government offices soon returned to their classrooms because they found "high society" unwilling to "extend the 'right hand of fellowship' to stenographers and clerks." To add insult to injury, their counterparts in the Women's Army Corps received praise for similar secretarial work. Juggling opportunities for personal economic security with pressures to uphold community responsibilities, African American women on the home front were in an exceptionally awkward position.[17]

Yet war work proved seductive for thousands. African American women in San Francisco's East Bay community felt a "social permission" to venture out and explore war mobilization work opportunities and enjoy greater freedom and independence not allowed by traditional gender boundaries, especially if they had moved to California from the rural South. In the New York metropolitan area black women took advantage of narrow openings in the societal fabric to assert themselves as both workers and consumers. One New York war worker wrote about living accommodations, "There are absolutely no vacancies. I wonder what the newcomer's [*sic*] are doing for sleeping space." About her search for a larger apartment to share with a friend, she said, "We knew others out of our set were having housing problems but we did not expect to join their ranks."[18] Housing proved one of the nation's biggest wartime challenges for young women engaged in pink-, blue-, and white-collar work.

Acute conditions in Washington, D.C., and other boom areas may seem exceptional given the concentrated influx of working women there, but they were indicative of a significant national problem: the exclusion from private housing faced by "young unattached" women in every region of the country during the first eighteen months of the war.[19] If they had not been lucky enough to find one of the few sympathetic if ever-watchful matrons who carried out their patriotic duty with middle-class propriety (as at the Lodge for Girls in Washington), women were forced to rely on typical households with advertised vacancies. And here they faced the worst discrimination. In Evansville, Indiana, where the number of female workers increased 450 percent from July 1942 to January 1943, landlords preferred not to rent to women because they suspected them of "immorality." Other Indiana observers claimed that women were "more work than men roomers" and "more 'trouble' around the house." In Scottsbluff, Nebraska, one respondent to a housing questionnaire wrote emphatically, "Give me *men* every time," adding that women were "harder to suit" and "not so tidy!!!" From Buffalo, New York, to High Point, North Carolina, and Casper, Wyoming, homeowners expressed unabashed prejudice against female boarders, and as a result, they would not rent rooms to them. Their reasons ranged widely—they claimed that women were more likely to get ill and "require attention"; that they were "careless" with the furniture, spotting sofas with soda pop or burning holes in chairs with their cigarettes; that some (especially office workers and college graduates) were too "particular" about the accommodations offered; and that unlike men, they expected "to use the whole house." Reasons for barring them were as specific as one woman's declaration, "Don't want other women in [the] house"; or they could be as vague as another householder's response: "the usual."[20]

One former rooming house operator baldly stated her complaints in an essay entitled, "The Awful Type of People That Clutter Up a House." Although she and her husband had rented rooms to married couples, as well as to unmarried men, her horror stories cast single women as the worst villains. In fact, apart from one couple who marred a good mahogany table by breaking ice on it every morning, the most despicable offenders were female. One had stolen the mistress's prized Italian cameo, another invited her boyfriend to spend every Sunday at the house, and three others "became ill from abortions." But the most sensational account described a seemingly "sweet and refined" woman who had arrived with three heavy suitcases filled, she claimed, with books. As the resident grew distant and reclusive, the landlady thought they were "housing a maniac" and so called the police. The officers determined the renter was not crazy but merely a "dope peddler." The boardinghouse keeper-turned-essayist concluded that "sweet and lovely" roomers were "surely in the minority." She signed herself "Mrs. Fair Minded."[21]

The colorful home front accounts of women's foibles, from the annoying to the criminal, illuminate the overwhelming desire of homeowners to keep women out of their houses and to justify their actions. But would male tenants not also be tempted to pocket a piece of jewelry or carelessly drop a cigarette butt or keep a sloppy room? Of course they would, but none of these weaknesses constituted a cultural bias against them, because they were not perceived *as a distinctive group* to engage in the most egregious and common offense committed by female roomers: too much laundry. From the East Coast to the West, from the South to the Midwest, one complaint about female residents dominated all others, making boardinghouse keepers "reluctant to accept" them. The transgressors "washed and ironed constantly." Men, on the other hand, "don't wash anything but themselves," reported one landlady. A Wyoming householder said that women caused "inconvenience amounting to nuisance" with their laundry. That they hung their "personal wash in conspicuous places" made a Petersburg, Virginia, landlord uncomfortable enough to avoid taking in female roomers again. After extensive research, the Women's Bureau officially identified female tenants' desire for such "privileges" as the chief reason for the "pronounced aversion" to them.[22]

If simple aggravation and embarrassing impropriety had been the only explanations that homeowners provided, the government's wartime propaganda machine might have been able to appeal to their patriotism during a time of national crisis. The OWI prompted the Outdoor Advertising Association of America to include small "Share Your Home" panels on billboards nationwide but particularly in areas with war industries. However, householders' frank opinions proved that they did not view their contribution as civically inspired volunteerism but instead as "a purely business matter." Margaret Ford, of the Baltimore Defense Homes Registry Office, stated plainly that landladies opened their homes because they wanted "the money." So, for these wartime entrepreneurs, renting to women was lousy business—they simply used too much water and electricity. And since they needed space to hang up their damp clothes, many refused to share a room with two or three other people, as landlords claimed men were willing to do. To counter this resistance and entice homeowners to take war workers into their homes, the federal government offered loans for home improvements. In several cities, local War Housing Center employees helped homeowners convert their properties into "rental quarters."[23]

Rules, responsibilities, and obligations dominated the American home front. Lists of "do's and don'ts" appeared everywhere, in store windows, local newspapers, national magazines, and on radio broadcasts. Boardinghouse culture reflected this larger trend toward tighter regulation of everyday life. The WB distributed to prospective female renters a list of "obligations of courtesy and consideration." Second only to keeping one's room neat was using care with one's laundry—the pamphlet instructed, "Do your wash at the proper time. Remember others must share the hot water." That laundry commanded such a prominent place in the prescriptive literature reveals its significance in young women's lives, as well as its propensity to agitate landlords. Radio announcer Kenneth Banghart's astute advice to prospective tenants included a strong suggestion that they examine the house bathroom before making a commitment to rent a room. If the landlord had posted little handwritten notes such as "No clothes drying on the shower rod" or "50-cent extra charge if light left on," then a roomer could expect an irksome existence. "He'll pester you all the time. Every day he will announce some silly-ass new rule," Banghart added. In one filthy, roach- and rat-infested Washington house, bathroom signs were "plentiful"; however, the landlady always enjoyed full occupancy. The house's proximity to government offices made it attractive, but perhaps even more important to its female tenants were the privileges offered: the landlady "allowed clothes to be washed in the bathrooms" and to extend her generosity further, she "levied no additional charge for hot water."[24] The women who lived in this house could overlook its squalor to enjoy rights that were denied them elsewhere. The trade-off must have seemed worth it. Looser regulations meant extended boundaries for women, including the freedom to perform what they considered ordinary tasks in daily living.

In the housing surveys distributed by the Women's Bureau through local American Association of University Women chapters, one respondent described washing and ironing as "a necessary part of a young woman's routine." Considered alongside the impassioned responses from other boardinghouse keepers, this acute observation helps to clarify the role of laundry in women's lives. That washing and ironing were deemed essential rather than optional to women suggests something about their perceptions of who they were or desired to be. In addition to the common cultural understanding that they needed and wanted to wash their clothes frequently was another practice identified and borne out by boardinghouse complaints as decidedly female: a propensity to take "long baths." Addressed as well by the Women's Bureau in its prescriptive literature to tenants, which recommended they show their "efficiency" in bathing, young women's habits could cause discord in a household, particularly if they disrupted the bathroom schedule.[25] Maintaining a surface tidiness appeared to be a vital responsibility for women, one duty among many in a variegated web of self-construction. The web contained threads that when woven together constituted an archetype of ideal femininity—a raced, classed body that might in reality be reachable by a few if only for brief moments. For most, however, the model stood outside their grasp. Deemed "others" due to lower socioeconomic class status, non-Anglo antecedents, or compromised sexuality, many women saw a goal that would require even greater effort to accomplish since they were working against well-entrenched cultural stereotypes rather than actual conditions. As Rickie Solinger points out, health workers and law enforcement personnel "used racist distinctions to draw a thick line between white, middle-class women and others. In professional journals, at charity agencies, in the courts, and elsewhere, experts described the sexuality of poor women and women of color as hot, rapacious, and dangerous." During the Second World War, black, immigrant, and working-class women contended against persistent images casting them as inherently dirty, smelly, and diseased.[26] By contrast, the feminine ideal depicted in mainstream discourse remained a fair-complexioned, fragrant, middle-class woman in her twenties.

Given the relationship between women and their personal laundry and bathing, several questions arise. What did the washing of clothes and bodies mean to them? Would regular and attentive cleansing take on greater import than indifferent care? Was there something beyond mere cleanliness to be gained by incessant laundering and extensive bathing? When viewed as "constraints" or compulsions, bathing and laundry habits reveal the lengths to which women went to establish their fitness for acceptance and full participation in mainstream heterosexual culture (fig. 31). In their desire to meet a preferred standard of womanhood, many attempted to create and sustain, quite literally, "bodies that matter[ed]."[27]

Messages regarding the "necessary" habits of young women emanated from many quarters. As we have seen, boardinghouse keepers' presumptions, their rules, and their resulting discrimination against women supplied one set of directives, while the U.S. government, in its attempts to assist both householders and female tenants, provided yet another group of prescriptions. But some of the most telling impressions were generated by corporate America in advertising campaigns. Product promotions directed at women, unmarried young women in particular, dramatize the potentially powerful force of self-regulation. To become a desirable player in one's social circle or in the larger culture, a woman needed to devote unyielding attention to personal cleanliness. Careful scrutiny was even linked to the extent of one's patriotism, although this connection was not widely exploited in advertising until 1944, where it flourished until long after Japan's surrender.[28] But in the first years of the war, amid rapid change and home front mobilization, corporate America's appeals to women about hygiene encouraged extensive use of

Figure 31. "Girl Chemists at Home. The apartment of Harriet Raynor and Mary Perta, technicians in the laboratories of the Standard Oil Development Company at Bayway Refinery, Elizabeth, N.J. Because she is very short, Mary Perta must stand on the wash basin to hang up her stockings." Esther Bubley for Standard Oil Co., May 1944. RG 208, National Archives Still Picture Branch (#LO-19J-7282).

soaps and detergents. While boardinghouse water could be monitored and limited by homeowners, soap was plentiful. In the midst of shortages and rationing on other fronts, cleansing products could be found on market shelves virtually untouched by government regulation. A War Production Board committee determined that despite the essential materials needed to produce it, soap could "well be considered next in human importance to food, clothing, shelter, and medicine," since it was "universally used daily" by all Americans "for the sake of cleanliness and health."[29] Government officials could hardly interfere with individual self-regulation if it helped to achieve weightier public goals, such as domestic social order in the midst of international crisis. Soap advertisements encouraged oversight, while linking cleanliness with traditional gender roles, consumer happiness, and national strength.

The desirable woman in the guise of a feminine archetype had proved a mainstay in advertising campaigns for several decades, for the J. Walter Thompson Company (JWT) in particular. Synonymous with women's products, the agency's name and storied history included such clients as the Pond's Extract Company, the Andrew Jergens Company, and Julius Kayser and Company, makers of silk gloves and underwear. The agency's unqualified embrace of female audiences began as early as 1908 when Helen Lansdowne went to work as the only copywriter in JWT's Cincinnati office. Three-and-a-half years later she moved to the New York office to plan national campaigns, while continuing to supply what she called "the feminine point of view," an attempt to ensure "that the idea, the wording, and the illustrating were effective for women," she said. An early example of her vision was the Woodbury's facial soap slogan "A Skin You Love to Touch," which according to Jennifer Scanlon introduced a "muted sexuality" that "created a sensation."[30] It also put forward a heterosexual model for romance and emotional fulfillment that would drive many of JWT's most successful advertising campaigns over the next thirty years.

A few months after Lansdowne married JWT executive Stanley Resor in 1917, she traveled to Washington to assist Food Administration organizer Herbert Hoover with a publicity campaign designed "to rouse every woman in America to a sense of her responsibility in winning the war." While Helen Lansdowne Resor helped shape propaganda for an ever-growing government bureaucracy in the First World War, she also breathed life into a new JWT account: Lever Brothers' LUX Flakes. Her strategy emphasized the laundry soap's suitability for "fine fabrics," linking it to elite customers whose clothing deserved delicate care. When JWT acquired the Lux Toilet Soap account in 1925, Resor put into motion the game plan for which she later became best known—using famous names and faces to sell beauty products to women. Her unwavering dedication to "believable" endorsement advertising carried JWT through a Depression-ridden American economy in the 1930s and into the war years, when an inspired cadre of female copywriters continued to generate the company's successful testimonial-driven ad campaigns.[31] In addition to using American socialites as advocates, JWT capitalized on the cachet of Hollywood celebrities and New York theater stars. The company's seductive images of film and stage personalities embracing Lux Toilet Soap clearly revealed what constituted ideal femininity in American culture in the early 1940s.

Lux Toilet Soap ads focused on body or complexion care and often a combination of both. A typical layout included a glamour shot of the star, a catchy headline followed by a brief instructional narrative, a small inset image of the product, and a picture of an "ordinary girl" who, after following the advice of a film icon, finds herself in the arms of an adoring man. The ad texts generated an air of authenticity, attributable in part to the star endorsements but also to the fictitious romantic encounters of the American Everywoman, who was often cast as a wide-eyed innocent needing advice from an older, experienced woman. Quantitative data added weight to the celebrity's testimonial, stating simply: "9 out of 10 Screen Stars use Lux Toilet Soap," a line first used in 1928 to link the product to the newest mass media influence.[32] Even if a viewer were not convinced by the actress's story or the anonymous young woman's smile, she might easily be persuaded by the more "scientific" evidence in the advertisement: the impressive numbers. The knowledge that such an overwhelming majority of desirable women used Lux would no doubt encourage her to join the preferred group, while at the same time she might wonder who constituted the other 10 percent, those who chose less popular brands. Should she risk casting herself in that small minority, siding with the sole one out of ten who did not use Lux soap? If she took that chance, what exactly did she risk, and would it be worth the cost? Beyond the numbers lay the irrefutable answer—her allure as a woman. Embedded in the Lux Toilet Soap advertisements' words and images, messages intimated how women could counter potential threats to ideal femininity. Allusions to a mysterious "charm" identified as "daintiness" appeared in each advertisement, promoting a powerful theme intended to resonate in a reader's mind long after she had tossed aside her magazine or newspaper.[33]

Among the many Hollywood stars who appeared in Lux Toilet Soap ads to extol the value of daintiness was Marlene Dietrich. Known for her sultry seductive characters in films tellingly titled *Blonde Venus* (1932), *The Devil Is a Woman* (1935), *Desire* (1936), and *Seven Sinners* (1940), Dietrich assumed quite different roles once the war began. Unlike the vamps she had portrayed earlier, Dietrich headlined the romantic comedy in 1942 entitled *The Lady Is Willing*. The protagonist is a stage star who yearns for a child, has an abandoned baby surprisingly appear in her life, and then learns she cannot adopt the child because she is unmarried. An attempted marriage of convenience eventually yields love, giving the tale and home front audiences a "happily ever after" conclusion. Such endings became a Hollywood staple during the war, as the OWI's Bureau of Motion Pictures reviewed every script, approved acceptable narratives, disapproved others, and made editorial changes necessary to keep American morale high.[34] In the Lux Toilet Soap ad starring Dietrich, steps to a "happy" ending appear in several places (fig. 32). In the image, the actress perches on the edge of a sleek, modern tub, wearing glittering high-heeled mules and a fur-accented bathrobe. In one hand she holds a bar of Lux Toilet Soap, the key to her "luxurious daily beauty bath." Dietrich's clothing and her surroundings bespeak material comfort, while her pose and slightly parted lips connote seduction. Her words, however, provide depth to this stereotypical image of modern

Figure 32. Lux Toilet Soap advertisement for magazines. 1942. JWT Archives, Hartman Center, Duke University.

feminine sexuality, in that they transmit a secret that movie stars possess—how to "protect" an "important charm" identified as "daintiness."

Although Dietrich does not explain what characterizes this physical state or allure, her prescription for achieving it demands that a woman bathe every day using Lux soap. Three separate references to a "daily" bath appear, two by Dietrich and one by an unidentified young woman in the lower right corner. To fail to carry out this necessary activity—to "neglect daintiness"—would yield grim consequences, since a woman could not then "expect Romance." Poor self-surveillance would result in loneliness, understood to mean the absence of male companionship and attention. The Lux advertisement iconically expresses a heterosexual model in the inset graphic, where the young woman's romantic fulfillment involves a male figure cast as a stranger. The viewer cannot see his eyes and therefore cannot know him. And since his chiseled facial features remain slightly obscured in shadow, mystery and a touch of danger characterize this section of the ad. The ordinary woman's contentment can be attributed largely to her earnest self-scrutiny, which has been guided by women who know well the formula for romance. After following their advice, she can proclaim their wisdom on this subject—"Screen Stars Are Right!"—suggesting that her own story has a happy ending.

Dietrich's testimonial claimed that Lux Toilet Soap removed "every trace of dust and dirt," easily discernible offenders in the quest for daintiness. Given the increasing presence of women in munitions factories, in offices and shops, and in train stations and bus terminals, their chances of accumulating dust and dirt had multiplied, as had the likelihood of their being seen in public wearing the collected grime. WAC mechanic Aileen Kilgore noted that long hours at difficult and dirty work meant that she and her fellow Wacs made their way around the base "saluting hither and yon with greasy paws and dirty faces." Women's military organizations remained sensitive to concerns about the cleanliness and appearance of their members, with recruitment literature emphasizing maintenance of a "well-groomed look" and the preservation of femininity inside a military uniform. If U.S. Marine Mary Cugini's reaction to "personal hygiene" instruction at Camp Lejeune, North Carolina, indicates the military's dedication on this front, then reality matched propaganda. Cugini wrote to her sister, "They teach you everything you can think of . . . forgetting nothing." Mary promised to let her sister in on the secrets after returning home since writing it "would sound vulgar." For women in military uniform, uncleanliness was linked to a disinterest in ideal womanhood and a propensity toward sexually aggressive behaviors. All of the services emphasized elements of femininity in troop training and in recruitment propaganda as a means of checking rumors about lesbianism on the one hand and heterosexual promiscuity on the other.[35]

What observers saw, however, would not be nearly as offensive as what they smelled, Lux storylines insinuated. Not only does Marlene Dietrich claim that Lux Toilet Soap guarantees "skin that's fresh and sweet," but the smiling young woman in the lower right corner of the advertisement tells readers they will "love the delicate perfume" it leaves. Fighting odors generated and emitted by the female body appears equally if not more crucial than removing surface soil, as anything ill smelling seriously challenges the desired state: daintiness. In *Femininity*, Susan Brownmiller identifies the ultimate feminine "aroma" as nearly impossible to achieve since "femininity exists on a plane of enchantment where the air is rarefied and sweet." Set against traditional views of the female body as it was perceived in most patriarchal cultures, femininity then would be a near-impossible achievement. As Janet Price and Margrit Shildrick point out, "The very fact that women are able in general to menstruate, to develop another body unseen within their own, to give birth, and to lactate is enough to suggest a potentially dangerous volatility that marks the female body as out of control." As a result it "demands attention and invites regulation." Cleansing rituals dating back hundreds of years attempted to check the elements that made women's bodies suspect.[36]

As a modern industrialized, urbanized America emerged at the turn of the twentieth century, working-class women were considered even less clean than their mothers before them and became identified as natural disease carriers. These stereotypes persisted through the 1920s and 1930s, and during the Second World War "the disease/deviance discourse expanded and was applied more broadly across race and class," argues Marilyn Hegarty. In part this was due to increased scrutiny and fear of women's sexual promiscuity, both imagined and real. Heightened awareness of sexual independence intersected with the nation's need to produce healthy male bodies for the military, leading to a discourse that "cast all women in the role of potential seducers, disease carriers, and friends of the enemy," maintains Elizabeth Clement. A bevy of government-issued posters warned against women who would spread venereal disease, exhorting men with such lines as "She May Look Clean—But . . ."[37] The senses could be fooled; eyes could only detect so much. For women, only their constant watch and preemptive care could counter the corporeal forces and fluids capable of altering them and potentially endangering men in uniform and ultimately the nation. Women could work against this, corporate advertising suggested, by carefully choosing soaps and using them often in an attempt to reach the standards for model womanhood. But the "charm" of daintiness remained ethereal and at the highest stage of femininity, unattainable.

Another layer of meaning in Lux Toilet Soap advertisements contradicted the notion that daintiness could be achieved by attentive daily bathing. For some women, daintiness was a natural state requiring protection. If lost or compromised, a woman's future could be changed, lessening or eliminating her chances of finding a suitable male companion. Although most viewers of the 1942 Lux Toilet Soap advertisements would not have known that the ad campaign's catchword, "dainty," originated in the Middle Ages, the text nevertheless hinted at a young woman's responsibility to "protect" something of worth that she possessed, cherishing it as a prize to be offered at an opportune time. Definitions of "dainty" highlight the genius of the Lux Toilet Soap campaign, which to some readers might have conjured visions of "something choice or pleasing," while to others it could have been something "attractively prepared and served." A more contemporary and common meaning would have appealed to most readers, though, who could have imagined a body "marked by delicate or diminutive beauty, form, or grace." Taken together, the definitions suggest anything to be appreciated or admired and therefore objectified; but delicacy required protection, lest it be defiled in some way or forfeited altogether. Yet only certain women could reach the feminine ideal where an illusion of cleanliness remained the principal measure. Others might strive—lower-class women, for example, or anyone considered socially inferior due to their identification with an African American, Native American, or Hispanic community—but since they stood outside the narrow confines of the dominant image of female beauty, daintiness would continue to elude them.[38]

Women who pursued the ephemeral quality of daintiness would presumably avoid "anything rough" by demonstrating a conscious effort toward delicacy in their bathing activities. Since Lux soap "gently caress[ed] the skin," it could cleanse a body without damaging it, as film icons made explicit. Actress Rita Hayworth, for example, referred to the "gentle, white" nature of Lux, invoking a decades-old pairing of two attributes deemed important to middle-class Americans and those who were climbing the socioeconomic ladder to join them. The virtues of "white" soaps had been touted since the mid-nineteenth century in consumer culture, but they developed widely during the height of the scientific racism movement that lifted Anglo-Saxon ancestry above all other genealogies in the late 1800s. Such ordering of human groups coincided with industrial development, the rise of the urban middle classes, large-scale immigration from southern and eastern Europe, and increasingly tighter social segregation rules for Americans identified as "colored." Political and social rhetoric about the inferiority of certain groups turned on varying degrees of "civilization," one mark of which was cleanliness. As Juliann Sivulka has argued, since "appearance and character were considered to be commensurate, the beauty of white skin and soap-and-water rituals expressed Anglo-Saxon virtues and civilization and marked a distinction within social classes." To strive for whiteness meant an embrace of middle-class moral standards and habits, including frequent bathing. Companies offered white soaps with seemingly magical qualities that promised to wash away dark skin and all of the dirt and roughness it presumably carried. Regular washing with a gentle, white soap, then, could bring users closer to a model of whiteness and civilization imposed by social elites. That "gentle" and "white" were linked together in soap advertising indicated the persistence of racial stereotyping in the 1940s.[39]

Pitched as a woman's ally in her daily campaign against signs of roughness, dust, and dirt, Lux Toilet Soap also claimed to make the battle relatively simple. The ad copy headline, in Dietrich's words, announced: "It's easy to make daintiness SURE." In other Lux advertisements that year, a focus on the near effortlessness of creating a desirable feminine body meant a great deal, especially when landlords and boardinghouse keepers limited one's bathroom time or rationed hot water. Using Lux Toilet Soap would guarantee the right sexual appeal as well as make a woman the ideal "paying guest" who showed her "efficiency" by finishing her bath "in the allotted time."[40] Relative ease did not signify carelessness, however, but certainty. To "make daintiness SURE" took little effort, the JWT ad campaign stressed.

How would a woman know if she had reached the desired state? The true measure would be determined not solely by her act of daily bathing, but by attracting and keeping a man. Lux Toilet Soap campaign headlines graduated from pressuring women "to make daintiness SURE" to instructing them on "how to win out" in the field of romance. Finding a man had become a competitive sport on the American home front, as thousands of men were mobilized, first leaving for stateside military camps, then shipping out overseas. Given the presumed scarcity of available men, Lux Toilet Soap could provide a much-needed edge in the struggle to snag one. New tactics in the evolving campaign reflected and promoted increasing cultural pressure on women to secure male companionship. In a widely distributed Lux promotion in the fall of 1943, the star endorser, Diana Barrymore, offers a step-by-step plan designed to help women succeed at romance (fig. 33). In the narrative, a woman receives a telephone call from a man she has "had [her] eye on." After he asks her for a date, she is instructed to "go into action" to prepare herself for the meeting. There is no suggestion that Lux helped her get the initial phone call, but it could certainly help her secure a relationship with the man on the other end of the line, if she chooses to enlist it as an ally. The first step then involves a conscious decision on her part to act so that she will "look irresistible" and, even more importantly, as the ad emphasizes, she will "*feel* it." Having made the psychological leap necessary to take the challenge, she then carries out step two of the plan, cleansing her body in a "refreshing Lux Toilet Soap beauty bath." Suggesting that a woman's busy schedule might not allow such indulgence, the actress's instructions recommend that she "take time out" for it. A boardinghouse roomer who took this step may have felt the tension between pursuing ultimate cleanliness and honoring the government's recommendations about "efficiency" in bathing. If she monopolized the bathroom, she could annoy a cranky landlord or frustrate her housemates. If she had to pay a few cents extra for her extravagant use of hot water, the trade-off of "feeling like a million" might have been worth it. But whether she

Figure 33. Lux Toilet Soap advertisement for magazines. August and September 1943. JWT Archives, Hartman Center, Duke University.

had achieved daintiness in the timely and costly process would be determined later in the evening and not by her.

As the advertisements made clear, once a woman found a suitable admirer, *he* would offer the final verdict on whether she had successfully achieved the ultimate objective. In "How To Win Out on Romance," the woman's bright smile gives way to a much more serious countenance, one that is both contemplative and inquisitive in the face of her companion. The caption suggests she is seeking his "approval," the true measure of whether her action plan will proceed successfully. Here the Lux ad defined gender role responsibilities as well as boundaries. Viewers learned that men did not use the word "daintiness." Instead, a man would likely utter, "You're sweet," or indicate approval "in his eyes" if his companion had eradicated offensive odors and surface grime. He may not have known or used the *language* of ideal femininity, but his judgment would determine it. His response, rather than a woman's opinion about herself, sealed her fate in the game of romance.

By 1943 the desired romantic tryst evinced in Lux advertising featured not a handsome dark stranger in after-six formal wear, but a man in uniform, and more often than not, an officer. The step-by-step plan of action described in the endorsement by Diana Barrymore included the outline of a man in military dress. Since he was not fleshed out with paint and ink like his female counterpart, he stood apart as a type even more than she did. One widely distributed 1943 newspaper promotion showed a smiling young woman embracing a man in uniform. The viewer saw only the back of his neatly barbered neck and his dress-whites, as the dreamy-eyed woman rested her head on his shoulder, her chin on his epaulet. The image bespoke a common theme that appeared more frequently in advertising after 1943—that young women waiting on the home front for returning or prospective sweethearts could expect them to show up as officers. Those who had sufficiently dedicated themselves to a U.S. military victory could even boost their respectability and socioeconomic status, if they needed to, by "marrying up." In wartime advertising, such success stories (whether fictional or real) often translated into text copy featuring wedding engagements of women to military officers.[41]

If Lux Toilet Soap ads linked women romantically with men of rank, Lux ads directed at men more often employed images of the ordinary enlistee or draftee. Issues of *Our Army* and *Our Navy* in 1942 reveal a large Lux campaign, complete with cartoon graphics and funny verses about why some guys got dates and others missed out. The key, Lux soap, was the only similarity these ads shared with the campaign targeted at women. The gender-specific promotions presented stark tonal contrasts; while a young woman without a date was a tragic figure, a young man similarly deprived was a comical character. Her situation implied loss in the guise of not winning an important contest, a fact that could seriously affect her future, but his situation appeared nonthreatening, a source of joviality for him and his merry pals, who planned to divulge the Lux "secret" to him. Throughout the war such hilarity characterized Lux ads geared toward men, especially those who read military magazines. For them, Lux soap was anything but gentle—"fast as a P-51, thorough as a bulldozer," promised a November 1944 advertisement.[42]

The gendered campaigns for Lux Toilet Soap clearly delineated the masculine from the feminine in perspective, language, tone, and iconography. Throughout the war these differences intensified, so that by the spring of 1945 a young woman who took a daily bath with Lux soap might still need additional assistance in capturing an officer (fig. 34). No longer content to wait for face-to-face approval, as were the female characters in earlier ads, one of the featured women prepares to pounce on an unsuspecting man in uniform with her large net. Perhaps the scene indicates cultural acceptance of independence for women or their ability to take the initiative in the romance game, but given the history of the Lux Toilet Soap campaign, it more likely encouraged women to take risks if they felt desperation in the quest for male companionship. In nearly every direction they turned, women saw or heard about a dwindling pool of marriageable men, leading to a "particularly pernicious fear" among young women that they "would lose out to their younger sisters if they deferred marriage very long." Experts lectured on grim "marital prospects." Popular literature created an atmosphere for such desperation with mid-1945 headlines warning women, "In Marriage, It's a Man's Market!" and "Somebody's after Your Man!"[43] The warnings simultaneously encouraged heterosexual relationships as the most desirable and most fulfilling in postwar culture, and not just because they resulted from personal initiative in hard-fought competition, but more importantly because these "romances" were rewards for correctly using the weapons of femininity—the right products—to achieve a larger victory. Following well-laid battle plans could yield satisfying results.

To strive for the ideal womanhood was a challenge posed to millions who saw Lux Toilet Soap ads during the war. If they aspired to enjoy romantic lives similar to the ones they viewed on the big screen or read about in popular fiction, they no doubt heeded the advice about daily bathing in order to fend off odors. But washing the body was only one half of the self-surveillance equation in the field of cleanliness. If the female body could wield such power, then it no doubt could contaminate whatever touched it, most significantly, intimate apparel. A woman's underclothes became potential adversaries; working against her, they could compromise her femininity and put her social life in jeopardy. They could block her efforts to create a body that mattered.

Where women provoked some of the most passionate responses about their efforts at cleanliness, as we have seen, was on the subject of their laundry. If board-

Figure 34. Lux Toilet Soap advertisement for magazines. March and April 1945. JWT Archives, Hartman Center, Duke University.

inghouse keepers railed against it, the WB tried to regulate it, and women expected to do it often, then where did wartime advertising come into the picture? Or more aptly, how did Madison Avenue's most powerful voice to women contribute to one of the sorest domestic squabbles in home front America? With a brilliant campaign for Lever Brothers seen in millions of copies of newspapers and popular magazines. A JWT account since the First World War, LUX Soap Flakes came to be known simply as LUX, a word so versatile that it saw use as noun, verb, *and* adjective. By 1943 a simple but suggestive ad copy announced, "She's a soldier's bride—she's a LUX girl" and every viewer knew what it meant. The happy bride had stepped into the much-anticipated world of marriage because she had been a dutiful laundress of her clothing, especially her undergarments.[44]

Long before the United States entered the Second World War, JWT had created a series of LUX ads focusing on the potential perils to a woman who wore malodorous lingerie. The dramatic elements in these promotions mirrored those appearing in the 1920s and 1930s for other personal products designed to eliminate body odor, halitosis, and other similar conditions. Many of these campaigns depended on sensationalism and melodrama to heighten a reader's worry. Ads for Listerine antiseptic asked pointedly, "Are you unpopular with your own children? Make sure you don't have halitosis. It is inexcusable. And unnecessary." A 1939 Listerine promotion featured a woman "discovering" her longtime boyfriend in the arms of another woman. "I only had myself to blame . . ." she thinks. LUX ads projected similar tones of caution. Throughout 1941 the promotions designed for magazines warned women to "avoid offending" people. If they kept personal odor at bay, women could prevent being shunned by spouses, friends, or family members, the advertisements assured. The key to success was clean underwear, guaranteed if a woman regularly rinsed her personal items in LUX. That her careful attention to the process might save an intimate relationship or preserve her social reputation was indisputable. A typical response to an issue of such import led one character to exclaim, "[H]ow thankful I am to LUX!" The woman's gratefulness, as she claimed, was due to the product's protection of "daintiness." Here, as in the Lux Toilet Soap campaign, the message to women was that damaging elements to their lives and futures resided in their seemingly uncontrollable bodies, especially their genitalia. Connections between clothes, body odors, and conscientious laundering had been forged and promoted in the domestic efficiency campaigns of the previous generation. But only in the 1930s, as home economics developed further and rural electrification spread widely, did the science of laundry grow popular. Cleanliness standards escalated, as did the accompanying quest for middle-class status. Laundry, traditionally women's most despised domestic chore, assumed even greater cultural and political import on the home front.[45]

Exerting personal control over one's own laundry could be empowering, LUX ads suggested to female audiences. Women would have to wage a tough fight against their underclothes, which seemed to take on lives of their own in JWT's wartime advertising. Animated lingerie starred in LUX ad copy in the early 1940s. Flying, chattering bras, slips, camisoles, and girdles claimed to harbor their owners' unpleasant secrets. In some promotions the sneaky garments threatened to release this information, while in other ads, they expressed pity for the oblivious young women who wore them. In one group of ads featuring the wily articles, a headline announced, "UNDIES ARE GOSSIPS!" The accompanying narrative then warned the reader that her underwear would tell others but not her. The ruse seemed deliberate, designed to render her powerless in her social circle until she discovered the secret. Once she did, she would act on the information immediately, the story suggested. In 1942 ads distributed to newspapers and magazines featured characters who appear horrified at the sight of their lingerie threatening to "tell everybody" that they have not been "LUXED." A talking brassiere asks, "WHY DOES SHE RISK POPULARITY?" Another ad shows the garments directly addressing a woman in the shower—"YOU DON'T NOTICE IT, BUT OTHERS DO"—then advising her to "LUX US AFTER EVERY WEARING OR YOU MAY OFFEND."[46] The women in both promotions "hear" the conversations before their clothes can jeopardize them. To be privy to such crucial revelations put each of the women in a position to change things if she took the initiative. But what if they had not been so fortunate to witness the spirited exchanges?

The LUX series also depicted underwear as conspiratorial snitches, working together against their naïve wearer. The best example in this genre circulated widely in the summer of 1942 in several magazines, including *True Confessions,* *Redbook,* and *Cosmopolitan* (fig. 35). In the ad copy image, an unsuspecting young woman lies peacefully asleep, while her lingerie deliberately plots, "WE WON'T TELL DOT. . . . BUT WE WILL TELL HER FRIENDS." Powerless, the character appears a pawn of those who possess information. Without the force of knowledge (in this case, her own "undie odor"), Dot will pay some undisclosed social cost, which is left to the viewer's imagination.

The "Undies Are Gossips" campaign radiated a core message familiar to Americans early in the war: the power of talk. U.S. government propaganda connected conversations with death and destruction for U.S. troops: "Somebody blabbed— button your lip!" and "A Careless Word . . . A Needless Sinking" warned viewers to check their conversations. One resonant quip suggested "Loose Lips Might Sink Ships." Reminiscent of the Committee on Public Information's propaganda campaigns during the First World War, in which U.S. citizens were warned about spreading rumors or chatting too much, the earliest World War II home front cam-

Figure 35. LUX advertisement for magazines. May and June 1942. JWT Archives, Hartman Center, Duke University.

paigns also homed in on the force of "secrets." The U.S. Office of Facts and Figures (OFF), which coordinated the government's initial visual information campaigns, organized an initiative a few weeks after the Pearl Harbor attack around the theme "The Enemy is Listening! He wants to know what you know. Keep it to yourself." One OFF administrator announced, "This one will be followed by a series of design posters on the same theme. The 'don't tell' message is the most urgent one right now, we feel . . . It's a question of first things first, at this stage." The USO instructed its junior hostesses to avoid asking servicemen any details about camps, assignments, or deployments. The young women were responsible "for shifting conversations from sensitive material to less dangerous territory."[47] Certain information conferred power; to divulge it could be ruinous. JWT's LUX ad writers followed Washington's lead in generating questions that would put Americans in a cautious mood. They asked: Who knows, and what do they know? Who shares information and in what ways is it imparted? How does one find out vital secrets? If disclosures are made, who suffers and how? What is the ultimate price?

The LUX talking underwear campaign managed to address all of these questions. As the analysis above shows, one group of ads in 1942 highlighted the knowledge itself, the nature of the secrets, and the prospect of sharing that information. The sensationalist, sometimes jocular, tone of these promotions gave way to more serious themes a few months later. In the new series, lonely young women suffering the consequences of offensive body odor seem unaware of the source of their unhappiness. Grave in mood, the stories reveal the costs of having one's secrets divulged (fig. 36). A June newspaper promotion announced: "Romance . . . but not for Joan." Viewers saw Joan wistfully peering out her window at a courting couple and were to understand that the damage had been done. Joan had missed her chance. The visual message implicitly cautioned readers against ending up like Joan, who, however attractive she might appear, had no special man in her life. The next month, a similar ad appeared in newspapers, raising the stakes even higher. In it a dejected woman glumly stared at a wedding invitation. A small sketch in a corner of the ad provided a glimpse into the young woman's imagination, a vision of the wartime dream she and others like her were encouraged to pursue—marriage to a man in uniform, marked by a stroll as bride and groom under the gauntlet of arched swords. The headline announced both her dilemma and her failure: "Wedding bells are ringing—BUT NOT FOR ELLEN!" While the respective ads made clear that Joan and Ellen were unaware of the problem that they shared, viewers were armed with necessary information to avoid such a fate. The increasingly serious tone of LUX advertising by the summer of 1942 was further intensified by the changing characterization of the undergarments themselves. The lively, chipper camisoles and bras of earlier ad designs gave way to ponderous lingerie claiming, "IT'S OUR FAULT JOAN'S SO LONELY. WE HAVE UNDIE ODOR." Humorless, the messages urged young women to take their personal laundry as a serious matter or be prepared to suffer severe emotional costs.[48]

Beyond the explicit directives in the LUX campaign, other more subtly couched hints for becoming the ideal home front woman lay embedded in the myriad words and pictures. The overwhelming message to female readers was that personal fulfillment came solely from male companionship. Any time spent with men could be gratifying, but walking arm-in-arm or dancing cheek-to-cheek seemed to elicit the biggest smiles, or as one girl claimed, "heaps of fun." LUX ads categorized solitary leisure pursuits—such as reading or working puzzles—as certain to induce boredom, as a somber reader named Connie soon discovered. Although the advertisement conceded, "reading is fine," the larger headline equated solitude with loneliness. Only after she began "LUXING" her lingerie did the friendless reader escape her destiny as a bookworm, transforming herself into a charming female companion. But as the illustrations pointed out, something else occurred in Con-

5334 (1942)
This advertisement appears in

Figure 36. LUX advertisement for newspapers. June 1942. JWT Archives, Hartman Center, Duke University.

nie's metamorphosis. She became an attentive launderer of her underclothes, smiling as she worked, clearly satisfied with her tasks. No longer a sedentary reader, but energized and purposeful, the new Connie spent time engaged in profitable pursuits—washing, wringing, hanging, and folding. The ad implied that such activities gave young women a sense of control in an arena that could determine their emotional health and future happiness.[49]

Women clearly responded to advertisements advising them on the vital role of laundry in personal cleanliness regimes, which boardinghouse owners detested. When the U.S. government finally completed duration housing projects, among the enticements touted were laundry facilities and spacious communal baths on each hall. An Arlington Farms insider found these residence halls for women lacking, however. Twenty-two-year-old photographer Esther Bubley documented life at the northern Virginia compound in 1943, finding residents' rooms "festooned with clothes" and their laundry rooms small and crowded (figs. 37 and 38). Bubley's fieldwork disclosed even more, as she explained in her notes: "Authorities say that hanging the laundry outside will make the project look like a tenement." The rules dictated that female government workers would be reminded constantly of their self-surveillance. They lived in close proximity to their daily laundry, forbidden to expose it, lest its public display indicate slippage from a plane of ideal womanhood. The U.S. government could not risk having watchful eyes believe that it sanctioned anything less.[50]

Characteristics of the feminine archetype in the 1940s abound in the LUX series devoted to undergarments. While some elements remained constant from 1941 to 1945, the overall campaign changed over those years to reflect the shifting cultural conditions and expectations of women on the American home front. The emphasis

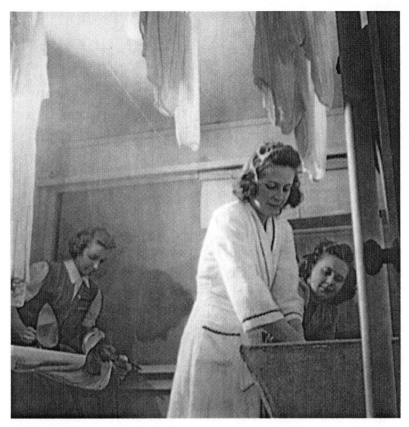

Figure 37. "Arlington, Virginia. Washing clothes in one of the laundry rooms at Idaho Hall, Arlington Farms, a residence for women who work in the government for the duration of the war." Esther Bubley, June 1943. FSA-OWI Collection, Library of Congress (LC-USW3–025730–E), digital ID: fsa 8d29012.

Figure 38. "Arlington, Virginia. A girl looking at snapshots in her room at Idaho Hall, Arlington Farms, a residence for women who work in the U.S. government for the duration of the war. A typical room scene since there is a shortage of space in the laundries and authorities say that hanging the laundry outside will make the project look like a tenement." Esther Bubley, June 1943. FSA-OWI Collection, Library of Congress (LC-USW3–026045-E), digital ID: fsa 8d29082.

on "daintiness" persisted, as did the notion that a LUX user was a conscientious consumer—a principal theme in all domestic advertising during the war.[51] Focal and tonal shifts in the series illuminated the more subtle pressures on young women to embrace measures to ensure their femininity and its rewards. A few months before the United States entered the Second World War, the LUX narratives featured as many married as single women. But from 1942 through the end of the war, unmarried women were pitched as those who had the most to lose from smelly undergarments. By 1943, when ad copy showed more than one officer boasting, "It's good to come home—to a LUX girl," viewers could know the woman had successfully completed one of her most important home front campaigns.[52] In

1944, as the talking underwear series continued, ad copy statements became even more explicit, the language more martial. One newspaper promotion declared, "Without daintiness, no other charm counts! Perspiration odor in underthings can kill charm, rob you of friends, romance." The blunt message was augmented by several illustrations, the most cogent featuring a perplexed young woman who stands at a postal box viewing the passersby: two men, a cheerful couple, and a well-dressed family (fig. 39). All of the men are in uniform, an iconic suggestion about the overwhelming number of U.S. troops in mid-1944. For over eighteen months, military men had been depicted in American advertising as the most desirable male companions, and since the number of draftees and volunteers continued to rise exponentially, it seemed logical that an unmarried woman's chances to meet a guy in uniform had greatly increased. If she lived near a training camp or in a port city, she enjoyed even better odds. The young woman in the June 1944 LUX promotion seems to be in such a position, given her surroundings. Personal frustration emanates from her failure to compete successfully: "20,000 MEN IN THIS TOWN— WHY ISN'T THERE ONE FOR ME?" A woman who could not manage to find a man for herself in such a crowd appeared naïve enough to remain unattached forever.

As the war drew to a close, the incisive, declarative nature of the LUX advertisements shifted to foreshadow postwar culture. Mirroring the growing pressure on American women to embrace traditional domestic arrangements, LUX ad copy borrowed themes familiar to any girl who had grown up hearing fairy tales. Language and scenery reminiscent of medieval folk tales and stories filtered into the advertisements. Romance was proclaimed the "enchantment of being loved," thus positioning women as passive recipients rather than active participants in intimate relationships. As the "birthright of every girl," romance seemingly fulfilled a natural entitlement if a woman became part of a heterosexual couple. As Carolyn Heilbrun argues, the prevailing narrative of women's lives in Western literature ended with a young woman's betrothal and/or marriage, as if there were nothing else to tell. American advertising during the Second World War reiterated the theme, pushing it even harder in 1945.[53]

Throughout the spring and summer that year, the language and imagery of chivalry further closed ideal women in, often placing them on a centuries-old pedestal. LUX promotions deemed women rather than lingerie (as in earlier ads) "precious." As an object of a man's desire, a woman could expect romance to follow if she seemed "wonderful in his eyes." The setting created in this series comprised an imaginary world of the pursuer and the pursued, he who hunted and then judged, she who waited and then withstood judgment. The pageant of words and looks and expectations came together in a universe of romantic fantasy. The extent of

Figure 39. LUX advertisement for newspapers. June 1944. JWT Archives, Hartman Center, Duke University.

the make-believe and concomitant fragility of late-war coupling appeared in the warning: "Even a hint of perspiration odor may break that magic spell." In a heterosexual couple the woman clearly bore responsibility for maintaining the mystery and illusion of romance; not for declaring it, but for sustaining its aura, a duty that would become paramount after the war.[54] Foreshadowing the dominant military emphasis in postwar political culture, images in late-war LUX advertisements focused on the kind of hero with whom a woman could most successfully fulfill her romantic fantasies: someone who had completed his missions in the air. In the ad designs, the long-awaited knight rescuing a LUX user from spinsterhood had barely distinguishable facial features, but his insignia marked him as an airman. That a pilot starred in the romantic dreams created by JWT ad writers gave the LUX series a contemporary edge; combined with the narrative elements from the war-torn Middle Ages, the ads cannily blended modern and traditional themes in an attempt to reach a wide audience. The pressure on women to adapt to elevated standards or be left behind grew more intense as the months passed, so that by July 1945, as thousands of American military personnel were on their way back to the

United States, LUX ads asked women to contemplate whether the "sweet promise of romance" would "come true" for them. By then, the answer was presumed to be evident: the promise would be theirs if they had made their bodies into what men overseas claimed they wanted to come home to.[55]

Print advertising campaigns for LUX (laundry soap) and Lux Toilet Soap illuminated and encouraged distinct gender divisions as well as a heteronormative home front society. Dominant themes in both campaigns stressed the consequential message that a woman's best hope for attaining sexual desirability depended on her unremitting self-regulation. If she seriously attempted to control her body's odors, she might well approach a state of ideal femininity, making her eligible for social acceptance, but more importantly, for exciting romantic encounters, a marriage proposal, or a long-awaited reunion with an absent partner. That women took such prescriptions to heart was borne out by boardinghouse owners' opinions about female housemates—that they did too much laundry and spent too much time in the bathtub. U.S. Department of Labor field researchers found these complaints to be the bases for homeowners' "general aversion" to women in all regions of the United States. In the home front equation, these profit-minded entrepreneurs challenged culturally accepted cleanliness standards by insisting that women's daily hygiene routines cost them too much. Given the emergency mobilization effort, one that depended on female workers, government agencies eventually distributed pamphlets with helpful advice about renting to women, and they offered financial incentives for home improvements. A woman who needed to rent a room during the war had to choose carefully, lest she be forced to jeopardize her attempts to create a body destined for personal success.

Large-scale migration irrevocably altered war boomtowns such as Evansville, Mobile, Seattle, and Washington, D.C. With many more women working, many more middle-class women doing dirty jobs in heavy industry, and many more women of color earning higher wages than ever before, millions of potentially dangerous female bodies abounded. They posed dangers because they represented myriad forms of independence—economic, sexual, social, and ultimately, political. To temper these disruptive forces, personal cleanliness standards rose to unprecedented heights. Indefatigable washing of bodies and underclothes served as a cultural grounding device. These demands would work in tandem with new ways and means of adornment, as wartime clothes and their relationship to female flesh shaped the modern twentieth-century American woman.

FOUR

Proper Attire and Streamlined Silhouettes

Clothing the Home Front Figure

In February 1944 writer Margaret H. Gammon offered a "consumer viewpoint" on women's wartime clothing. "Isn't it time to stop treating women like nincompoops? Isn't it time to consult them about their tastes in fabrics, color, fit, becomingness . . . ? They are the buyers and users and they might have some useful words to say, even in the fashion field where they are supposed to leave matters in the competent hands of masculine esthetes." Gammon's indignation over current styles seemed less important than her concern about the silencing of women in an arena that clearly mattered to them: how they covered their bodies. Identifying "signs of restlessness and revolt" in American women who felt patronized, Gammon issued a warning to policy makers who might wish to run a postwar domestic economy in the same manner as they were currently operating the wartime economy.[1] Although she didn't employ the ubiquitous wartime phrase "for the duration," she implied that women would challenge condescension and caricature after the global crisis ended. To what extent was Gammon onto something? Had women really been treated like fools in the clothing department? What had they been offered in terms of style and coverage, and how did these garments reflect public needs and cultural desires?

In Gammon's lifetime, clothing had increasingly contributed to the identification and judgment of American women. The domestic's aproned uniform and the shop clerk's shirtwaist in the teens, the flapper's chemise in the 1920s, the androgyne's tuxedo a few years later, and by 1941 the sweater girl's "sweater" all helped to categorize and define certain groups of women.[2] As modern consumer society developed in the same period, prevailing images of the ideal female body as a decorative model became more sophisticated. The term "figure" had come into use many years earlier to suggest an attractive corporeal outline; but its meaning in the field of geometry applies more aptly to the idea of the body as a site for decoration, specifically "a definite form constituted by a given line or continuous series of lines so arranged as to enclose a superficial space, or by a given surface or series of surfaces enclosing a space of three dimensions." Particular points, lines, and surfaces on the body could be accentuated or minimized by materials operating in conjunction with the body itself, thus reflecting current tastes or generating new ones.[3] From the Victorian hourglass silhouette to the slenderer, more athletic Gibson girl in the 1890s to the boyish flapper of the 1920s, the combination of points, lines, and surfaces shifted starkly and quickly from generation to generation and intra-generationally as well. And by the time actress Lana Turner made her first "sweater" appearance in the late 1930s, the body and its fabric covering were inextricably bound.

Conflation of the female body and its clothing was far from a new phenomenon during the Second World War, but the public emergency generated some fresh ideas about it. That a grid superimposed over an image of Betty Grable wearing only a man's army shirt and high heels could be used to teach American soldiers map-reading is perhaps the most literal example of the official use of a woman's points, lines, and surfaces (fig. 40). For many Americans this was the only way that women should have appeared in military garb; to put them in uniforms of their own seemed a dangerous social experiment. But millions of women donned uniforms and other clothing indicative of the war's demands. The resulting anxieties on the home front produced new means of judging women. Clothes working together with corporeal shapes and sizes redrew cultural boundaries and possibilities for women.[4]

Even before the war, as Americans were seduced by the sleek lines and smooth curves known as "streamlining" in everything from pencil sharpeners to railway locomotives, the ideal female "figure" took on a similar appearance. Dictated by a whiteness quotient, the ideal manifested itself in urban America where partygoers and trendsetters bought close-fitting gowns to reveal slim outlines with long legs, narrow waists, and flat chests. Stereotypes of women of color as well as immigrant

Figure 40. Grid superimposed on an image of actress Betty Grable for U.S. Army instructional purposes. USAAFTC, Library of Congress.

women helped promote whiteness as an ideal. That Ziegfeld's dancers were "leggy" distanced them from the urban immigrant communities from which many came, while placing them nearer a goal of assimilated American womanhood. By the 1940s U.S. government agencies addressing women's issues described the "problem figures" of "immigrant" women, a reference to rounder and stouter female bodies that designers constructed as different from Anglo-American models. Roberta Pollack Seid notes that the wartime generation's notions of the slender or thin female body stood apart from those in the postwar generation who witnessed the beginning of a "real war on fat" in 1950. However, the arsenal for that war was stocked in the early 1940s, with some battles staged earlier than Seid suggests. By 1944 American designers were calling for trimmer bodies on which to hang their creations.[5]

American women who adopted novelist Margaret Mitchell's heroine Scarlett O'Hara as a model in the late 1930s knew that one of her greatest attributes was her "seventeen-inch waist, the smallest in three counties." Even if readers had missed this fact on *Gone With the Wind*'s first page, they could easily recall an early scene in David O. Selznick's popular Academy Award–winning film that had played to packed houses in the months following its December 15, 1939, premiere. In the scene, Scarlett argues with her family's house slave, Mammy, over a tightly laced corset, a young woman's display of appetite, and what constitutes proper upper-class white womanhood. Literary critic Deborah McDowell has read this scene for both its dichotomous imagery and its statement on African American women and girth. "While Scarlett's seventeen-inch waist is one fetishized mark of her sexual desirability, Mammy's mammoth body has long since foreclosed on all of that. It's plain to see that she has helped herself to heaping plates of food." Scarlett, however, remains small throughout the narrative, reiterating the modern notion that "[t]hinness is prototypically embodied by the white woman." The scene raises questions not merely about race, class, and American womanhood in the late 1930s, but about the ways in which appetites and bodies figured into the larger wartime culture that emerged a few months later.[6] The conflagration of flesh and material underlay an environment where political needs pressed deeply into Americans' private lives. How then could articles of clothing hide, enhance, or expose female bodies amid a flurry of messages about sacrifice, patriotic duty, economic opportunity, and postwar promise?

Given the war emergency, how did U.S. policy makers, advertisers, and cultural commentators speak to women about clothing? In what ways did they use assumptions about women's attachment to clothing, even the seduction of certain designs, in order to attract, persuade, or admonish them? How could women be made or unmade by their clothing choices? The answers to these questions matter in a context where appetites were judged only in part by eating habits but more universally by the ways in which clothes—as political statements—defined the female body.[7]

Scarlett O'Hara's corset produced an illusion, an ideal form. During World War II, conservation of fibers and fabrics intersected with conservation of food products, and a thinner female body emerged as a sign of both patriotic devotion and private desire. The tight conflation of clothing and bodies mattered in a culture where appearances more than sexual acts determined femininity and sexuality. Messages abounded on how women could make themselves into the right kind of home front fighters by adorning and streamlining their bodies appropriately. At home, on trains and buses, in food markets and department stores, and at USO clubs, women—some real, some imagined—received widespread media attention for their uniforms, work togs, and leisure apparel. In a high-tech age where the glorious attributes of machinery were signs of cultural superiority, the streamlined body could also be interpreted as an "efficient" and productive one. Mass-market advertisers and U.S. government war agencies introduced techniques and themes heralding clothes to serve several interconnected purposes—conserving valuable resources for troops abroad, perpetuating a healthy consumer ethic among women at home, while ultimately safeguarding gender boundaries and promoting femininity. The adorned or "decorated" body emitted signals about American women in wartime culture, among them its relationship to government policy, political standing, socioeconomic status, sexuality, and sexual availability. In the end, women wore the war, while literally embodying its demands.

Immediately after the U.S. declaration of war, the American garment industry stepped up to preserve itself by linking fashion to victory. One of the industry's new and increasingly powerful voices, the New York Dress Institute (NYDI), encouraged apparel producers as well as the public to temper their desire to sacrifice too much too quickly. In one appeal it urged, "[F]or patriotic reasons we should give up only those things that need giving up." The NYDI had been organized a year earlier, in an unlikely collaboration between the garment workers unions and dress manufacturers, to ensure that New York remained on its path to become the fashion capital of the United States. With Paris couture houses and designers inaccessible due to Nazi occupation, New York designers were trying to establish themselves in an American market where they had previously been anonymous. The war "gave them an opportunity to take center stage," argues Sandra Buckland.[8] While recognizing the clothing industry's responsibility to outfit American military personnel on the battlefronts and elsewhere, the NYDI put much greater emphasis on the role of fashion for women. To defend its position on limited sacrifice, the institute pointed to Great Britain, where after the outbreak of war "English women, in eagerness to get down to serious work, found themselves adopting drab uniformity of dress." The trend led to "depressing" effects, "thereby serving the enemy's purpose." Only a dispositional shift prompting British women to embrace "colorful and gay" clothes corrected their path and generated better spirits nationwide.[9] And this, the NYDI insisted, was women's principal role during the crisis. In a preemptive advertising blitz, the institute issued an "arresting series" of messages articulating the inspirational function of women. The centerpiece of the series announced, "More than any other group, the women of a nation carry the delicate flower of morale in their hands. *From them*, as ever, must come the fragrance of a life worth fighting for. *With them* must be found surcease from strain. *On them* is the burden of relief from the tragic, the grim and the drab." Illustrating its message not with contemporary faces or designs, but rather a two-thousand-year-old icon—the Nike of Samothrace—the NYDI declared: "It is no accident that the Winged Victory is a feminine figure."[10] Enlisting classical cultural expression, archetypal behavior, and form, the ad designer invoked timelessness and universality. From this launching point a decorative purpose for wartime women could be firmly established without appearing frivolous.

The NYDI and its partners flooded the trade with similar directives compressing all women into a safely gendered imaginary. Bonwit Teller department store bought space in the December 21, 1941, issue of the *New York Times* to announce, "America doesn't want its women dreary. It wants you looking nice." The advertisement suggested such a course would not only be good for them and for "the boys, God bless 'em," but more importantly, for national morale. The NYDI similarly situated women in a communiqué that concluded: "a woman in war must be more than the equal of a man. She must be his guiding star. Whatever war tasks she undertakes, she must still shine forth as Woman." While the narrative recognizes the possibility of social change, it articulates a clear imperative. "Woman" (with a capital W) is an immutable ideal, and real women were responsible for keeping it that way. The fashion industry planned to help them meet the challenge.[11]

Capitalizing on a moment of crisis, the industry was determined to heighten consumer sensibility by developing a "greater clothes consciousness among women of America." Designers, producers, and consumers were urged to consider apparel designs that combined "Beauty and Duty." Fabric and apparel makers hoped that American women would not heed the advice of a well-known "society matron" who had announced in a major newspaper that "all patriotic women should have only one dress, a black dress of general utility." *Women's Wear Daily* responded that such a course would ensure "a Nazi victory." American women, it was argued, could keep morale high just as they had done during the First World War by realizing that "to dress well and smartly, with charm and color" was their "patriotic duty."

Town & Country readers learned that "lightness of heart and beauty of dress" were "woman's greatest contributions to the spirit of her country at war." It appeared the industry would have its way, as a January 1942 report in the *Journal of Commerce* noted signs of "glamorous femininity" in spring fashions. Writer Alice Ten Eyck pointed to the season's "shock" colors and "brilliant plaids and checks" as indicators of a plucky approach to wartime pressures. She also commended "[t]he verve and dash of capes on coats and on dresses—full-skirted, short-jacketed suit-like dresses reminiscent of the Godey demureness of another day are highlighted and jabots, frills and ruffles are repeatedly emphasized. . . . Peplums, tiers, pleats and still more pleats, overdrapes, side drapes—all are the keynote of the day." The reference to the nineteenth-century American women's fashion arbiter, *Godey's Lady's Book*, may have reassured some readers that the recent declaration of war would not interrupt the flow of fabric and design.[12]

The excess that Ten Eyck described would soon go out of fashion, however, as home front style was forced to take its lead from the War Production Board (WPB) rather than the New York Dress Institute. Lively colors, pleats, and ruffles became quaint memories for the duration of the war. The WPB's regulations on excess were clear. General Limitation Order L-85, announced in April 1942, sought to conserve natural fibers, such as cotton, silk, and wool.[13] It also limited the domestic use of nylon and rayon. The policy demanded that dresses have narrower skirts and fewer decorative touches requiring extra fabric. A two-inch limit applied to hem depth and same fabric belts; jacket length could not exceed twenty-five inches. Balloon sleeves, turnover cuffs, double material yokes, and attached hoods and shawls were prohibited. A jacket could feature only one patch pocket. The WPB committee that developed the policy included representatives from the government as well as the textiles industry and apparel industry. H. Stanley Marcus of Neiman-Marcus Department Store in Dallas served as a principal design consultant as well as the WPB's Apparel Section chief. His committee intended for the policy to save 15 percent of yardage in current use, but the members also hoped that style changes would remain as inconspicuous as possible, so as not to shock or discourage American consumers by making their current wardrobes obsolete.[14]

Marcus wanted L-85 fashions to be "fresh-looking but not so new that you feel you have to discard your last year's little black dress or your favorite tweed suit." Fashion writer Ethel Gorham went even further, contending, "You don't have to be a slave to the government rulings." Since WPB orders applied to clothes manufactured *after* the regulations took effect, women could still purchase the previous year's fashions remaining in stores. Giving a nod to official needs, corporate desires, and consumer wishes, Gorham advised, "The best trick of all, in the eyes of the government, would be to make your existing wardrobe look new and fresh."

One way to keep fabric consumption down was "not to buy anything new at all," but she recognized how importune such a suggestion would be to all constituencies. She concluded, "[E]ven the government knows you can't keep a nation of best-dressed women (that's what they always said about American women, you know) from hankering for clothes, war or no war. The best they hope for is that you work on a kind of clothes diet built on leftovers." Marcus and his WPB committee members hoped women would not rely solely on leftovers but would instead embrace the new lines as acceptable changes and continue buying mass-produced dresses, skirts, blouses, and jackets as they always had.[15]

To standardize conservation in all domestic fabric use, Marcus also promoted Order L-116, regulating women's and children's lingerie, which included slips, gowns, and pajamas. He made the case to his superiors by emphasizing his expertise on women's thoughts about apparel: "Women will feel that, since their outer clothes are under restriction, their underclothes should be also, if there is a real need to save fabrics." He also iterated the government's role in guaranteeing "consistency" if it wanted to convince the public of "the necessity to conserve." Marcus's committee recommended changes similar to those outlined in L-85, projecting approximately 15 percent savings in fabric consumption. More than anything else, the focus was on eliminating excess material—belts, ruffles, and balloon sleeves from nightgowns, and cuffs and extra pockets from pajamas. Endorsing L-116, WPB officials promoted Marcus's message of consistency while also acknowledging the drawbacks of altering "functional" garments. He noted that the "restrictions [could] not be so stringent as to cause impracticability." A woman would find newly manufactured slips without the "sweep" they were accustomed to and without double yokes and decorative hems. But the slips would complement the narrow-skirted L-85 dresses they would be made to serve.[16]

Consumer thinking mattered, but manufacturers' tempers also had prompted the WPB Apparel Section to act decisively. Marcus justified the L-116 order request to his superiors by pointing out that lingerie makers could not be trusted to regulate themselves "due to the highly competitive nature" of their business. High-end producers who made the most expensive lingerie, considered "the most extravagant users of material," were not exempt; the committee agreed that L-116 restrictions should be felt across the board. The fierce competition in the lingerie business would provide natural enforcement of the policy, one administrator suggested, since each manufacturer would naturally serve as "a checking agent" to other manufacturers' compliance with the new regulations. In addition to the producers' surveillance of one another, retailers would recognize whether merchandise met wartime restrictions. The principal overseer, however, would remain "the general force of public opinion." Marcus claimed that "fashion and consumer publications" would educate and "mobilize" Americans to recognize apparel made to government specifications.[17]

Fashion magazines immediately covered the coming changes in mass-manufactured clothing. *Women's Wear Daily* published a diagram of the new dress suit design with specifications clearly outlined (fig. 41). *Vogue* editor Edna Woolman Chase had told a group of fashion magazine editors as early as January 1942 that their opinions mattered more now than ever in "helping to shape the views of many other women in America." In an eight-page photographic essay, *LIFE* magazine's spring fashion issue revealed what soon would be *in* and what definitely would be *out*. "Women Lose Pockets and Frills to Save Fabrics," the story headline announced. In *LIFE's* photographic coverage, models standing side by side set the prewar styles against the new wartime looks. If the narrower, shorter, frills-free clothing juxtaposed against the fuller, longer styles did not offer enough contrast to educate viewers, the photo captions pointed out what was "illegal" or "prohibited." In a matter of months, American fashion would be inextricably linked to conservation, maturing inside a home front culture destined to herald its new designs, above all, as practical and functional.[18]

The simple lines of L-85 design influenced all women's suit manufacturing, including the newest site for American style: the military. Nearly every ad designed to attract women to military service depicted the advantages of wearing a uniform, which became synonymous with high fashion in recruitment literature. The USMCWR used an haute couture angle to highlight the Marine olive and scarlet piping: "It was Elsa Schiaparelli, Paris couturier, who first convinced American women that a combination of green and red needn't make them look like a Christmas tree, provided the combination was subtly made. That was back about 10 years ago, and it's been a favorite color combination with smartly dressed women ever since." The WAVES attracted enlistees with uniforms designed by Mainbocher's in New York, a fashion house "patronized by the Duchess of Windsor and Hollywood stars." In 1944 the U.S. Cadet Nurse Corps promotions in national magazines relied on endorsement testimonials such as one from a new recruit who gleams, "The Cadet uniform is so smart! It's for outdoor wear, and I don't think there's a better looking one in the women's services." As the WAC stepped up its recruitment in 1944, official literature highlighted the organization's stylish clothing. A promotional headline circulated by the OWI promised "Fashions for a Woman with a Future!" Pitched as the "smartest suit in the world right now—to be worn every season," a WAC uniform transcended the fleeting nature of fashion. Instead, as the message implied, the suit meant long-term stability for any woman who put it on. A "high-style" handbag to match ensured adventure: "You'll cram it with post cards of new cities you visit, snapshots of new friends to proudly show the folks back

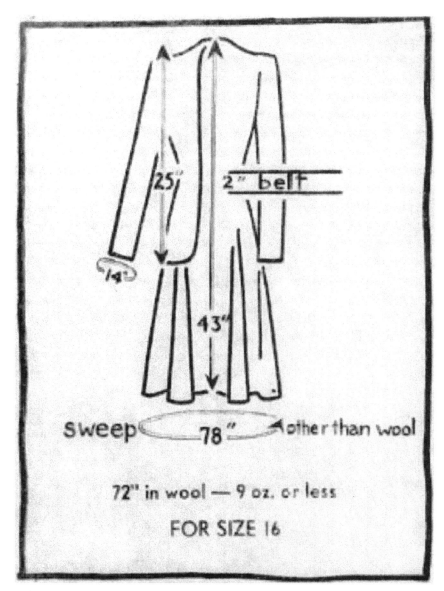

Figure 41. WPB regulations as outlined in *Women's Wear Daily*. 1942. Costume Collection, Division of Social History, National Museum of American History.

home—and every so often, a wonderful week-end pass!" If clothes were considered a medium certain to entice women to join the military, WAC officer Elizabeth Hampton promised her African American audience that the government would supply not just uniforms and accessories but any clothing soldiers might need for special assignments or leisure activities.[19]

Proper fit of uniforms mattered to wearers and observers alike. U.S. authorities recommended and in some places demanded that women's suits be tailored. Such messages implied that alterations were to announce female silhouettes to the public, making bust lines and waistlines visible. Yet garments had to remain loose enough for women to carry out active work. A Marine Corps pamphlet promised volunteers that "expert tailors" would make sure they got "a perfect fit." WAVES enlistees were guaranteed "trim" and "smartly-styled, comfortable uniforms." While a USMCWR volunteer could take pride in clothes "identical" to those of "combat Marines," she received reassurance that the standard uniform had been adapted "to preserve [her] tailored femininity, to flatter [her] face and figure." Detailed narrative descriptions and extensive photo illustrations informed recruits about the various wardrobe components they would be expected to wear, leaving no room for shock or surprise once they arrived at "boot camp." The recurrent motif in USMCWR literature was the deliberate effort to adapt Marine Corps traditions, colors, and overall appearance to a contemporary crisis that required women's participation. Uniforms, both stylish and practical, were described as mere variations of what men in the corps had worn for decades, encouraging women to think of themselves as actual marines, not auxiliaries. And yet the attention paid to details of style and fashion in their recruitment suggests something quite different. No materials distributed to male marines pointed to the advantages of wearing jackets with "slightly built up shoulders, shoulder straps, pointed lapels, slash breast pockets and welt hip pockets." Nor were men promised overcoats "fitted to your figure" with "notched lapels, flap pockets and pointed cuffs." Such details presumably would entice women volunteers who wished to look stylishly feminine.[20]

The U.S. Coast Guard went one step further by engaging one of the war's premier pin-up artists to portray the organization's female contingent, known as SPAR (Semper Paratus Always Ready). *Esquire* magazine illustrator Alberto Vargas created the energetic, smiling enlistee who confidently strode on the cover of the official publication in April 1943 (fig. 42). Vargas's distinctive vision of the ideal female body—broad shoulders, long legs, and narrow waists made to look even more so by substantial bust lines—grew in popularity during the war years. Given their avid reading of *Esquire*, American women could recognize the artist's outline of the physical ideal if not his distinctive signature.[21] What messages lay behind such a magazine cover? Could joining the SPAR transform a woman into a pin-up? Perhaps so, if her uniform enhanced her shape and announced a female body without sexualizing it too conspicuously. Striking a balance would be a challenge for the women's armed forces.

To fit thousands of women in such unconventional clothing was an unprecedented task for the U.S. government. Large American mail order companies de-

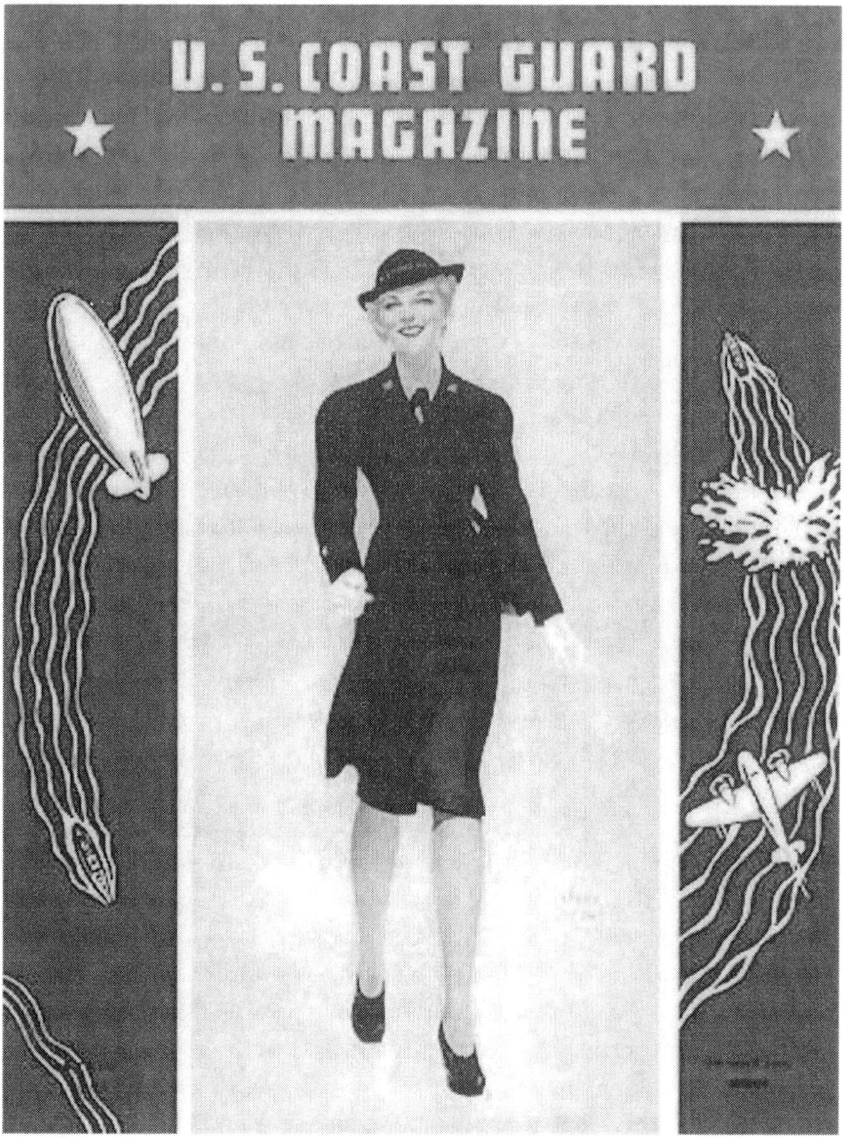

Figure 42. SPAR volunteer. Illustration by Alberto Vargas. *U.S. Coast Guard Magazine* cover, April 1943.

veloped size charts for the WAC to assist in clothing thousands of female soldiers, but as historian Leisa Meyer points out, "the Philadelphia Quartermaster's Depot for most of the war based its patterns and sizes for women's attire on male models." Wac Aileen Kilgore wrote to her parents the day she received her uniforms at Fort Oglethorpe, Georgia: "Every thing fit me well except my two winter skirts had to be taken up, and there wasn't an overcoat small enough for me. The ones I tried on weighed a ton. We got two fatigue dresses of green striped seersucker (some were brown stripe) with voluminous bloomers to match." Four days later, she eagerly reported that they had received additional "extra nice" clothes, including "cotton vests, two long cotton underpants, a sweater, three coats" as well as "5 shirts, 2 winter uniforms, 3 summer skirts, one summer jacket, 2 ties, 2 pairs wool socks." In her twenty-two months as a soldier, Kilgore wrote a great deal about her various uniforms, their fit, comfort, upkeep, and degree of popularity among her fellow soldiers. Eunice McConnell wrote to her parents about the "BIG day" that she and other WAVES had anxiously awaited at their Bloomington, Indiana, training camp. Looking forward to the first uniform shipment, they prepared to follow an order to "try everything on to be sure they fit."[22]

The operation's magnitude exposed weaknesses in a burgeoning wartime bureaucracy, the blurring of lines and categories as large numbers of bodies had to be quickly processed. Fort Des Moines supply sergeant Edna Floyd described the "hopeless muddle" in the supply house after new companies of women arrived at the camp. Yet Floyd reveled in the demands of her job—both physical and organizational—noting there was "never a dull moment" at the warehouse. WAC mechanic Kilgore made several trips to the Ellington Air Base Alterations Department to get an overcoat fitted to her small 104-pound frame, but the tailors never got it quite right; even worse, she had to wear size 48 coveralls that made her look "like Charley Chaplin," she said.[23]

At WAC camps, racial segregation dictated clothing distribution. Individual platoons were to visit the clothing warehouse separately, with African Americans scheduled to arrive after white soldiers had selected their uniforms. The plan presumed that black bodies would not touch garments to be worn eventually by white bodies; it also meant that black soldiers received leftover uniforms that had been tried on and discarded by their white counterparts. But, as Charity Adams reported, the well-intentioned program broke down since "so many misfits requiring adjustments" meant that rarely was anyone "completely outfitted on the first round." So as Jim Crow segregation was tested on many better-known fronts during the Second World War, it was also challenged in places as seemingly insignificant as a supply room.[24]

The organization culture so carefully constructed by Progressives earlier in the century, and instituted by President Roosevelt's New Dealers during the Great Depression, got its true test as the U.S. government attempted to quickly mobilize bodies and resources in the early 1940s. The bureaucracy's attempt to maintain order with strict boundaries and categories could not withstand millions of small decisions that had to be made on the spot. Where supervisors insisted on "proper channel" approvals and requisite paper shuffling, the effort stalled. The results of this monumental clothing operation left plenty of women not as neatly attired as advertisements had promised.[25]

What uniforms might do to the women who donned them was anyone's guess, but attempts to shape reactions abounded. *Good Housekeeping* offered women a "little list" of suggestions on how to wear military uniforms, hoping to generate approval from American men who had not yet warmed up to women's newest clothing options nor (although left unsaid) to the jobs, salaries, titles, and opportunities requiring such apparel. The magazine's lists of "do's" and "don'ts" addressed elements of a woman's body more than the actual uniform, revealing an indistinct line between flesh and garment. Suggestions about hairstyles, nail polish, cosmetics, jewelry, and personal hygiene made important top-of-the-list spots. A woman's behavior and attitude while in uniform could also determine her approval rating. Women were advised not to wear their uniforms into bars or nightclubs. Smoking and drinking in uniform were discouraged; these admonitions were followed by "Don't swagger or stride along in masculine fashion," a clear connection made between the behaviors. *Good Housekeeping* warned against anything that seemed to indicate inappropriate gender crossing. That *Good Housekeeping*'s editors compared service women with other *women* rather than other military personnel reminded female readers that gender defined them first and foremost. Encouraging other traditionally "feminine" traits, *Good Housekeeping* also recommended that a uniform be worn "modestly, simply, and unself-consciously" and never with a "self-righteous air, as if you were doing more for your country than other women are." Getting out of uniform and into "civvies" immediately after work would help a woman keep her position in the service separate from her personal life, the article implied. The sentiment closely followed a *Women's Wear Daily* prognostication that "women who either wear uniforms or adopt masculine strides during wartime work will feel the urge of contrast to look more feminine when working hours are over."[26] Behind this and similar advice dispensed during the war years were echoes of a nagging fear that military service had the power to so confuse gender boundaries as to yield irrevocable cultural change.

The U.S. military assumed, then, its greatest home front challenge—to make women "soldiers" while simultaneously reassuring the public that "woman" *as an idea* remained clearly distinct from "soldier." By the fall of 1944 thousands of women had joined the WAC, WAVES, SPAR, and USMCWR, with hundreds more serving as military nurses. American society was saturated with women in uniform, a discomfiting reality for many civilians as well as some military personnel. The Wacs' reference to formal dress uniforms as "pinks" seemed to offer little consolation. A smear campaign generated by male GIs kept WAC administrators busy in

What the Wacs Wear

the good soldier dresses the part

A Wac WEARS a uniform for the same reasons Army men do — it's efficient for the work she has to do. It marks her as an Army person — a person who is doing her full share in helping America win the war.

When a Wac arrives at the Training Center she is issued complete clothing and equipment. If you were to buy these things in a store, at retail prices, they would cost you about $250.

When a Wac becomes an officer, she is given a clothing allowance of $250 cash to cover the purchase of her uniforms.

DRESS AND SERVICE UNIFORM is olive drab woolen

UTILITY COAT has removable wool lining and rain hood

WORK DRESS is seersucker, easily laundered

RUSSET LEATHER HANDBAG to match shoes

WORK UNIFORM is worn in motor mechanics Air Force jobs

COTTON SUMMER UNIFORM is cool and smart

OLIVE DRAB WOOL OVERCOAT is warm, but not heavy

NEW PUMPS — russet with Cuban heels

NEW WAC OVERSEAS CAP. wool khaki, khaki-colored, tropical worsted. New WAC scarf and glove set in chamois

Figure 43. "What the Wacs Wear" from "A Book of Facts about the WAC." 1944. JWT Archives, Hartman Center, Duke University.

1943, the year the organization discarded its "auxiliary" status to become an integral part of the U.S. Army. Initial rumors about Wacs serving as prostitutes for male soldiers gave way to more intense and prolonged concerns about a "lesbian threat" in the organization. American medical opinion as well as public opinion in the 1940s based female sexual "deviance" overwhelmingly on a woman's appearance. The more androgynous or "mannish" a woman looked, the greater likelihood that she would be viewed as dangerous, since she challenged the rules of femininity that presumably grounded heterosexuality and maintained social order. Laws against cross-dressing had existed for generations, in Europe to ensure class divisions as much as anything else but in the United States to distinguish women from men. To challenge those codes, to blur "the sartorial signposts" could "inspire hostility and rage," Susan Brownmiller reminds us. With the stakes high during the war years, as social and economic shifts threatened to upset traditional domestic structures, the prospect of gender disguise seemed even more perilous.[27]

To counter criticism of the diverse organization she headed, WAC director Oveta Culp Hobby instructed female soldiers "to avoid rough or masculine appearance which would cause unfavorable public comment." In the spring of 1944 WAC mechanics at Ellington Air Base got a serious lecture about "proper dress for work" with a warning not to "roll up" the legs or sleeves of their coveralls. Aileen Kilgore told her parents, "We are now buttoned and covered from tip to toe." The instructions would ensure for Kilgore and her fellow Wacs a long, hot Texas summer. The OWI instructed advertisers to depict Wacs in "complete G. I. uniform" in all graphic designs featuring female soldiers. In another media guide, the OWI urged all commentators to accept and transmit the government's official line: "Women in uniform are no less feminine than before they enlisted." A two-page fashion spread in the recruitment pamphlet, "A Book of Facts about the WAC," cast female soldiers in the poses of runway models and department store mannequins (fig. 43). Even if women didn't care for the featured styles, they might be enticed to join after learning they would be outfitted at no personal cost in a new wardrobe worth "about $250." The public relations effort addressed doubters who continued to question decisions allowing American women into the U.S. military.[28]

The prospect of female civilians in uniform also set opinion makers abuzz. In early 1942, as American women were urged to volunteer in whatever capacity they could, the question about uniforms surfaced on a regular basis. In the handbook *Calling All Women*, author Keith Ayling identified a few Civilian Defense positions that demanded special attire. Prospective volunteers learned that "five attractive uniforms" had been "officially adopted for wear by those *who are trained and qualified in their jobs.*" Presumably clothing would set apart air-raid wardens from canteen hostesses and both from nurses, allowing each to be easily identified. The message also suggested that only those women serious enough about volunteerism to undergo rigorous training or endure long hours would enjoy the privilege of wearing uniforms. Others were encouraged to take positions even if they had to wear their own clothes. "Martha" jobs, such as sewing, patching, and darning, and similar volunteer work, required no special attire; nor did maintaining morale, which required a woman only "to kill rumor with intelligent optimism." And as the guide assured them, "[Y]ou don't have to wear a uniform or take a course of training to do that." Given the growing popularity of martial style in fashion, however, some women wanted clothes to herald their home front contributions. According to Ayling one prospective volunteer "swept in with considerable enthusiasm" to commit to wartime duty but then quickly left the office after learning that her chosen job required no uniform. The woman's motivation for home front work made her appear suspect, too superficial to carry out necessary, even if unglamorous, tasks. Yet propaganda writers continued to use clothing as an enticement if they thought it would lead more women to volunteer.[29]

The notion of civilian women in uniform remained unsettling, however. Uniforms could signify assumption of duty or commitment of time and resources, but as some worried, perhaps merely an opportunity to show off a developing trend in fashion. Civilian women who needed to wear uniforms or wanted to don uniform style in their leisure time did so at their own risk. Department store Bonwit Teller's Ethel Gorham advised women who planned to undertake volunteer work, "Even if it is permissible to, but not required, don't wear a uniform. If it is both required and necessary, just wear your uniform during the allotted time and change back into ordinary clothes as soon as you can." In her book *So Your Husband's Gone to War!* Gorham implored wives to make as few changes as possible in their newly altered lives, particularly if change meant assuming a more public identity than before the war. In a chapter devoted solely to clothing decisions, Gorham recommended that women not rush to buy new suits even if they were all the rage in fashion. "Don't you feel that after seeing suits, suits, suits going up and down again, there's been too much stress on them, useful as they are? . . . You don't want to get bored with yourself and your clothes by seeing yourself coming and going on every street in the land. Neither do men want to see you regimented into stand-bys that all look alike. (They are probably sick of themselves in uniforms, like peas in a pod, and feel enough is enough.)" Gorham's sentiment was felt widely. Apparel was supposed to separate women from men. The USO organizers certainly agreed, as junior hostesses had to dress like the "good girls" they were supposed to be and stand as far afield as possible from military styles and colors. As Meghan Winchell reports of a Baltimore club's dictates to its young entertainers: "Khaki, blue, and gray were 'out,' while pink and white were 'most appealing.'" True femininity was outfitted in dresses rather than WPB-cut suits, even though women continued to put their consumer dollars toward suit purchases.[30]

American fashion dictators turned away from martial style very soon after Allied Forces staged a successful invasion of France in the summer of 1944. With optimism high on the political front, cultural arbiters looked toward postwar style. *Harper's Bazaar* boldly announced the fall of 1944: "The G.I. look is gone." Zeroing in on two characteristic elements of uniform style—shoulder pads and sharp lapels—the fashion arbiter noted that "broad-shouldered masculinity" had been replaced by "smooth and rounded" shoulders and "small, high, pushed-out, and rounded" lapels. The look, it was suggested, would be complete with a final touch to enhance a female body, where "under the jacket your waist is hugged like an hourglass." Such deliberate exposure of the female form would supposedly counteract what uniforms had done to American women during the war. However carefully tailored the military "look" (for both soldiers and civilians), it remained a uniform. As Paul Fussell argues, the point of military uniforms is to separate those who wear them from the larger culture. He relies on modernist writer Hermann Broch's explanation that a uniform "provides its wearer with a definitive line of demarcation between his person and the world" concealing "whatever in the human body is soft and flowing, covering up the soldier's underclothes and skin." Given the popularity of the "G.I. look" in civilian clothes on the American home front and the enthusiastic embrace of martial style by women, something had to be done to renegotiate femininity after an Allied victory seemed within reach. In many ways, the efforts to impress upon women new designs that enhanced the "soft and flowing" corporeal characteristics could be viewed as recovery missions. If uniforms and uniform styles had erected barriers between women and the larger culture, these were to come down. To suggest that women could hold onto the garments that separated them from society and protected them, in part, from its gaze would allow them too much autonomy; after all, in the end women's bodies belonged not to themselves but to everyone. Postwar fashion would work to promote this assumption.[31]

While martial style for civilian women may have waned in the last months of the war, one traditional male garment that so many of them bought and wore in the early 1940s would remain in their wardrobes indefinitely. Narrower skirts, frills-free dresses, and "military style" suits generated some consternation, but they were no match for the most shocking new item in women's wartime wardrobes: slacks. Pants had appeared earlier in lounge clothes and leisure wear, but World War II made them both a fashion statement and a necessity. Cultural historian Elizabeth Wilson claims that "the advance of the trouser for women" was "the most significant fashion change of the twentieth century." Early in 1942 *Women's*

Wear Daily and *Vogue* informed their upscale readers about the advantages *and* drawbacks of slacks. *Vogue* even offered instructions on "How to Wear Them." *LIFE* magazine featured a model in slacks on the cover of its spring 1942 fashion issue. To accompany it, the magazine's main story examined the trousers fad in an article entitled, "Men Lose Their Pants to Slack-Crazy Women." The photo-essay reveals the title to be mere sensationalism, as the images show ordinary women going about normal activities—strolling down city streets, walking to school, and socializing with one another. They simply carry out their daily routines in slacks rather than skirts. Although *LIFE* warned that "such spectacles will increase," its message indicated that women remained safely in their places even if they dressed differently. Only a couple of the dozen images in *LIFE's* narrative point to a new trend in American life—women working in heavy industry. One woman steadies a drill with her knee on the factory floor, the pose revealing the necessity of wearing pants on the job. Although just a hint in *LIFE* magazine, such images proliferated in subsequent months as women flooded into U.S. munitions plants (figs. 44 and 45).[32]

Soon after the 1942 mobilization efforts began, what women wore into the factories stimulated nationwide discussion. Cluett, Peabody & Company, known best for manufacturing men's shirts, offered their line of War Work Garments for Women. The company stressed the functionality of their single-style uniforms, noting that they would "eliminate the urge for 'out-dressing' fellow-workers." Cluett, Peabody officials urged that designs vary only by department or division, so that "feminine workers" could be "quickly identified when they wander from where they belong." The concern discloses the cultural belief in the early 1940s that women were generally undisciplined when it came to paid employment. Every effort and ploy would be needed to keep them on task, it was assumed, especially if they had not worked outside the domestic arena. Conformity could stimulate production and keep female workers focused on their assignments.[33]

As early as September 1942 the Ford Company required its female employees to wear slacks on the job. Some companies, such as Curtiss-Wright in St. Louis, offered cheap and fashionable work clothes. Even though it didn't require female employees to wear uniforms early in the war, the aircraft plant encouraged their use by providing a "well-cut, washable navy blue slack suit, trimmed with yellow braid and a Curtiss-Wright insignia" for just $3.41. Boeing Aircraft Company approved certain coveralls designed to protect women's "regular clothes from wear and tear." One government report warned against a single style or color, announcing unequivocally, "Women dislike too much standardization and insist on the right to keep themselves attractive, even at work. Brown-eyed girls and those with auburn hair may resent blues while blue-eyed girls may resent browns. Give them

Figure 44. "With nearly 1,000 Negro women employed as burners, welders, scalers and in other capacities at the Kaiser Shipyards in Richmond, Calif., women war workers played an important part in the construction of the liberty ship, ss *George Washington Carver*, launched on May 7, 1943. Welder-trainee Josie Lucille Owens plies her trade on the ship." E. F. Joseph for owi, 1943. RG 208, National Archives Still Picture Branch (#28671).

a choice of colors." D. H. Davenport, a Labor Department official, recommended to owi photo division chief Roy Stryker that he send photographers to the Briggs plants in the Detroit area, where they would find aesthetically pleasing scenes of women in aircraft manufacturing. They would satisfy the camera eye and the viewing public as well, he argued, since Briggs employees did not wear uniforms but "slacks of different colors," which "add[ed] considerably to the picturesqueness of the factory." The wmc argued that creatively designed ID badges worn on the upper chest served a dual purpose, "to mark women war workers and make working both patriotic and fashionable."[34]

This urge to maintain a decorative function for women workers coexisted uneasily with government clothing regulations. In suggesting specific ways that local institutions—from churches to women's clubs to radio stations—could encourage women to seek paid employment, the War Manpower Commission often mentioned apparel. Retail store managers were told they could help by arranging

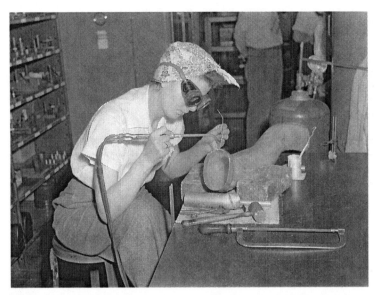

Figure 45. "Steady of eye and hand, women workers at the great Willow Run bomber plant are among those throughout the country who are relieving serious shortages of skilled workers by doing such semi-skilled jobs as the one shown here. She's welding parts of the cooling system direct to the supercharger. Ford plant, Willow Run [Michigan]." Ann Rosener, July 1942. FSA-OWI Collection, Library of Congress (LC-USE6-D-005688), digital ID: fsa 8e11141.

"displays of good-looking work clothes for women" in prominent places in their stores, primarily as a means of "selling the idea that proper working clothes promote *safety, neatness, health*, etc. Women should be convinced that overalls, slacks, and sensible shoes are the order of the day." The Women's Bureau of the U.S. Labor Department spent months campaigning nationwide for protective clothing in all war industries. Even after the WMC sent directives to companies to enforce safety standards on all fronts, some Labor Department inspectors found that industrial managers would not comply until threatened with prosecution.[35]

Despite their growing appeal in popular culture and the government's recommendations about slacks for war work, some commentators capitalized on women's insecurities about their newest clothing option. The makers of Tampax pointed out that slacks could be "very revealing if worn over any bulges or wrinkles," and that women who desired a "smooth and slick" appearance needed to wear internal absorption products during menstrual periods. A 1942 newspaper advertisement announced the endorsement of a burgeoning demographic in its headline, "Girls in Slacks at War Plants Hail Tampax." Fashion writer Ethel Gorham discouraged the wartime trend for aesthetic reasons, announcing, "Most women look like the devil in slacks. . . . For the one long-legged, rangy, stomachless girl who looks like Marlene Dietrich in trousers, there are all the ninety-nine others who simply look hippy, bulgy, and sloppy." If women could not live without pants, she insisted that they have them altered just as they had their skirts fitted to flatter their shapes. But Gorham also argued against women wearing trousers for political reasons, asking, "[W]hy do you have to wear slacks on city streets just to show you're all-out in the war effort? Why do you have to get into pants to prove your loyalty?" In the end, gender definition guided her most vehement criticism of the new fashion trend, noting that men were "violently anti-slacks" and laughed bitterly at women who wore them. She explained such mockery as resentment at what slacks represented, specifically, "all the 'mannish' jobs" that American women had assumed. Suggesting that men worried about "their own masculine supremacy in the future," Gorham admonished her readers, "Why rub it in?"[36]

Such threats to the gendered social order surfaced regularly and in various quarters. A *Los Angeles Times* promotion ran a photograph of female airplane builders alongside the headline: "Now she REALLY wears the Pants." The quip's message goes beyond the actual garment to the power accorded the worker by the nature of her paycheck. Readers in the retail trade, the main audience for the advertisement, could understand the announcement as a consumer call. The woman in pants signaled a new social phenomenon, certainly, but more important to them, she wielded even greater purchasing power than before she put on a worker's trousers and collected steady and solid wages. Constance Bowman, a high school teacher who spent the summer of 1943 working in a San Diego bomber factory and kept daily notes on her experiences there, illuminated the public's reaction to women in trousers. She was shocked by the treatment she got in public when she wore slacks—catcalls, whistles, pawing, and suggestive comments from strangers like the marine who stalked her after her swing shift had ended, heckling all the way, "How about a little war work, Sister?" Bowman got a small taste of what working-class women had endured for decades—harassment sanctioned by the stereotype that working women were sexually available due to their public visibility. Although Bowman's hourly wage of 68 cents set her above many of her working-class counterparts, such as textile mill laborers and domestic servants, she could no longer enjoy the cultural insulation protecting white women who remained at home or who had appropriately "feminized" pink- and white-collar employment as teachers, nurses, secretaries, or social workers. When she submitted a book manuscript about her experiences a few months after leaving the factory, Bowman only half-jokingly suggested as her title, "*We Were Available*." Trousers marked millions of women during the war, opening the floodgates of anger and resentment by those who could not abide gender role redefinition in such a public manner.[37]

Bowman attributed the insults and abusive treatment she and a coworker received largely to the fact that they had to wear their work slacks to and from the factory. She could not believe that "people who knew us acted as if they didn't" and "people who didn't know us whistled as if they did." Bowman claimed that women in skirts received much better treatment in department stores, on the streets, and on public transportation. After just a few days on the job at the B-24 plant, she and her coworker and fellow schoolteacher Clara Marie Allen "were beginning to hate women who could wear skirts to work." Men would give up their bus seats to such women and assist them in other ways, while Bowman and other female factory workers were ignored or looked at with disdain. To test their theory about trouser-clad women, Bowman and Allen spent their first free Sunday out, dressed up in linen suits and high-heeled shoes. On a city bus, no fewer than eight servicemen offered them seats, which they gratefully accepted. One of Bowman and Allen's most telling lessons in the summer of 1943 was the "great shock" at learning that "being a lady depended more upon our clothes than upon ourselves." Bowman concluded, "[W]e found out that it was not our innate dignity that protected us from unwelcome attentions, but our trim suits, big hats, white gloves, and spectator pumps. Clothes, we reflected sadly, make the woman—and some clothes make the man think that he can make the woman." Bowman spoke, of course, as a white woman. Dressing up failed to protect women of color against men in uniform who groped, abused, and attacked them in public. The symbolic meaning of garments worked for some but not all American women.[38]

Slacks sent other messages about literal or potential gender crossings, especially where women participated in activities traditionally identified with men. Since the All-American Girls Professional Baseball League organizers sought to promote "neatness and feminine appeal" both on and off the field, it prohibited players from wearing slacks in public. Team members could don sportswear for leisure activities such as tennis and golf, but otherwise, they were to appear in skirts, blouses, and jackets, and, at special social functions, in dresses. That they took the field in short skirts revealed the league creators' goals of entertainment and spectacle more than anything else. Hoping for a serious approach to the game, Indiana sportswriter Jim Costin had disapprovingly predicted when the league was formed that the players would "wear scanties, if that's the word for the abbreviated softball uniforms that girls wear." Costin's prediction came true, but he was able to look beyond their attire to encourage the public to attend games based on "the quality of ball played by the girls." Sliding into third base barelegged could indicate toughness or competitive spirit, but off the field, a player reminded her public that she was first and foremost a respectable young woman, and baseball merely a game.[39]

Because pants became "acceptable garb for women" during the war, "a distinctive lesbian 'style'" developed around them, Lillian Faderman argues. Before the war "butch lesbians understood that while they might wear pants at home, they had to change to a skirt to go out on the street—unless they were able to pass as men." While pants became a symbol of identification for some gay women, Faderman suggests that the popularity of slacks assisted the lesbian community in role definition, in that "butch and femme distinctions in style could be more pronounced, and the roles became very clear-cut for more lesbians." With lesbian sexuality considered "the ultimate promiscuity" during the Second World War, any woman wearing pants in public might find herself a target of epithets and other abuse.[40]

The U.S. government offered assistance on the clothing front to women pursuing traditional routes in gender role definition. The WPB's decision to exempt wedding gowns and maternity clothes from textile conservation measures demonstrated official commitment to marriage and motherhood as social pillars. Clergymen had argued that white wedding gowns helped to ensure religious solemnity and reinforce tradition, while the apparel industry contended that "long white gowns were vital for morale." The U.S. Census Bureau estimated "more than a million more families were formed" between 1940 and 1943 than would have been under "normal" conditions. Along with soldier–sweetheart liaisons, marriage in defense boom areas rose sharply: Cincinnati saw a 51 percent increase, Baltimore underwent a 47 percent rise, and in San Diego, "marriages doubled and even trebled in those first hectic two years of mobilization for war," Mercedes Rosebery reported. Many brides chose not to wear traditional gowns, but for those who did, the nation's official sanction of a sacred ritual shored up domestic femininity.[41]

The cultural whirlwind caused by new government-regulated styles, the range of uniforms, and the rapid mainstream acceptance of slacks gave American women apparel options that they and their ancestors had never before enjoyed. But they were advised overtly and covertly to exercise these options with care. In traditional male arenas—heavy industry, professional sports, and the military—they needed to deflect criticism by shedding their "duration" apparel as soon as they could. Wearing the right clothes when it mattered most—in their leisure time, off the job, with friends or family—indicated that war work was temporary. It could be boxed off, categorized, punched in and out, without irreversible effects. Connie Bowman's decision to wear her trousers to and from work unnerved those around her because she blurred gender lines. In this and millions of cases like hers, an item of clothing could be interpreted in disparate ways, as a mark of independence, mobility, nonconformity, or comfort. If a public slacks wearer did not neutralize her choice with feminine "embellishments" such as colorful accessories and decorative shoes, to show, in Susan Brownmiller's words, her "heterosexual good will," she could expect intense criticism.[42] Attire marked as "feminine" could help keep sexuality safely circumscribed. As more women filled men's jobs, occupied men's spaces, and participated in men's activities, how they chose to cover their flesh mattered more than ever.

Beneath the apparel visible to the gazing public lay more challenges for policy makers and ordinary citizens. Wartime "foundations"—brassieres, corsets, and girdles—frustrated women who relied on these items to safely and dependably sculpt their bodies. Changes occurred just a few months after Pearl Harbor, as the WPB moved quickly to address materials shortages. Declaration L-90, the keystone in the U.S. government's corset and brassiere policy, reduced the availability of rubber in "foundations" manufacturing but deemed the garments "essential." Since East Asian rubber supplies had been blocked and the remaining sources were needed for war materials, women soon discovered that their newly purchased underclothes lacked two valuable qualities: durability and flexibility. With the brassiere and corset industry's elastic allowance cut in half, new foundation garments yielded indiscriminate results. The synthetics that became available in the United States to replace rubber, including neoprene and nylon, failed to meet standards American women had come to expect in their intimate apparel. Commentator Janice Griffiths wrote that as "guinea pigs for new and substitute products," women had been subject to "interesting, annoying [and] downright exasperating" experiences that were simply "hell in the lingerie department." The poorly constructed new foundations included girdles with little "give" and garters with too much "grab." The WPB advisory committee responsible for the initial policy in early 1942 met again in the summer of 1943 to address "the materials situation." After congratulating itself on the "generally satisfactory manner in which L-90 [was] operating," the committee—comprising twenty-four men and three women—acknowledged the industry's problems and anticipated policy revision as soon as additional synthetic rubber sources were released. While most discussion centered on practical matters such as fabric weights and weave designs, a few members expressed concern about "stiff and uncomfortable" garments that might irritate skin or worse, not "be successfully moulded [sic] to the figure." The committee concluded that wartime foundations had caused "considerable dissatisfaction among all classes of women."[43]

If women had known they faced a future with precarious garters and stiff girdles, they might not have so readily and enthusiastically given up their old things in salvage campaigns. Americans went through closets, basements, and attics to find galoshes, gloves, old doormats, hot-water bottles, garden hoses, and more. Children donated their rubber toys, swimmers gave up their rubber suits, and office workers turned in their rubber stamps. The most titillating stories of sacrifice, however, focused on women relinquishing their "unmentionables." The *Washington Times Herald* identified four local dancers as "patriettes" after they gave up their garters to a rubber drive. The story's accompanying photograph showed the young women with skirts pulled thigh high, unsnapping their donations. The photo caption sanitized the image while simultaneously making it more provocative: "This isn't a strip act, but a scrap act. . . . Nobody asked for their girdles, but if the girls want to stretch that point, well and good." The rather innocuous encouragement to the young women to rid themselves of other binding garments implied further unleashing of female flesh. The guise of patriotic duty mitigated the inherent dangers in such deeds—namely free bodies and enhanced sexual awareness and availability. Women who wanted to exercise more corporeal freedom used the environment of national need to test and expand prewar gender boundaries. But even if they eliminated constrictive undergarments from their wardrobes, they came up against a cultural standard that held firm on the ideal female figure as a slender silhouette.[44]

The most logical result of women's surrender of their intimate items failed to transpire. Freeing the literal body from its artificial constraints did not prompt acceptance of looser or larger torsos and hips. The prized corporeal design instead remained slender in waist and hips and smooth in appearance. Roberta Pollack Seid argues that early twentieth-century industrialization, technological development, modernization, and "the ideology of efficiency" all contributed "to reinforce the slenderized ideal" of the human body, thus establishing "the framework for our prejudice against fat." Industrial design in the 1920s and 1930s pushed these ideas further, refining and shaping structures large and small, from skyscrapers to pillboxes, inspiring a machine age aesthetic enthusiastically perpetuated in the midst of the Great Depression. Sleek machines matured with modern architecture as well as women's apparel, allowing the literal embodiment of new design. Women's dresses in particular depended on body-skimming textiles and cuts that required smooth corporeal outlines to achieve the desired effect. Undergarments became the unseen helpers in accomplishing the requisite smoothness. In 1941 the Vassarette Company promised its products would offer "smooth re-drawing" of the wearer's body to effect "one long, liquid line." Despite the War Production Board's declaration on undergarment limitations, the girdle industry touted its products as more necessary than ever, arguing "L-85 dresses require a more perfect silhouette." As Farrell-Beck and Gau point out, "Women had to have good shapes under dresses that molded closely to the body and lacked the distraction of extensive trimmings." Those who had given up their rubber-based garments as an expression of patriotic duty found little of substance to replace them; they had lost a trusted ally.[45]

Editors and designers emphasized ways that women could and should control the sizes, shapes, and other attributes of their bodies. More than ever before, mainstream women's magazines promoted the shrinking female body as something to strive for. Numerous articles offered tips on weight loss. *Harper's Bazaar* had to reprint a diet published in a 1943 article entitled "Reducing with Meat" after the issue sold out on newsstands. Daily newspapers urged the weight-loss trend as well. In May 1943 the *Pittsburgh Sun-Telegraph* boasted the newspaper's devotion to women who wanted to "safely slim down" by promising, in an echo of the U.S. Navy tune, "Hips Hips Away." Alongside the promise a revelatory image featured a woman on a scale with a tape measure around her hips; recording her "progress" on a weight wall chart, she had begun at 140 pounds but was poised to mark the 105-pound line. The newspaper claimed that 235 women had written to its editors in the last month to find out about losing weight. *Woman's Home Companion* told women: "Change Your Food, but Keep Your Figure."[46]

With substandard, unreliable wartime undergarments, the corporeal ideal would be harder to achieve. Some dressmakers touted designs that could be comfortably worn without girdles, including one rayon set dubbed a "duration suit." The garments boasted adjustable waistlines and bust lines. Despite these options, *McCall's* editors suggested a "Self-Mortification-for-Victory" program, noting: "Just what the lack of girdles will eventually do to styles is anybody's guess, but Washington's experts don't hold out much hope for a return to solid, hefty bulges. Stay slim for healthy beauty and morale—that's their advice. . . . Go slow on fats and sweets. And take exercises.'" If wartime undergarments could no longer do the job, women would have to shape themselves from within—minimizing food intake and maximizing physical activity. While most studies of fad dieting and eating disorders among American women have focused on the postwar era, evidence suggests that wartime policy and cultural expectations also encouraged women to hide or eliminate excess flesh. Brownmiller identifies the 1940s "campaign of diet and exercise" in martial terms, casting it as a "full-scale battle." While "chubby" girls and teens continued to be recognized by the WPB as a viable group who deserved certain allowances in their clothing, young and middle-aged women were to maintain a smooth, sleek appearance if they desired affirmation on the home front.[47]

Women's military organizations used a trim, healthy body image as recruitment fodder, and some of their claims were borne out in actual servicewomen's lives. One award-winning advertisement played on a soldier's exhilaration at her physical transformation. In a letter to a friend, she proudly intimated: "you should see me now, since the Air-WACS have remodeled me. Three inches gone from my waistline. Appetite terrific." The quintessential Wac in H. I. Phillips's *All-Out Arlene* stood 5 feet 8 inches tall and weighed 132 pounds. Many women who joined various branches of the military happily reported the changes in their bodies to their families and friends. Marine Mary Cugini wrote to her younger sister Dena about physical training at Camp Lejeune, North Carolina: "These exercises certainly streamline our figures. My legs have nice muscles in them now." A few weeks later Cugini assumed her new bookkeeping assignment in Arlington, Virginia. The shift from training outdoors to a desk job indoors prompted her to take stock of the physical changes she had undergone since joining the USMCWR, intimating that she had gained ten pounds. Aileen Kilgore, who just barely earned a spot in the WAC due to her low weight, assured her parents that she had "plenty" to eat at training camp, noting "My little belly feels like it might explode any minute." Food was a major theme in her letters home, reflecting her amazement at its variety and abundance, the experience of thousands of soldiers who had suffered lean years as children and teenagers during the Great Depression. Early on she concluded, "Good food is the outstanding thing about the Army to me." During her nearly two years in the WAC, Kilgore's weight fluctuated from 99 to 116 pounds and hit various points in between, which she carefully recorded and reported to her family. The trend began just a few weeks into her training, when she wondered, "I look at my legs and suspect I'm getting fat." To her own diary she confided a week later, "We tear around here at such high speed I'll never get fat." Newspaper columnist Keith Frazier Somerville assured her Bolivar County, Mississippi, readers that local women who had joined the WAC reported "the food good" at their Florida training camp. SPAR enlistee Pearl "Perla" Gullickson described "a typical Army mess" as "too heavy" for her. After only two months in the Women Airforce Service Pilots (WASP) training at Sweetwater, Texas, Marion Stegeman wrote to her mother another self-described "slap-happy" letter, which she concluded simply, "I'm so healthy and feel so good that it's revolting. . . . EEEEEEEE, law! What a life!"[48]

Besides military service, war work encouraged awareness of prospective and actual corporeal changes. A New Yorker who identified herself as "one of a great company of brown women working from 12 to 8" said of her late-night shift: "[U]nusual hours are broadening both my outlook and my figure. Positively I have gained five pounds this month!" She claimed to have been eating "really nourishing food instead of 'trash.'" Southern Californians Connie Bowman and Clara Marie Allen had heard rumors about swing shift weight gain and were worried that they might succumb to the temptation of eating four instead of three meals a day, a change recommended by nutrition experts during the war. Food icon Betty Crocker insisted on "a light extra meal" for swing- or night-shift workers due to fatigue from "broken sleep." After taking summer jobs at a San Diego aircraft plant, Bowman and Allen "took a solemn vow" to "never, absolutely never, under any conditions, not even as a special celebration on pay night, take *one* small bite after work." As Bowman wrote, "We thought bitterly that it would be *too much* to work on the production line all summer and get fat *besides!*" She observed that her coworkers ate "*all* the time" but she managed to stay trim. After just a few weeks on the job, Bowman and Allen were happily "pounds lighter and inches thinner." Their transformation invited welcome compliments. An acquaintance they saw one day on the street looked them over "admiringly" and "enviously," exclaiming: "'What are you doing this summer? You must be having a wonderful time!'" Leotha Hackshaw, an African American ordnance inspector on the East Coast, got quite different reactions to her dramatic weight loss. Dropping twenty pounds during her first month on the job, Hackshaw got a stern warning from her doctor to quit work that was clearly "much too hard" for her. She "needed every pound," her doctor insisted.[49]

To celebrate African American women working in industry and to encourage more to apply for factory jobs, the *Brown American* claimed that industrial labor "streamlined" the body, touting: "Surplus weight is discarded, and abdominal muscles, unrestricted for the first time in years, tend to be firm and shapely." As African American female bodies grew slimmer and tauter, they defied the stereotype of the rotund black woman, thus moving real bodies into a realm of whiteness. The *Brown American*'s verbal encouragement of streamlining did not square, however, with an image the editors chose to illustrate a feature story on industrial workers (fig. 46). The figure's pear shape emphasizes instead the kind of "plumpness" traditionally seen as a symbol of "health and prosperity" for African American women. Among the many wars fought on the American home front in the 1940s were those inside the black community as a better job market challenged tight class strictures and popular culture wrestled with racial boundaries.[50]

Degrees of whiteness were adjudicated in many wartime venues, with thinner female bodies garnering awards for ideal femininity. *Crisis* covers in the early 1940s revealed the magazine's embrace of a thinness standard for African American women that lined up closely with the white women who competed in the annual Miss America Pageant in Atlantic City. In July 1944 *Crisis* featured on its cover a swimsuit-clad woman identified as "Tan Tidbit—Summer Style" (fig. 47). Identified inside the issue as Priscilla Williams, she was one of several "gorgeous lassies" in similar attire who filled the pages of a story on the Sepia Miss America competition, a "nationwide series of contests to select the outstanding Negro beauty in the country."[51] In other photographs, the young women paraded in lines arranged for viewers to compare their physical attributes. The activities mimicked Miss America "walks" and revues. The annual Atlantic City affair influenced many similar competitions. At the University of Georgia, Sigma Chi fraternity members selected not only their annual sweetheart but also a female classmate they deemed "Modern

Figure 46. African American war worker.
Brown American, Summer 1943.

Venus." Women competed in a variety of games and races to win the Sigma Chi Sweetheart title, but they had to submit to a tape measure and scales to attain the rank of goddess. The fraternity men themselves took each woman's measurements in order to see who came closest to the "ideal" standard set by Miss America each year. Sigma Chi's Modern Venus for 1942, Blanche Wallace, stood 5 foot 5½ inches and weighed 120 pounds. As the years passed, the "ideal" American woman for the Delta chapter had grown smaller. An early Miss America in the 1920s, Mary Campbell, had stood over an inch taller and weighed 140 pounds.[52]

That some women chose to limit their food consumption during the war reveals one of many home front incongruities. While modern middle-class women had been denying themselves food for decades, such behavior could be linked during the 1940s to fulfillment of public duty. Self-inflicted hunger persisted in the face of widespread nutrition campaigns designed to increase the overall health of Americans. Joan Jacobs Brumberg argues, however, that "dieting seemed an

The CRISIS

July, 1944 • Fifteen Cents

TAN TIDBIT—SUMMER STYLE

Sepia Miss America

Figure 47. Sepia Miss America contestant. *Crisis* cover, July 1944.

inappropriate and silly preoccupation in the midst of scarcity and a compelling national emergency. . . . During the war women who waited in line for a weekly ration of butter and sugar were more likely to savor than to reject items made from these hard-to-get ingredients." Food historian Amy Bentley points out that "cultural latitude regarding body shape and size" in the 1940s meant "women with fuller figures did not necessarily feel the pressure to diet."[53] Dire economic and political conditions no doubt prevented self-starvation from playing the same role among women that it did in times of peace and prosperity, but those who aspired to achieve a modern standard of physical beauty and style during the war needed to limit their food intake. Magazine and newspaper advertising, posters, car cards, and billboards all revealed the ideal wartime female figure—that of "discriminating women"—as svelte. With women's fashions shorter and briefer than ever before, American women were pressed to recognize standards of clothing designers such as Nettie Rosenstein, whose "perfect world" had all women possess "high, well-rounded breasts, slim waists and gently curving backsides." In 1944 Elizabeth Arden, a cosmetics guru who had expanded her business to include fashion, introduced her vision of "the new American figure," where a "rule of proportion" with "ideal measurements" dictated whether a woman would be able to carry off sartorial splendor. The wartime silhouette equated clothes, bodies, and food in an unprecedented new formula.[54]

Women who bought food for their own households may have been more practical about rationed items, but those who boarded at someone else's table or ate their main meals during a work shift or at a government-run cafeteria did not have to consider bulk food purchases as seriously as did homemakers. And for a young woman weighing the costs of sexual availability or aggressiveness against the strictures of middle-class respectability and attendant chastity, a safe middle ground may have been in one of the few areas over which she had control—food intake. Amid rapidly shifting political, economic, and social templates, those who ate little "could dissociate themselves from sexuality and fecundity," thus using their bodies to express much more in the ways of "intelligence, sensitivity, and morality." The *Washington Post* told local war workers who were "fat and dumpy" to take action in order to experience the "satisfaction" from "cutting a fine figure."[55]

Thin wartime bodies—those created by designers and artists and those inhabited and controlled by women themselves—emerged from the rhetoric of political sacrifice, home front conservation, future prosperity, and modern style. To limit personal food intake, to measure waists and busts and hips then wrap them in "foundations" without much foundation were ways that women could test their patriotic mettle. The Second World War, like all wars before it, depended on sacrificial bodies. Those who were not engaged in combat could fight in other ways, turning their bodies into battlegrounds worthy of notice.

Among the images of malnourished women during the war, those whose hunger appeared most noble were service wives. The kind of concern expressed in the media for poorly fed working women extended as well to military spouses, becoming a usable theme on the home front. Zelda Popkin illuminated this sentiment in an early scene in her novel, *The Journey Home* (1945). In it her protagonist, Air Force lieutenant Don Corbett, observes a military family standing on a train platform. Of the four—the sailor, his wife, a toddler, and a baby—the woman quickly attracts Corbett's attention: "She was thin, he saw, as service wives are, because they're so young and worry so much and don't eat enough since there's no man coming home for a meal and it's much too much bother to cook for yourself."[56] Corbett's evaluation failed to confront one of the realities that many such women faced—making ends meet on paltry military salaries, and for some, on or near defense camps far from home and extended family. The typical U.S. Army PFC who landed overseas made about seventy-five dollars per month. Soldiers' and sailors' wives had to scrimp and save and share housing with friends or family or strangers to be able to feed themselves and their children, especially if they were not earning wages themselves. Countless military spouses accompanied their husbands to training camps and embarkation points, many of them living in substandard housing with limited cooking facilities, if any at all. In *The Journey Home*, Corbett sees the sailor's wife's need or desire for good nutrition as inextricably linked to that of her husband: as he ate, so did she, unconcerned about her own health as separate from his. For women who lived on the margins of stateside military camps, food was not as plentiful as that provided by the U.S. government to their husbands inside the gates.[57]

Early in the war, advertising executives had identified a national nutrition problem, pointing in particular to those who could afford food but chose "to exist on cheese sandwiches and pie, paying scant attention to such necessities as vitamins." One cultural critic described Americans as "unimaginative" eaters who always sought "chain restaurants" when they ate out. The war emergency gave the American advertising industry an opportunity to work with U.S. government agencies in the area of nutrition education "to increase the health of the nation." Home front propaganda employed the image of the military wife as thin and sometimes hungry but not by her own choice. Not disinterested in cooking or eating (as Popkin and others depicted her), she was instead an innocent victim of consumer corruption—by other women who literally and figuratively took food from her table. In appeals to advertisers nationwide, the Ad Council's agencies recommended certain images in the sample advertisements they distributed for national anti-inflation campaigns. A pervasive theme in the agencies' "copy slants" pitted women with money against soldiers' wives. In one scene a mother and her two young children sit quietly in their living room, at the center of which stands a framed portrait of the absent father in uniform. The domestic scene is made more poignant by a headline warning grocery shoppers, "DON'T MAKE IT ANY HARDER FOR THEM." The family would suffer if food buyers, most of them women, ignored Office of Price Administration (OPA) regulations on food prices. Shoppers were also encouraged to keep grocers honest by reporting any errors in a store's posted price listings, and if these were not corrected, to report the violation to their local rationing board. With nutrition identified in the private sector as "one of the most vital arms in the entire defense program," those who bought and prepared food on the home front became warriors in their own right. By taking a Home Front

Pledge—to pay "no more than ceiling prices" even if they had the means to do so and later to "accept no rationed goods without giving up ration stamps"—homemakers could ensure a fair food economy.[58]

Government propagandists used hungry bodies and women's clothes as signs to educate women about home front overindulgence. Official messages insinuated that apparel could betray status and moral behavior. The woman most likely to be victimized in the food economy, the service wife, wore plainly tailored L-85 dresses, simple hats, and sensible shoes. The woman who stood to abuse her, marked by privilege, wore furs, jewels, gathered gloves, showy hats, even ruffled collars—a forbidden extra under WPB domestic textiles regulations. Any analysis of "food and eating in America has to confront the complex interaction between production, consumption, and identity," argues Joan Jacobs Brumberg, who implores us to look at "the culture of women, a culture that made food suspect because of a deeply rooted aversion to any form of sensuous self-indulgence." If, as Brumberg argues, women's "displays of appetite" were considered "dangerous," then these appetites presumably mattered more and came under greater scrutiny during a political crisis where civilian decision-making centered on the theme of sacrifice. Although Brumberg focuses on individual food consumption, her theory can be applied more broadly to female consumer culture during the Second World War. Graphic designers for the Ad Council and the OWI pushed the appropriate emotional buttons in their images of greedy women whose voracious appetites manifested themselves not necessarily in food intake but food purchase. Overindulgence came not at the table but in the store, where money empowered them to control food in a different—in fact, illegal—way. *Gourmet* magazine ran full-page ads cautioning those who could afford to pay more than OPA ceiling prices: "Maybe *you* can, but how about the millions of soldiers' families who must live on Army allotments?"[59]

After the D-Day invasion in 1944 and subsequent Allied successes in Europe, the Ad Council, working in cooperation with the OWI and the OPA, intensified the "Food Fights for Freedom" campaign. OPA administrator Chester Bowles expressed concern that advertisers might use the "recent good news from the battle front" to ease their sponsorship of war programs, thus generating high inflation, which could ruin the domestic economy. Advertising motifs designed specifically to target "greater public compliance with price ceilings in the food field" set well-dressed women against humbly attired military wives. In one November advertisement, readers saw the warning: "Don't Outbid a Soldier's Wife . . . Her husband fights for the things we celebrate this day—thanksgiving for American plenty—deliverance from oppression. He fights to protect *our* freedom from want!" In another ad design, a haughty, pretentious protagonist remains indifferent to a military wife, who in a posture of prayer, casts a serene presence over her domestic environment. The angelic figure serves as a foil to the finely attired cheater who appears not merely unethical but evil. In a national context where government propaganda explained the war itself in terms of "good versus evil," the Ad Council's designs defined adversaries and battle lines. In the war agencies' food campaigns, courage, patriotism, and moral integrity were firmly planted in modestly attired female bodies facing literal or potential hunger. In the competition pitting women against women, apparel marked battle lines. The image of a U.S. military wife served as a perfect site for the intersections of food scarcity, corporeal thinness, and textiles conservation.[60]

As women continued to wear the war, all of their clothing choices were affected by closed-door discussions in Washington. Style coexisted with conservation, but for women working in heavy industry, safety also played a role in the national conversation. With wpb committees deliberating the domestic use of leather for shoe construction and textiles for millinery design, the government considered every item a woman put on from head to toe. Shoe retailers' influence in Washington meant that most of the high-level wpb talks focused on women's "desire" for stylish after-hours shoes rather than functional shoes for daily use or work. Promoting the notion that women in factories would get by during their shifts wearing "whatever they can use," even moccasins or platforms, the wpb failed to address what U.S. Secretary of Labor Frances Perkins found most alarming in occupational safety reports—the numerous industrial accidents among women in the "slip, fall, and stumble categories." Her insistence upon shoe designs to help women prevent such accidents failed to take hold, as leather supplies dwindled and fashion trumped safety.[61]

Despite the wpb Women's Millinery Advisory Committee's defense of hats as "strictly utilitarian," scarves, snoods, and other "hang-downs" disappeared from hat brims for the duration. Deemed "non-essential" by the wpb, women's hats came to match in brevity the simpler, trimmer wartime suit designs. Ethel Gorham suggested that American women show the same persistence in finding, decorating, and wearing beautiful hats as their British counterparts had done in the face of much harsher clothing restrictions. She insisted that cost mattered little, since a cheap hat could be embellished with "a cluster of violets and a length of veiling from the five-and-ten." *Advertising & Selling* contributor Margaret Gammon identified the home front bandana and headscarf craze as a revolt against the horrible hats available to American women. But bandanas, turbans, and similar designs also allowed millions of working women fashionable hair coverings (fig. 48).[62]

The Labor Department tried to convince American women workers to don safety hats rather than cloth coverings. wb analyst Margaret Mettert reported that "the most distressing accident" in war industry resulted "from hair catching in the

Figure 48. "Production. Willow Run bomber plant [Michigan]." Ann Rosener, July 1942. FSA-OWI Collection, Library of Congress (LC-USE6-D-005687), digital ID: fsa 8e11140.

moving parts of machinery." Gruesome stories made the government's case: one spinning machine operator was totally disabled for sixteen weeks and partially disabled for another forty-five weeks; an ordnance factory worker who lost a "large clump of hair" on a barrel-turning machine suffered as much from the shock as from the actual wound; and a Rhode Island woman was "completely scalped" after her hair caught on an assembly line belt. Debate centered on whether frightening employees into covering their heads would be more effective than threatening their employers with arrest if they failed to make their workers comply with safety standards.[63] Movie star Veronica Lake, whose blonde tresses became her trademark in the 1930s, posed for a graphic wartime message, warning the estimated twenty thousand women who chose to wear "peekaboo hairstyles" on the job that they were flirting with danger. In the image, Lake's platinum locks wrap easily around a drill press, revealing the kind of quick and painful accident that government officials warned against (fig. 49). In a subsequent *LIFE* magazine photo-essay, the actress wore a "swept-up hairdo" to educate and influence women in industry. OWI photographer Ann Rosener completed an assignment at Bendix Aviation in Brooklyn with a similar message. Her series on "how NOT to wear your hair" included captions reinforcing the government's official message about protection: "Woman's crowning glory is distinctly out of place in a machine shop—and

Figure 49. Veronica Lake poses on behalf of industrial safety. *LIFE*, March 8, 1943.

decidedly dangerous besides, unless completely tucked away beneath a safety hat."
(fig. 50). Arguing for hats rather than bandanas, the War Manpower Commission
announced: "An over-abundance of *cloth* on the head is just as apt to get caught
in machinery as an over-abundance of hair!" A few large industrial plants, such as
Lockheed, built beauty salons on site to assist women with both safety and style.[64]

But to what extent could the U.S. government force workers to wear safety hats
and caps? WB pamphlets warned managers not to impose a single hat style on all
women in their factories or send out a heavy-handed order; ideally female supervisors would broach the subject since as the WB emphasized, "women resent
admonitions about clothing from men." Unable to endorse specific companies'
designs, the Labor Department nevertheless distributed a poster showcasing a variety of styles in an array of fabrics. Without decree or coercion, the poster recommended appropriate designs for specific tasks, in general suggesting that women

Figure 50. "Eunice Kimball, with hair dangerously disheveled, poses in Bendix Aviation Plant to illustrate how the safety-conscious woman worker will not look. Bendix Aviation Plant, Brooklyn, New York." Ann Rosener, March 1943. FSA-OWI Collection, Library of Congress (LC-USE6-D-009755), digital ID: fsa 8b06437.

could make choices based on their individual needs and preferences.[65] Yet however diverse the designs, their characteristic practicality set them against the most widely circulated images of wartime "Rosies" as well as real workers' desires. One factory superintendent's frustrations mirrored those felt nationwide when he said, "We have tried all sorts of things and are still seeking a satisfactory arrangement to cover women's hair completely and have it stay there." That Connie Bowman devoted so much attention to the dilemma suggests it weighed significantly in the daily power struggles between female aircraft workers and their male supervisors at Vultee Aircraft. After Bowman told a bus driver about her supervisor reading a safety cap order aloud on the factory floor, the driver responded, "That'll be harder

Figure 51. "Cotton stockings. Lana Turner inspecting the ankle-flattering bracelet design embroidered on dressy, fine point lisle cotton mesh hose." October 1941. FSA-OWI Collection, Library of Congress (LC-USE6-D-001605).

to enforce than prohibition." Bowman recounted the struggle that ensued over the order: foremen calling out women who had exposed their hair, sending some of them home, giving others warning slips, and directing a few to rewrap their hair in scarves, towels, or whatever they could find. After a seventy-two-hour struggle and lost production time, the women won their fight. Overseers realized that enforcing the cap and hair coverage edict had become a fulltime job in itself and so gave up. Bowman's coworkers celebrated their victory by flaunting their individual hairstyles the next day.[66]

Although all women's apparel came under scrutiny during the war, nothing increased in value and assumed such a mythic place as stockings. Silk had begun to disappear in 1941 after the U.S. embargo on Japanese supplies. The policy led to greater dependence on nylon, which had contributed to 20 percent of hosiery before it, too, became an essential resource for parachute construction. Since nylon manufacturing required phenol, another valuable wartime industry resource, women's hosiery saw dramatic changes. Rayon was an alternative, despite its needs elsewhere (as in tire making), but stockings in rayon never became as popular as dresses and blouses in the fabric because the material did not lend itself to a sheer, sleek covering for legs. Ethel Gorham advised women early in the war not to buy up silk hosiery stock they might find left over from pre-WPB regulation days: "It's silly from a style point of view. If silk and nylon hose are going off the market entirely, and every shop is going to carry cotton and rayon and lisle instead, the fashion will be cotton and lisle. You'll look dated and dowdy wearing silken hose in a world where the men ogle the ankles in cotton mesh" (fig. 51). Ignoring such advice, women stormed hosiery counters in cities and towns all over the country. Police had to shut down a Pueblo, Colorado, department store after seven hundred women rushed in to buy the thirty pairs of nylon stockings that had just gone on sale. In a move to spur purchases in the first War Bond Drive, Bloomingdale's in New York announced it would allow each person who bought a bond to purchase two pairs of nylon hosiery. In fifteen minutes, ten thousand women came through Bloomingdale's doors. Within the hour, three thousand pairs of hosiery had been sold, but many customers went away empty-handed. Such scarcity inspired romantic tales of soldiers and sailors securing silk stockings overseas as special gifts for the women in their lives.[67]

As the hosiery business suffered, American women were impelled to consider hosiery's role in the overall scheme of the decorated body. The increasing popularity of slacks helped some solve their hosiery problem. If the makers of Lux soap promised to help women "cut down on [their] stocking bills" by preserving elasticity and fabric strength in the garments, they claimed even more boldly that regular use of the product would amount to "getting an extra pair of stockings!" And in a consumer culture offering poor and unattractive substitutes, an extra pair meant a great deal. WAC lieutenant Betty Bandel wrote enthusiastically to her mother about birthday gifts from fellow officers, with "2 pairs of nice stockings from Patty" topping the list. WAC enlistee Aileen Kilgore bragged to her parents about her first military hosiery issue, which included "4 pairs cotton stockings (for every day wear)" and "4 pairs handsome rayon hose (worn only with our dress-up uniform)." In December 1944 she decided to send stockings to her sisters as Christmas gifts. Promising her family even more hosiery in the near future, she reported months later, "The cotton hose have been taken off our records. Everybody hated them so much I should be able to collect more from the girls who don't want theirs." Kilgore's story reveals a minor yet telling benefit of her wartime military service— provisions for her rural southern family. She remained grateful for the clothing the army provided her, even the items considered unfashionable by most women.[68]

The bonds linking women's clothes, their bodies, and the ideal female form were tightened by brassieres, breast enhancement products, and the sweater girl phenomenon. The 1942–43 Sears Roebuck Catalog offered breast augmentation devices, and the Charmode Company sold its "Flatterettes" for seventy-seven cents a pair. The foam inserts offered women with "'under-developed breasts'" the opportunity for "a 'new, attractive figure' in a culture that placed value on women's breast size." Signature brassiere colors distinguished women underneath, a Warner's advertisement suggested: "Nurse's white, Army tan, Air Corps grey, and Civilian nude." In 1943 the *Corset and Underwear Review* attributed the growing popularity of brassieres to fashions worn regularly in southern California, proclaiming that everyone there "from 13 to 90 wears brassieres, except perhaps a very few flat-busted women." The next year *Vogue* magazine revealed the importance of the increasingly popular undergarment in its fall 1944 fashion preview by promising "full coverage" of new styles. But none of these consumer trends would have taken hold without the sweater girl image.[69]

Real sweater girls on the big screen had their influence curbed by Hollywood's Production Code Administration director Joseph I. Breen. In 1941 he advised movie studio heads to dispense with the recent trend in "sweater shots," clarifying his reference as views "in which the breasts of women are clearly outlined and emphasized." They violated the Production Code's restriction against close-fitting garments that might suggest to viewers an outline of "intimate parts," he argued. *LIFE* magazine mocked the ruling in a follow-up photo-essay featuring a wide range of women wearing sweaters, from Wellesley College students to stage and screen personalities. While the college women donned "blouses, bras or both" underneath their sweaters, entertainers such as dancer June Preisser wore a sweater that, according to *LIFE*, gave her "an aspect of bouncing good health." The story generated quite a response, as the magazine's letters to the editor revealed in subsequent issues. One reader criticized Breen's office for "undoing" what the "immortal" Florenz Ziegfeld had accomplished in the 1920s. After consciously selecting women for his shows who were "bustier than the fashionable ideal"—a minimum chest measurement of thirty-six inches—Ziegfeld had been instrumental in refocusing his audience's gaze upward beyond women's legs and torsos. In the 1930s Lana Turner became so clearly identified as "The Sweater Girl" that she had trouble shaking the moniker when she wanted to be taken seriously as an actress. Form-fitting sweaters remained popular throughout the war, satisfying some Americans while upsetting others.[70]

Sweater girls complicated the wartime workplace. A 1942 government report suggested to employers: "Lay down the law . . . no sweaters allowed. If a pulchritudinous girl wears one she can usually demoralize the plant in ten minutes. Not only will the men have a hard time making their eyes behave but the other women will rise up in indignation." Was there more danger in a woman's corporeal display if she riveted, welded, or sanded on a munitions assembly line than if she typed stock orders, filed payroll reports, or took dictation at a desk? Clerical workers enjoyed greater freedom on the fashion front, a privilege the United Auto Workers pointed out in its defense of fifty-three Vought-Sikorsky Aircraft employees who were sent home for wearing sweaters to work. The UAW local made its case by asking why no woman at a desk job had been similarly singled out on "moral" grounds. Beyond the principal issue of inconsistent and discriminatory standards, the case revealed how Americans grappled with the intersection of production mobilization demands, women in traditionally male workspaces, and personal clothing choices. The punished workers had worn sweaters to work because they disliked the "baggy old slack suits" the company demanded they wear; as one woman explained, "the jackets are too bulky and expensive, and you can't roll up the sleeves to work easily." Practicality and appearance were inextricably bound for this war worker, who represented many other thousands who knew efficiency and thrift could coincide comfortably with style.[71]

For all of their imagined or actual trouble making, sweater girls spurred a consumer market. They helped to inspire and promote not only sweater sales but undergarment sales as well. These women "epitomized the achievements of brassiere makers," who could thank the war itself for popularizing their product, making it "the support garment of choice." By 1945 women "had grown more comfortable" with brassieres than corsets, indicating the shift toward bustline enhancement and control. Film critic André Bazin argued that U.S. servicemen during the war gradually turned their gaze toward women's breasts instead of legs. The move from one site of objectification to another would develop fully in the postwar world, morphing into the phenomenon that film historian Marjorie Rosen dubbed "mammary madness." Not merely "for the duration" but into the second half of the twentieth century, female breasts would take the place of female legs as principal sites of erotic desire and pornographic voyeurism.[72]

Shortages, competition, and more relaxed social rules on the home front yielded incongruities on the fashion front. Of women's clothing options, historian Geoffrey Perrett concluded: "On the one hand, it was all severe uniforms and work clothes. On the other, it was all frills, fluffiness and bareness." He lamented women's "unrelenting search for ways to expose their bodies." But home front political culture made the search easy. Even WPB director Donald Nelson's national scrap metal initiative generated skin-baring antics, after a Colorado woman donned a "skirt" made entirely of old keys strung together. Posed in the key skirt, a bandeau top, and high heels, she brought new meaning to the "decorated" body in war. On hers, conservation, loyalty, and sexuality could coexist comfortably. While Washington bureaucrats debated the "essentiality" of various textiles and the New York apparel industry sought to hold its ground, American women's fashion took cues from a Southern California climate where new brief designs showed a lot more than one's patriotism. "Hula bathing suits from California" had been seen on American beaches as early as 1941, but during the war years they grew even more popular. California's "year-round indoor/outdoor lifestyle" proved fertile ground for more leisure styles, even "play clothes" similar to children's shorts and shirts.[73]

During the war years these casual clothes found a receptive national market, especially among women who wished to show more skin. The Catholic Church took its stand against such styles, disapproving of "the scantiness in women's dress." Pope Pius XII had warned Catholic Action Girls against "daring" dress in a May 1941 speech, but that was months before a U.S. declaration of war allowed patriotic fervor and a range of other emotions to compete with religious conviction. The National Catholic Women's Union declared at its 1943 annual meeting that wartime fabrics had been "diabolically employed to create a sensual allure." Narrower skirts and V-neck blouses were particular targets of criticism. Not only did they "offend against the Sixth and Ninth Commandments," the women complained, but these "progressively more offensive" designs represented "an act of treason" rather than patriotism. By 1944, as Los Angeles promoters raised funds in order to sell the city as "the style capital of the world," Hollywood's influence on women became further entrenched in American culture. A self-help manual suggested that women study certain movie stars' individual styles to replicate "The Sophisticate," "The Gamine," and "The Exotic Woman," among others. From Tokyo Bay in 1945 Ewart Shuler wrote to his sweetheart about seeing a movie with women "all clad in tight, black, scanty bathing suits," then implored her to get one. Visual images, warm climates, limited fabric, and erotic longings helped to establish where American women stood in relation to their clothes as the war ended. The *New Yorker* cartoonist Sam Cobean set up a gendered binary that perhaps drew too sharp a distinction between clothes and bodies (fig. 52). But we will never know what lay buried in the realm of imagination.[74]

American women on the home front during the Second World War witnessed unexpected and astounding changes in clothing styles and requirements for their bodies at work, at play and at rest. They were offered an array of new clothing choices, some of them with big price tags. Materials restrictions meant more skin exposure. Closer-fitting L-85 dresses with fewer "distractions" demanded more perfect silhouettes, since neither the fashion industry nor the culture at large relaxed their demands on the ideal feminized body marked by race and class. Some women clung to the sculpting support offered by undependable garters and girdles

Figure 52. Cartoon by Sam Cobean. *The New Yorker*, November 24, 1945. © Sam Cobean/ Condé Nast Publications/www.cartoonbank.com.

manufactured according to WPB guidelines. The shrinking female body became an ideal image of femininity at the same time some women freed their hips from restrictive sub-par "foundations" and encased their breasts in brassieres. Trouser-clad women caused all manner of confusion, since the popular fad blurred gender lines as no other trend had done in modern American fashion. Marlene Dietrich and Katharine Hepburn could make trousers a personal trademark, but as Hollywood stars they stood apart. From head to toe and hat to shoe the WPB determined what women would be able to purchase and wear for the duration; its policies largely put style before safety, comfort, or functionality. By 1944 distinctive American design had taken hold in the United States. Some women loved the fresh trends and new rules and what they represented, while others scorned them.[75]

Military uniforms for women signified patriotic duty, yet they also inspired fear, since "a body at war" had typically been male, and in *this* war it was idealized as hypermasculine. This tension would greatly influence women in military service. The emphasis on the cut and tailoring of their uniforms bespoke a need to construct a clearly gendered, in this case, feminized, body. H. I. Phillips's fictional soldier, Arlene Applegate, insisted that her military service was temporary by promising at war's end to rush out and buy "the frilliest dresses on the market, the silkiest lingerie known to girlhood, a collection of nightgowns right out of Hollywood, a white evening gown, oodles of gold-and-silver slippers with French heels de luxe, and a half-dozen of the goofiest hats in town." She would be finished with clothing she considered too masculine, namely "pajamas" and "flat-heeled shoes."[76]

Unlike the fictional Wac who could not run away from soldierhood fast enough, WAC private Aileen Kilgore planned to wear her army issue after her discharge, telling her parents, "Don't be alarmed at the GI clothes I send home. They're legally mine. The supply sergeant gave me the field jacket. The long underwear and woolen socks came from girls who don't wear them. I'm taking all they give me— if we can't use them, somebody else can." Lieutenant Colonel Betty Bandel also hoped to use her army apparel in postwar life. Even with the GI Bill benefits she expected to receive, Bandel foresaw difficulty making ends meet, identifying her "biggest problem" as "getting a wardrobe, from the skin out!" She planned to alter her uniforms by cutting off the tails and collars and dying them different colors, intimating to her mother, "That isn't exactly legal, but I don't think after the war, anyone will recognize it for army stuff."[77] The glossy portraits that soldiers had posed for would become historical artifacts just like the uniforms themselves, relics of a near past where war emergency made the unthinkable possible. As the war neared its end, the overwhelming messages from Washington, Madison Avenue, Hollywood, and everywhere in between suggested that normal women should not want to wear uniforms any longer.

In 1945, anxieties over postwar gender boundaries and women's power permeated American culture. The all-knowing Nina in Popkin's *The Journey Home* aptly reveals the tensions and unease in a monologue about her own choices. After her new acquaintance, Lieutenant Don Corbett, teases Nina about her appearance, carefully constructed to pick up a man, she throws it back at him. Asking why he chose her of all the women on the train, Nina persists in answering her own question. She tells him what the two of them and millions of Americans already knew, that she upholds an ideal image seared in the minds of servicemen: "You picked me out because I had all of that glamour you boys have been dreaming about. Because I make it my business to look well and dress well and even smell nice." Acerbically she describes the circumscribed role women had taken on during the war—and boils it all down to appearance: "It's no less than our duty, our patriotic duty, to keep things going the way they were before, the way you expect them to be. I suppose you'd like it better if you came home, saw us dowdy and shapeless." Nina's speech offered a foil to Ethel Gorham's earlier warning to women whose husbands were away not to "surprise" them by changing their overall appearance. Gorham wrote about a woman who typically wore casual clothes at home, but for her husband's first leave donned "a black satin nightgown, a negligee with froufrou of lace in the wrong places" that only embarrassed him. The man "had hoped that at least one thing in this changeable world had remained the same," Gorham reported. Her example reveals the confusion and conflict American women faced during the war over how to decorate, cover, and uncover themselves. Clothes and the bodies in them could inspire, arouse, protect, and offend, all at the same time.[78]

What novelist Zelda Popkin and writer Ethel Gorham illuminated in their fiction and reportage were the ironies in attempting to keep things "the way they were before." To have maintained a static existence mimicking the trends, tastes, and codes of prewar life was impossible. The decorated body proved an important vehicle through which the fashion industry, the U.S. government, and media convinced the public to assume tasks and challenges necessary to ensure Allied victory. How American women embraced the messages, manipulated them to their advantage, and ushered in unprecedented possibilities revealed their collective mettle and creativity in the face of home front needs. Inside their decorated facades, they developed attitudes and bearing to meet and surpass the nation's demands of them, building a wellspring of resolve for subsequent generations to draw upon.

FIVE

Sacrifice and Agreeability
Cultivating Right Minds

In the spring of 1943, a manuscript copy of a brief essay by writer and raconteur Dorothy Parker circulated behind closed doors in Washington. The sharp-edged story criticized American women who refused to take up "paid" work for the war effort. In the acerbic tone for which she was famous, Parker railed, "Inside many pretty heads, where there is plenty of room, there still runs the notion that war is conducted rather like a charity bazaar, with the workers—close quotes—giving their services in the booths for a couple of hours around cocktail time." She admonished such women to "lose [their] amateur standing" by filling positions left empty by men who had entered the military, then asked: "If he can do what he is doing now, certainly you can do what he used to do. For God's sake—are we women or are we mice?" She warned them they would not be sought after by photographers or showered with gifts or parties for assuming such responsibility; instead, "saving" the future would be their reward. Giving up "Glamour girl" status to embrace the title "Miss Brass Tacks" would be worth it, Parker promised.[1]

The story impressed some readers and put off others. Mary Brewster White at the U.S. War Manpower Commission (WMC) wanted "this 'make-'em-squirm' type of literature to be circulated as widely as possible" and attempted to place the essay in national magazines with general readership. When the piece was initially rejected by a *Readers Digest* editor who labeled it "a bit too 'specialized'" for their audience, White concluded: "It seems to me that pretty much the whole country has specialized, brilliantly, in misunderstanding womanpower. A quick right to a few well-chosen feminine egos would help a lot." In the summer of 1943 labor mobilization proceeded but not at the pace U.S. government officials had hoped. The questions asked by the agencies involved varied from "Who is to blame?" to "How can they be brought on board?" One respondent to White's memo pointed out, "it may well be that a substantial body of editorial opinion on [*Readers Digest*] secretly shares the view that the woman in uniform or overalls is betraying her sex." The discussion around Dorothy Parker's essay, which was published first in *Mademoiselle* and eventually condensed for publication in *Readers Digest*, illuminates the disagreement and confusion over how best to appeal to American women to contribute to the war effort. But it also reveals them to be likely scapegoats for

failures in that effort. One Washington official declared: "Women who psychologically hold themselves aloof from war work or feel superior to it are unconsciously
lending themselves to the Nazi propaganda machine." Full industrial mobilization
depended upon women. But so did many other components of the home front
economy and social structure. Whether they would embrace these emergency duties was crucial, but *how* they went about it seemed almost as consequential.[2]

From all quarters, women were reminded that the war would be won or lost
based on their attitudes. They were to embrace change when necessary, remain
static where prudent, exhibit shrewdness and humility as workers, consumers,
wives, mothers, sweethearts, lovers, daughters, and citizens, and exude a spirit of
sacrifice without becoming parsimonious or bitter. Cheerfulness, optimism, and
patience ranked highly in the morale-building game, while efficiency and fidelity
rounded out the profile of the model female citizen. Magazines, newspapers, posters, billboards, car cards, elevator signs, cookbooks, pamphlets, and store displays
revealed the mental and emotional dispositions women were to assume on the
home front if they wanted to help ensure U.S. victory abroad. Wavering attitudes
could be costly, they were reminded at every turn. On the other hand, inflexibility
could be just as harmful to the nation's cause. Ideal women would adjust according to the political culture's needs, knowing their outlook and behavior reinforced
what U.S. troops presumably were fighting for. From the inside out, women were
measured by the ways they served their partners, children, soldiers, bosses, coworkers, the larger community, the marketplace, the "race," and the nation.

As various war agencies organized in 1942, questions about "women's roles"
abounded. Looking for "the woman's angle" early in the war, ad writer Sylvia
Carewe suggested to her colleagues that they "appeal to women's basic instincts—
mother love, self-preservation, the search for happiness, [and] the desire to improve their lot in life." Identifying these as "emotions" that could easily be linked
to victory, Carewe insisted that this was "the starting point of powerful advertising
to which women will react." Several months into the war, women had hardly been
tapped as a morale-boosting influence, Carewe argued. "By morale, I don't mean
just dressing up pretty to gladden the eyes of our fighting men on leave. Although
that has its place," she qualified. Instead, women needed to see and hear messages
about their role in helping to solve current "labor problems." Tight production
schedules and increased hours and shifts had led fatigued male workers to become
negligent at work. Their wives needed to forestall further factory downturns and
mishaps, Carewe claimed, by cheering on "these potential assembly line heroes."
Wartime advertising could encourage women in their roles as boosters: "Tell the
wife her man is just as much a hero as if he were flying a plane, as if he were

commanding a ship in battle. After all, she's responsible for feeding him, for seeing that he gets enough sleep, for waking him to go to work in the morning, for jollying him along when he is tired. She'll see to it that he doesn't lay down on the job."[3]

Wives' responsibilities at home took on greater import as they directly affected industrial production lines. Male workers who sloughed off could evade blame, it seemed, as women were held accountable for producing healthy, happy, well-rested laborers every day. In 1942 the *Woman's Home Companion Cook Book* insisted that homemakers' greatest contribution to the war effort was "a healthy nation." The Kerr Glass Corporation, whose name was synonymous with jars for home canning, informed American women that properly feeding their families was their "sacred duty." In 1943 Kerr saluted American homemakers for serving "without banners" but inspiring men with their "courage and devotion." As "proud daughters of the builders of America," their duty reflected a long "heritage" that they were to uphold. Aunt Jenny, the face of Spry Vegetable Shortening, told women: "It is our patriotic duty to feed our families well." To create "a strong, invincible America" she insisted they think beyond "wholesome, nutritious, well-balanced" meals to making food "look good, taste good." Aunt Jenny's product, of course, would help women prepare "light, delicate cakes" and "tender, flaky pies." The desserts themselves reflected the attributes synonymous with femininity and those most desired in American women—tenderness, delicacy, and sweetness. Presumably women who put themselves into their desserts would spread good feelings beyond their own kitchens.[4]

Morale rested squarely on women's shoulders. Since modern communication systems linked Americans as never before, argued Margaret Culkin Banning, "the spirit and mood" of various groups could affect others. She warned: "By indifference, by unsuitable desires, by complaints, even by the lack of realization that every mood and habit is important, women can sabotage civilian morale and have a serious effect on the morale of the armed forces." In the early wartime propaganda treatise *Calling All Women*, author Keith Ayling told women that beyond volunteering, consuming wisely, and spending disposable incor. e on the government, they could challenge "defeatists" in their midst by refusing to repeat gossip; they were to "kill rumor with intelligent optimism." In fact, a woman's preeminent duty, Ayling reiterated, was to maintain morale on the home front: "[Y]ou don't have to wear a uniform or take a course of training to do that. You just have to be a good talker, and as convincing as the person who takes a delight in spreading bad news. You can do it." Encouragement emanated from many print sources, reassuring American women that they had the tools to adjust to the demands of war. Those who stepped a bit further and took risks for a larger cause got early notice in the American media, helping to shape the criteria for ideal womanhood.[5]

Typical or "ordinary" women could excel in new and sundry fields, Americans learned early in the war. Magazines featured women managing to balance work and family, American companies highlighted their female employees' accomplishments, and U.S. government agencies generated stories starring women. In no arena was this celebratory mood more prevalent than industrial work. Ohio labor official George Strain announced, "I have sufficient respect for the patriotism and the physical stamina of the women of America to believe that the glorious pattern set by the people of Russia can be matched by our own women."[6] More often, the British were used as a basis for comparison, but in the end American exceptionalism trumped all comparisons to allies or enemies. Two wartime stories reveal what the nation heard most about "everywoman" on the assembly line. While Mary Godfrey Berckman and Freda MacArthur lived three thousand miles apart—Berckman in New England and MacArthur in the Pacific Northwest—both women contributed to the war effort with a similar spirit of pluck and practicality. For each, deference to a larger idea made her notable, Berckman to her family, MacArthur to the nation. Both served to instruct other women about attitudes necessary for sustaining a home front esprit de corps.

As one of the first women hired at the Colt Firearms Manufacturing Company in Hartford, Connecticut, Mary Godfrey Berckman was held up as a model for other middle-aged American women considering war work. An October 1942 *LHJ* story depicted her as an enthusiastic, good-natured employee and devoted wife and mother. A favorite of male coworkers due to "her quick laugh and Irish tongue," Berckman found that working outside her home kept her spirits high. She told the *LHJ* reporter, "You get irritable sticking with housework, especially with a lot of children. I know women who've gone so stale raising a family and polishing furniture they won't give you a civil answer to a civil question." Since paid work allowed women to "meet a different crowd," home life became "much easier," Berckman reported. She had entered the workforce out of necessity, however, after her partially disabled husband could not work full time. Berckman's story was designed to show readers that a normal life could be maintained as long as one's husband was "sporting enough" to allow it and, even better, if he helped with typically woman-centered duties such as washing, ironing, and cooking, as Fred Berckman did. Any personal ambition or ego that Mary Berckman might have felt as the household's main income source was outshined by her dreams for her four children. She hoped her three daughters would go into teaching or "nurse-maid" service, which she had briefly enjoyed as a young woman, while she wanted to see her only son become a priest. The Berckmans' devotion to their Catholic faith ran throughout the story, showing that the family had sustained values congruent with mainstream America's ethical framework despite their unusual domestic arrangements. That they saved scrap metal and contributed regularly to war bond and stamp drives secured their all-American identity. The Berckmans had mastered the correct approach to wartime necessity, the story insinuated. Mary realized that getting away from her home daily made her a better mother, and her agreeability in the workplace made her a model blue-collar employee.[7]

Across the continent in Seattle, Boeing's Freda MacArthur possessed a winning attitude that garnered notice. Even though MacArthur had been singled out for making a practical workplace suggestion, Boeing and the War Manpower Commission admired her general enthusiasm as much as her ingenuity. Her recommendation for a worktable tool drawer was attributed by the company to "the housewifely principle of a 'place for everything and everything in its place.'" MacArthur was marked as singularly creative since Boeing engineers had been, in one representative's opinion, "waiting quite a while for a woman worker to show up with an acceptable idea." But more impressive was MacArthur's spirit, the report emphasized; having been at Pearl Harbor on December 7, 1941, she possessed a "hatred for the Nip attackers and a deeply-rooted desire to do whatever she could to speed production of Flying Fortresses." MacArthur's persona, or her employer's knack for fashioning it with a little hyperbole, revealed a desirable characteristic in any American war plant employee—a spirit of revenge strong enough to inspire serious attention to her work.[8]

Both Mary Godfrey Berckman and Freda MacArthur had cultivated attitudes proper for middle-aged working women on the home front: cheerful, helpful, dependable, and perhaps most important, aware that they were working for causes larger than themselves. In addition, their stories highlighted appropriate places for "older workers"—defined by government agencies and the advertisers who served them as "women over 35"—a demographic targeted even more intensely as the war continued. Many middle-aged and older women needed an extra push to enter the work world, since they had lived through a Great Depression culture that had mobilized against them. The overwhelming message throughout the 1930s, but especially early in the decade, was that working women took jobs away from those who needed them most, namely male "breadwinners"; some organizations made it official policy, while others kept it unspoken that women would be terminated from employment upon marriage. So by 1942 enticing these same women into the workforce required special media initiatives. In its "human interest" report to the WMC, the Federal Shipbuilding and Dry Dock Company in Kearny, New Jersey, chose to highlight its "Federal grandmothers," those the business identified as "old-fashioned" enough "not to tell their ages." The company reporter played up the industry's preference for "more mature" workers, proudly stating: "Federal isn't going in much for flappers." The *Evansville Courier and Press* celebrated the Servel

Company's chapter of the War Working Grandmothers of America in a Sunday edition feature, headlining a photo, "Granny has gone to work in the war plant." On the WMC billboard, "Grandma's got her gun," a white-haired, double-chinned, deeply lined face appeals to viewers to fill positions like those at Servel and other industrial production companies (fig. 53). Designed to inspire women who "had never done anything but housework" to step into the "foreign" territory of wage labor in 1944, the oversized message allowed American businesses to make direct appeals to prospective employees by alleviating their hesitations about "job hunting." The design's accompanying instructions iterated that such women "must be told where to go, and must be impressed with the patriotic reasons for their taking war jobs." The U.S. Employment Service encouraged older women to join or rejoin the nation's workforce for several reasons; but its ideological mainstay in announcements small and large was an appeal to patriotism overlaid with preservation of the American family. Since older women presumably had no young children at home, they could step in to fill positions that their younger counterparts with children might be tempted to take.[9]

Industrial work posed numerous physical, mental, and emotional risks that women had to weigh against possible gains and losses. Their approaches to some risks earned them accolades. Machine tool shop foremen at a New Jersey shipyard claimed that the women in their section were "a source of inspiration to men

Figure 53. Recruitment billboard. Design by the Outdoor Advertising Association of America for the War Manpower Commission, April 1944. H. E. Fisk Collection, Hartman Center, Duke University.

workers" because of their "extremely enthusiastic" approach. When asked about workplace relations between male and female employees, the men reported that women who got along best were those "not too inhibited and shy in their attitudes towards the men—the ones who start out with 'Hello, Frank, you are going to teach me the job' attitude." In this and many similar cases, deference proved the best diplomacy. Even though most of the women at the shipyard had college degrees and had undergone rigorous training to undertake their specific responsibilities, yielding to male experience won them more points than anything else. Beyond diplomatic skills, in some shipyards sheer grit was necessary. A Women's Bureau "confidential report" noted conditions at one New Jersey operation where 40 of the 120 women at the site had been "sent to the sick bay" after working "for at least five hours in the extreme cold." Describing the work environment as hazardous at every turn—with conditions "tough" and "dirty" and in temperatures "16 degrees below zero"—the WB field worker concluded: "[T]heir job is certainly one that has teeth in it." In Arkansas an arsenal worker who "twice rescued fellow workers from burning to death" in her plant became the War Department's first female recipient of its highest civilian honor, the Emblem for Exceptional Civilian Service. The New York City welder named "Miss Negro Victory Worker" in 1944 said in her award acceptance speech that war work "must be well done, because the stake in getting it out is perhaps the life of some boy fighting on the beachheads." Other women won titles based not merely on perfect attendance and production records but activities demonstrating their patriotism—war bond purchases, salvage drive contributions, and impressive Victory Gardens. Lauded in the African American press and by the U.S. Department of Labor, these women revealed the spirit and stamina that working women were to exhibit.[10]

African American women were encouraged to curb any ill feelings about racial discrimination and support the war effort wherever possible. In the spring of 1943, Anna Rosenberg at the WMC appealed to black women to join the workforce secure in the knowledge that although discrimination still existed it would soon be eliminated. And their efforts would secure it: "As you advance you must fortify and solidify your gains," Rosenberg told them. Noting the needs in ordnance, aircraft, iron, steel, and shipbuilding industries, Rosenberg then shifted her focus to farm labor, pointing out that by the end of the year, women would constitute 10 percent of all agricultural workers. African Americans "familiar with rural conditions, especially in the South" should assume most of "the burden of raising the food to feed wartime America, its fighters, and its allies," she argued. Recognizing that black womanpower remained "largely untapped," Rosenberg told readers to take advantage of free government-sponsored training courses as well as any vocational classes to solidify strides made during the war.[11]

Black women workers faced an uphill climb toward equal rights, though. NUL executive secretary Lester B. Granger praised those who enrolled in defense training and nurses' aide training even while they were unwelcome in some industries and hospitals, reminding them that "not only Negro Americans, but America herself reaps the rewards of this devotion and preparation." A few months later the *Brown American* offered a glowing tribute to women of color for all they were doing and had done as workers in warehouses, steel mills, and numerous other venues, especially since the "Four Freedoms" remained beyond their reach. The "American Negro Woman" deserved recognition for many sacrifices, the editor contended, but particularly because she "steels her face to the insults, implied and spoken, which attend her every path, that people throughout the world might have, in greater abundance, from our American hands, that to which Negroes in this free land still aspire."[12] Those aspirations energized African American women to interpret their efforts as part of the Double V Campaign, a national program to ensure victory over racial discrimination at home while defeating global fascism abroad.

The inextricable bond between black women's approach to wage labor and the Double V Campaign shone through in an essay contest sponsored by *Opportunity* magazine, the NUL's chief publication. Both the first- and second-place essay award winners emphasized their upbeat attitudes in helping them confront difficult work as inspectors at ordnance plants. In the winning essays, the writers recognized hardships as a natural part of a woman's wartime work experience, which included strange schedules, long commutes, physically taxing labor, unreliable childcare, and interrupted sleep, among other things. Both essays insisted that black industrial war workers did much more than make and inspect war machines and munitions. Leotha Hackshaw, whose essay won the contest's second place, pondered her formal education after her first day on the job, realizing with disappointment, "One did not need a college degree to do this!" But she grew to see her daily work as an optical lens inspector as more serious than she had first imagined. In her narrative, she described the lens metaphorically, using it to peer back into the long history of African Americans and the particular sacrifices made by slaves, soldiers, abolitionists, and the first black congressmen during Reconstruction. The slaves' "hope of deliverance" inspired her to carry on courageously in her work, which she identified as "more than just livelihood," but instead as "a sharp weapon" to bring "the day of victory nearer" and as "the means of preserving our very lives." Similar approaches toward industrial work earned African American women attention, including two who attributed their promotions to "learning the names and positions of those in authority, making friends with workers in the preferred section, becoming familiar with the work routine, keeping up with plant bulletins, and staying on the job." In addition to their activities, they thought "tact" also played a role in their success.[13]

Some black women measured their efforts against those of soldiers and sailors. In a lively essay, Hortense Johnson described a typical day at the Picatinny Arsenal in Dover, New Jersey, as "exciting" and "plenty complicated" much like "jungle warfare must be, hard and painstaking and monotonous—until something goes off with a bang!" Johnson elevated women's work with her comparison, cataloguing as well her off-hours challenges. With a realist's eye and tone, she admitted: "It never occurs to you to figure out how much money you're making, because it isn't much anyhow—after you've had your victory tax deducted, paid for your war bond, set aside money for your bus commutation ticket. By the time you've given grandmother the food and rent money, and paid the doctor for helping you to fight off your frequent colds, and bought the extra-heavy clothes the job calls for, you're just about where the boys in New Guinea are. Don't let Senator Wheeler fool you with his talk about 'high wages for war workers!'" She then asked why any woman would want to continue such a schedule, answering, "We brown women of America need victory so much, so desperately." Johnson's fight was personal; and in her attempt to inspire her readers, she invoked internal fortitude, pleading, "it's one thing to resent and fight against racial injustices; it's another thing to let them break your spirit, so that you quit this struggle and turn the country over to Hitler and the Talmadges and Dies' who will run this country if Hitler wins." The United States could defeat fascists at home and abroad, Johnson insisted, but only if "the labor and sacrifice of her brown daughters" remained an integral part of the plan.[14] When the Women's Bureau published its tribute to African American women workers, it pointed to their selflessness and spirit of sacrifice, acknowledging the discrimination they faced in industries that had hired them "chiefly as cleaners and maids."[15]

Like their blue-collar counterparts, African American professionals who aspired to join the U.S. civil service ranks faced ongoing discrimination in major metropolitan areas despite the great need for federal workers. New York sustained "an alarming picture of exclusion" on this front, Elmer Henderson reported. Greater strides toward equity in white-collar federal employment across the color line had been made in Washington, D.C., than in any other American city, but employees stepped tenuously in their office environments, instructed to be vigilant about their demeanor. African American professionals in U.S. government offices were encouraged to shoulder the burden for continued hiring progress by countering "existing stereotypes about Negroes." They could challenge workplace prejudice as long as they pursued it "without assuming a chip-on-the-shoulder air." Given their responsibility for lifting up all African Americans, black federal workers were not to appear "careless or indifferent," two attitudes judged the worst possible signs of race neglect.[16]

The greater presence of women in the workforce encouraged close scrutiny of their motives, approaches, and attitudes toward newfound opportunities or responsibilities. Among the most closely watched women were those who had not typically worked outside their homes, in particular middle-class mothers. While social conservatives could abide grandmothers working for wages—even those who had never before done so—the prospect of their daughters seeking employment left the middle-class American family not only embattled but endangered. In early 1942 Keith Ayling insisted on the maintenance of domestic life even if volunteer opportunities arose, telling women that no work they undertook "could justify neglect of the home." He identified a "deep-rooted respect" for the home as paramount in "the American way of living." Media pressure on mothers to assume full responsibility for their children's development intensified during the war, as reports of increasing juvenile delinquency appeared in magazines and newspapers. Philip Wylie's work, *A Generation of Vipers* (1942), criticized "Mom" for many "social discomforts and ills," particularly the problems of American youth. FBI director J. Edgar Hoover instructed mothers to stop "the drift of normal youth toward immorality and crime," telling them not to take war jobs if employment meant "the hiring of another woman to come in and take care of [their] children." Hoover's argument countered those of other Washington agencies clamoring for women to join the workforce. One poster message appealed to the civic-minded: "If you can't leave your children alone during the day, maybe you can free another woman for war work by taking care of her children." In some defense boom areas, staff members at schools and agencies devoted to child welfare criticized women who chose to work, believing that "additional income and a too great readiness to evade full responsibility for their children" were more likely inspirations than "patriotic motives."[17] The greatest challenge for women was reconciling home life and work life. Cartoonist Bob Barnes put a humorous spin on the all-too-real environment for those who needed or wanted to work in 1943 (fig. 54). The wartime "superwoman" belied the fact that American society, despite the current emergency, would not budge on its expectations of working mothers to fulfill needs all around—to their families, to their communities, and to the nation.

The OWI artist's multitasker, Wylie's "Moms," and all others presumably encouraging juvenile delinquency coexisted with the preeminent image of ideal motherhood on the home front—"The Greatest Mother in the World," an American Red Cross highway billboard (fig. 55). Within six weeks of its introduction, American companies purchased over 17,000 copies of the "Greatest Mother" image. The monthly cost of keeping the billboards up exceeded $250,000, paid by American

Figure 54. "And then in my spare time . . ." Bob Barnes for owi, ca. 1943. Prints and Photographs Division, Library of Congress (LC-USZ62–97636), digital ID: cph 3b43729.

businesses on behalf of the American Red Cross. In 1944 the outdoor industry posted the same image at 29,000 sites across the country. The design's central figure, a woman draped in a white gown and veil, points to death and destruction in the distance while pleading for support from viewers. An angelic figure, the "Greatest Mother" was one of the few nationally distributed poster images of American womanhood mirroring those distributed for the Red Cross in the First World War. With its symbolic value intact, the visual construct appeared outdated, however. Too many images of modern women had already circulated. Wearing coveralls and uniforms and L-85 dresses, women in advertisements and public

Figure 55. American Red Cross War Fund Drive billboard. Design by Lawrence Wilbur, February 1943. OAAA Archives, Hartman Center, Duke University.

service campaigns possessed qualities that took them beyond allegorical representation. Wartime graphic artists and ad copywriters had striven to create female figures that might in fact be archetypes but still retained enough characteristics of flesh-and-blood women to be believable. In a popular culture teeming with images of sexualized female bodies, the "Greatest Mother" not only belonged to another war but another century. And given all of the literature designed to frighten Americans about neglectful mothers, overprotective mothers, and otherwise dangerous women with children, the "Greatest Mother" appears an ironic figure; she might be an angel of mercy but she was nobody's mother. The Red Cross's emblematic figure had transcended real motherhood in its selfless devotion to all suffering people on war fronts, yet the woman on the billboard remained two-dimensional.[18]

Real mothers on the home front made sacrifices under more complicated conditions. Columnist Keith Frazier Somerville hailed Annie Tutwiler of Bolivar County, Mississippi, as "our six star [N]egro mother" whose "American soldier-sons, each [write] longingly of the day when they'll return to their homes in the deep South." While Tutwiler and her sons may have, from Somerville's point of view, reconciled their Jim Crow world with a fight for democracy, other African American mothers wrestled with these contradictions. "Georgia" wrote to *Redbook* to say that her job as a black mother was even more challenging than that of "some mothers" because she felt a heavy burden in helping her nine-year-old son, who collected scrap metal, to maintain a "pride and eagerness to help his country win this war." Her job seemed daunting, she intimated, due to occasional "resentment and discourage-ment." The U.S. government's upbeat messages about the Allies' fight for freedom weighed against those who tried to dash her son's dreams—"fanatics" on one side who told him he could not achieve them because he was black and "fanatics in [her] own race" who questioned African American war efforts as pointless in their struggle for opportunity.[19]

Psychological appeals in home front propaganda emphasized women's worry, guilt, and fear over their wartime decisions. One eerily spun advertisement fea-tured a woman haunted by a talking clock ever since her husband left home to fight. To confront her madness, she got a job: "Not very glamorous. Just a job. Last night I looked into the mirror. No outward change. No halo. No resemblance to Joan of Arc. But the clock knows the difference. It won't frighten me now . . . Last night I heard it using Jack's words—words spoken for millions of our men out there who are counting on us helping here. 'Good-girl! . . . Good-girl! . . . Good-girl!'" Anti-hoarding campaigns also played on women's guilt, portraying the lunacy of consumers gone wild. In a Scott Paper Company advertisement, "The woman who FORGOT Pearl Harbor!" secretly and greedily stacked Scott products in her attic. Another design in the series featured the three Axis dictators singing to a hoarder, "For She's a Jolly Good Fellow," and reminding readers: "Yes, Hoarding gives comfort to the enemy." The Office of Price Administration sent out bulletins warning women: "Panic-buying merely clutters a woman's closet with a lot of out-of-date clothes, clothes you won't want to wear next year because they'll brand you as a hoarder." Late in the war when emotionally charged appeals to recruit military nurses grew more graphic, one asked women: "Is Your Comfort as Important as the Lives of 15 Wounded Soldiers?" The OWI attempted to provoke guilt among women whose "apathy" had kept them from taking their places in industry. In its "Final Push to Victory" campaign, the organization announced to print media outlets, "Hundreds of thousands of women who *could* do this work are unmoved to do so because they do not understand the urgency of the need." Women had to be re-minded to seek employment actively rather than wait for "a war job to find them."[20]

If pricking a woman's conscience about her full participation became common-place, whether to appeal to her self-interest was controversial. Advertisers could remind prospective military volunteers of substantial base pay in addition to food, lodging, clothing, and medical and dental care; promotions meant pay raises. But this information came with a warning: "Don't limit recruiting messages entirely to the self-interest approach. Include an appeal to patriotism and the desire to help our fighting men." However personally exciting or enticing military opportunities might appear, women were not to sate selfish desires; their motives needed to be purer.[21] One popular line encouraged women to put their extra wages into war bonds. Earning money, then, would be less likely to encourage a sense of financial independence, dangerous in its potential to generate feelings of independence in other areas. As Elaine Tyler May states, "too much money, strong women, and too much sex" was a deadly combination that could easily "destroy the dream of the [postwar] good life." Women's contributions to government initiatives put extra dollars in safe places. Anyone who had a few pennies could contribute meaningfully, Keith Ayling told women, since a ten-cent war stamp would purchase "a set of insignia for the Army" or "five .45 cartridges for the Marine Corps" or an item of equal significance. Those with more were encouraged to give more; one thousand dollars would buy "a reconnaissance car," they were reminded. In 1944 the 6th War Bond Drive included a "Pin Money War Bond" promotion for women who previously had been unable to afford their own bond buying; whether unemployed or underemployed, they could spend pennies and nickels filling a "stamp" album, eventually convertible to a war bond. Eleanor Sewall, a Lockheed Aircraft employee whose husband was captured on Bataan, was singled out by the company for her willingness to contribute 50 percent of her salary in payroll deductions toward war bonds. Beyond the investment's practical value in assisting the government, less disposable income for women meant greater control over them and any self-serving desires they might entertain.[22]

Just as every penny mattered to the war effort, so did every job. Women were urged to consider civilian work as vital as war production, especially since not everyone would get an opportunity to build bombers. Beyond riveting and welding, other tasks required even more hands and minds nationwide. Telephone operators, laundry workers, food servers, bus drivers, and childcare assistants were needed nationwide, even more so in industrial boom towns where services were stretched beyond their limits. Although the U.S. government had promised to set up day care centers in these areas, the project was not funded until 1943, and "even then, the centers provided care for only 10 percent of the children who needed it," notes Elaine Tyler May. WAC officer Betty Bandel discovered low morale among her troops soon after their switch to regular army status, much due to Wacs being assigned jobs similar to those they had held in civilian life. Despite their specialized training in radio, mechanics, and chemistry, many women were given traditional gendered work instead and unable "to use their training." Bandel confided to her mother: "Even skills that Wacs bring with them from civilian life are often not recognized and made use of by the army: language skills, for example. Some [Army Air Force] commands request Wacs for such unsuitable duties as laundry and troop entertainment." African American army wives who accompanied their husbands to Fort Huachuca, Arizona, lived in a squalid "unconverted barrack" outside the camp's gates, and during the day they served on the base as secretaries, janitors, cooks, food servers, launderers, and maids in white officers' homes. One reporter praised them for making "the morale of their menfolk" their main priority.[23]

Motivating women to develop right minds for the war effort meant balancing personal enticements with patriotic duty. In early 1944, after absenteeism among women in the war plants had become a chronic problem nationwide, the OWI decided to prepare its first general campaign to counter it. Grappling with how to appeal to women to stay on the job, the organization's initial program contained hard-edged literature designed to stimulate feelings of guilt. The nation "desperately" needed them, with "womanpower" the only solution to war production needs. The appeals stated bluntly to women that their refusal to work would translate into too few bombs and tanks, punchlined with "*You don't want that to happen.*" Several reviewers had serious reservations about the OWI's first attempt. Bureau of Manpower Utilization representatives warned that if published, the messages would be "dangerous to the morale of the entire country." Other reviewers thought the campaign plan needed a more "positive" edge, appealing not only to women's patriotism but their self-interest. The WMC's Women's Advisory Committee responded to the program with an explicit directive to appeal to "personal gain." Although such an approach could be tempered by suggesting to women to save their earnings "to buy the things [they] wanted in the post war period," more practically, the committee noted, women needed to know they could learn skills or trades that would be useful later. Work could "represent a type of insurance to women." More controversial than any issue the propaganda makers grappled with during the war, the appeal to self-interest might just create a generation of ambitious independent women who would resist leaving well-paid industrial work or white-collar positions after the war ended. To appeal to "personal gain" was dangerous business in 1944, and every company or agency attempting to talk to women had to temper their messages accordingly. By the summer of 1944 the OWI had put together a workable document that acknowledged the importance of appeals to women's self-interest in recruitment publicity but instructed designers to balance this message with other appeals. Women were not to be encouraged to consider themselves independent operators separate from a larger national cause.[24]

Self-interest could be a selling point, however, if couched within the framework of marriage and domesticity. Cadet Nurse recruitment ads appearing in magazines such as *Collier's* and *Look* assured hesitant parents: "When she marries, she'll be a better wife and mother for the training she's getting now, and if she wants to stay in nursing after the war, it's a field in which a girl can go a long way." The 1945 military nurse campaigns depicted her as "what he's been fighting for—the tender touch of a woman's hand—peace and understanding—all the things that mean America to him." As a profession already feminized, nursing did not challenge a gendered professional structure, but public reminders helped to reinforce the status quo. In several Outdoor Advertising Association of America (OAAA) billboards, a "dark" world characterized by battle scenes was offset by "tomorrow's brighter world," peopled by newlyweds and other couples exercising their freedom to buy. Consumerism appeared seductive, the carrot in front of a wartime population prompted to save through war bonds so that they could purchase household goods later. Phillips's *All-Out Arlene* directed prospective military recruits to think along similar lines. After her promotion to sergeant, Arlene pondered her post-military life. Writing a list of women's desires for the local newspaper, Arlene included "cradles, baby carriages, and diaper services" and the "return of a time when a girl can concentrate on such simple things as how a man likes his eggs, whether she can afford a new electric icebox, how to meet the installment on the vacuum cleaner, and what's wrong with the cat." Her new "America" would be "a world of romance, sentiment, and love," not one where promotions like hers created ambitious women in uniform. The protagonist's bold pronouncements about her aspirations were designed to generate sighs of relief among the skeptical and the scared.[25]

While official recruitment literature drew safe boundaries when predicting the military's possible effects on women, other home front media addressed public apprehension about women in uniform more subtly. Highway billboards advertising Krispy Crackers featured a woman in uniform saluting with one hand while holding a plate in the other. Her domestic posture and promise—"Always ready to serve!"—softened both her uniform and her salute; the soldier remained first and foremost a server of food. Keith Frazier Somerville reassured readers of her weekly newspaper column, "Dear Boys," that femininity could be maintained in a uniform. Somerville's lively reports about local people and places urged comfort in the face of dramatic social change. In a clever twist, she chose to emphasize how Mississippi women would transform the military rather than the other way around. Of a soldier at a Florida training camp, she contended, "with her voice and her piano playing and her capacity to make friends, she'll be a marvelous W.A.C.!" One local woman trained in "home science" would be "a big addition to the Women's Army," while another headed to Alexandria, Virginia, to become a "decoder" would excel since, as Somerville concluded, "All women love secrets and I'm sure [she] can keep Uncle Sam's well!" Colonel J. Noel Macy similarly praised African American Wacs for carrying out their duties within a feminized framework, describing the ideal African American soldier as one whose "valuable work" was conducted "[q]uietly, efficiently" and without any interest in "personal glory."[26]

Tempering military women's ambitions was a tall order since military life fed them. Wac Dorothy Muni expressed her enthusiasm at military service, telling a friend: "I'm nuts about all this stuff. . . . Of course, after the war, I'll be a bore to all my friends—women don't like this stuff and men prefer to be masters at war interpretation. . . . For quite a while after the war, civilian life will be very, very dull. Suppose they'll keep on us females?" Muni's excitement and confidence echoed the wartime feelings of many young women buoyed by their military experience. WASP pilot Marion Stegeman wrote to her mother, "Nothing is such a gauge to the spirits as how well or how poorly one has flown. . . . Oh, God, how I love it! Honestly, Mother, you haven't *lived* until you get way *up* there—all alone—just you and that big beautiful plane humming under your control." One Wac told a U.S. Army survey team in 1943, "I feel competent for the first time and independent. It is a good feeling to be able to take care of yourself." Twenty-year-old Mary Cugini, whose early weeks in Marine Corps training had changed her, claimed, "I feel like a woman of the world and I'm not afraid of anything or anyone." A year later, having risen in the ranks, USMCWR corporal Cugini intimated to her sister, "I am getting too independent for my own good. Maybe it's a good thing, because now no one pushes me around and if I don't like the way people treat me, I tell them so. The Marine Corp[s] sure has done wonders for my character." Jess Rice told a confidante in 1944 that she had joined the Women's Army Corps in order to "know what the conversation [was] about after the war." Her desire to understand postwar discourse indicates some self-interest but also a hint that unless she operated on the inside at the height of the crisis, she could be relegated to the periphery later.[27]

But how would such women assimilate into postwar civilian culture? Dorothy Muni's trepidation about it reveals the transformative effects of military life on women, as well as her understanding of what would be expected of *all* women once the war ended. While Jess Rice may have been more prescient than many women who read hope into promises of postwar careers or stable employment, her comment suggests that whatever went on inside traditionally male preserves would dictate a postwar world. To inhabit one of those places would secure her a desired social and intellectual position. That women simultaneously reveled in and worried about their military experience and its rewards shows the complex psychologies for which recruitment literature could not fully prepare them, their families, or American society.

Homemakers during the war years were bombarded with messages about how to buy, what to buy, whether to share, and how, both practically and emotionally, to handle wartime changes in their households and communities. Grappling with the consumer economy tested their reserve, but they could confront challenges by executing their duties with efficiency and sustaining an atmosphere of fairness, propaganda makers told them. One writer contended early in the war: "If [women] have been allowed to spend in peacetime they must accept the responsibility for what is spent in wartime, with all the inevitable adjustments and sacrifices that will be entailed." Touting its ability to speak "a universal language to the educated and uneducated alike" and to reach people of all races and creeds, the OAAA targeted homemakers on behalf of the War Food Administration. Creating impressions with visual images "over and over again, day after day," billboards filled the mind's eye with ways to win the war at home. "FAIR PLAY" could be urged on "all of the people of [a] community," the OAAA argued, but in the realm of food consumption, appealing specifically to women made sense since they did "most of the buying."[28]

A long term result of the Progressive Era consumerism and efficiency experts' influence, advice on practical living meshed well with wartime emergency conditions. Women could save time in the kitchen, preventing "a lot of last minute hustle and bustle," if they planned well, began preparing meals days ahead, or chose "one dish" meals. Frigidaire's publications on using refrigerators wisely during wartime showed women how to get the most out of their food and time. They could prepare meat loaves and stews in advance, keep bread dough and waffle batter ready to go, and store gelatin puddings for several days. Even if a woman did not earn wages in an industrial job, she could mimic that kind of work by keeping her kitchen appliances in working order—the refrigerator alone demanded that she clean the condenser, oil the motor, check the seals, and repair rust spots. Charles McGovern has argued that private enterprise won the battle for industry during the war by paying for materials that kept their names alive even though they had little to offer a domestic market. While companies certainly did make their products known, the elaborate instructions about efficiency, conservation, and rational homemaking drew heavily on Progressivism's entrenchment in American society by the 1940s. Progressives' traditional views of gender roles, borne of their middle- and upper-class backgrounds, nineteenth-century Protestantism, and two generations of activism driven by their beliefs in essential differences between women and men, surfaced in advertisements small and large.[29]

A woman's use of food resources indicated the extent of her patriotic fervor. General Mills icon Betty Crocker said, "In war-time, more than at any other time, we need friendly get-togethers to keep up our morale, give us refreshment and relaxation." She encouraged a combination of "cooperation and simplicity" on the home front. Creative community gatherings ranged from the "Victory Garden Supper" celebrating neighborhood foods to a fund-raising "Basket Social."[30] Other advertisements offered sober warnings. Kraft cheese spread promotions advised: "Waste is 'Sabotage'—Millions of Americans are working hard to produce more food. But at the same time, millions are thoughtlessly wasting food . . . a little here, a little there. . . . Don't waste *any* at your house." A textbook encouraging women to can fruits and vegetables noted that "spoilage is worse than uneconomical—it is unpatriotic . . . there must be no waste." In consideration of the hungry world beyond U.S. borders, American women were to follow recipe directions carefully and "never, never cut down on the processing time." To prevent drudgery, women could actually make canning a "glamorous" affair. Even if family members chose not to help, the ideal homemaker would not be "a martyr about it." Instead, she "prepared a cool drink and a snack ahead of time. . . . She took an occasional lick of salt to ward off heat exhaustion. She liked what she was doing and she looked pretty doing it. And come winter she had gleaming rows of home canned fruit." The Ad Council sent out an appeal in April 1945 to encourage women to save and turn in tin cans since their kitchens represented "America's only 'tin mines.'" With the nation's stockpile of tin decreasing rapidly, private home spaces became war fronts as well; the "ranking officer" in charge of such a space would demonstrate her devotion to the nation's goals by guarding against waste, inefficiency, and unfairness.[31]

In all work that they undertook—paid or unpaid, at home or away, in cities or in rural areas—wartime women were supposed to cultivate the habits of patience, cheerfulness, and optimism. WAC officer Betty Bandel took pride in helping fellow soldiers understand government bureaucracy and not become overwhelmed by "the immensity of the system." *McCall's* published an illustrated guide entitled "This Woman Needs Help" to show the ad industry how to assist women who were being bombarded on all sides with rules for wartime living. Frances Harriet Williams urged fellow African Americans to cooperate with the government on rationing and price control not only because it was "easy" to embrace but because regulations ensured fairness across color lines, class lines, and all other barriers that separated Americans. In small matters such as local distribution of sugar ration books, people worked willingly together, she reported. In Washington, D.C., for example, "White people stood patiently in line to receive their sugar books from Negro school teachers." Williams reported that even in Alabama, black and white teachers called to meet about rationing policies sat together, and "small petty acts of segregation were forgotten." Americans had to be prepared to stand in long lines everywhere, because they had become commonplace. Pitched as virtues, patience and tolerance appeared frequently.[32]

Women's patience assumed mythic proportions during the war. One commentator reinforced the stereotype, claiming, "Women excel in patience and thoroughness. Repetitive, monotonous tasks fail to break down this care taking attitude." He also noted that women wanted to like their colleagues to be satisfied with their work situation, whereas men could enjoy their jobs even if they disliked the people around them. Employers criticized women as "creatures of habit" who rarely introduced new ideas in the workplace. The U.S. War Department cast women workers in similar terms, alerting prospective employers to what they could expect: in addition to their adaptability and dexterity, women were "accurate—precision workers [and] good at repetitive tasks." Beatrice Candee challenged wartime testing used to determine what kinds of work best suited women. She argued that men and women showed many more points of overlap than difference, conceding that some evidence suggested that women were better on "fine dexterity operations" while men excelled in "spatial relationships." The assumption about women that she challenged most forcefully was female "patience," pointing out, "There is little evidence from tests on the often heard observation that women have more patience with monotonous jobs, since most tests are too short to involve this factor."[33]

To augment their patience, women were to cultivate and exhibit cheerful spirits. A 1943 exhibit celebrating "Women in War Work" sponsored by *LHJ* and the Franklin Institute of Philadelphia (and given the stamp of approval by the WMC's Women's Division, the Labor Department's Women's Bureau, and the OWI) included a panel describing black women as "efficient, careful, and cooperative." Those who worked night shifts "with no complaints" received special praise. Cheerfulness and optimism resonated as habits worth cultivating on the home front. But by mid-1944, African American women in both the blue-collar and white-collar sectors voiced concerns about their "duration" jobs. Most wanted to continue working at or above the levels they had reached but could sense that doors could close near the end of the war. At USO-YWCA counseling sessions they wanted to know about additional training in fields they now populated, about sharpening their typing and other clerical skills, about taking business courses, and about making careful choices regarding jobs in which they could remain long after the war ended. A less than optimistic realist asked, "'What can be done to make domestic jobs more attractive for those of us who may have to return to them?'" *Opportunity* magazine advised every female worker to make "planning for her future a part of her daily routine," identifying it as a mental habit to be undertaken in the "same spirit" as her current war work.[34]

A woman's good spirit and cheerfulness rested in part on her function as an intent listener and reserved but pleasant conversationalist. Identified as "one of the greatest female man-catchers of all time," listening grew in importance during the war. Ethel Gorham informed wives of soldiers and sailors that they would have to "listen hard," since conversations would be quite different from those they enjoyed before their husbands left for military service. U.S. Marine Mary Cugini noticed that she lost her "civilian attitude" and became more "reserved" after a few weeks in training at Camp Lejeune. Her "tone" changed in part, she wrote, due to public scrutiny of "gals in the service." *Photoplay* magazine instructed its readership: "Listen to your laughter . . . let it come easily, especially if you're with boys who have had little to laugh at for too long. Laugh at the silly things you used to do together. . . . And if you hear your laugh sound hysterical, giddy, or loud, tone it down. . . . Serenity is the wellspring of the romantic look." Reserve, lightheartedness, and agreeability were worth cultivating, women learned from many sources.[35]

Cheerfulness could win for women the kinds of accolades they were thought to desire. A high profile series of wartime advertisements for 7-Up suggested that a woman's attitude was perhaps her greatest asset—and that drinking the product regularly could help her cultivate and maintain it. An April 1945 newspaper ad headline linked a woman's "good disposition" directly to her ability to build "a happy home." In the adjacent image a 7-Up bottle nestles in alongside the accoutrements of domesticity—a pincushion, spools of thread, bits of lace, and other scraps of material (fig. 56). Suggesting the drink could help women cope—"when things go wrong and you need to smile"—the promotion indicated a valuable therapeutic function that would secure a woman's place. In the end, women were to "get the habit of smiling!"[36]

An extensive series of 7-Up product promotions in magazines drove home the importance of a woman's "good disposition." Each full-page, full-color ad focused on a different smiling woman or man, whose rewards for amiability varied according to gender expectations. A woman who drank 7-Up could expect to have friends, well-behaved children, a happy home, or a reputation as "the favorite [mom] of the neighborhood." Her worth depended on others' responses to her. A man who drank the soda would be a better decision maker, would have greater control over his energies, or could concentrate more intensely. An independent entity, he became the sole beneficiary of the drink's properties. 7-Up promotions hit certain buttons hard in 1945, as the war drew to a close and American society was being redrawn to settle gender boundaries in comfortable places. One ad reminded women: "The first requirement of an attractive personality is to be pleasant and considerate at all times. Intelligence, vivacity and high ideals add to your charm, but a good disposition comes first!" Those who tried to "build a happy home" would naturally have the "determination to magnify the pleasant things and forget the unpleasant." Cultivating a postwar trend where children's power over their mothers was celebrated, wartime 7-Up ads appealed to mothers to guard their moods according to the "likes and dislikes" of their children, who would "resent" an uncheerful mother. The 7-Up advertisements that appeared in American newspapers and magazines during the war suggested a firm binary, revealing what were considered basic mental and emotional differences between women and men.[37]

a good disposition helps to build a happy home...

Happy homes are built on a determination to magnify the pleasant things and forget the unpleasant. Keep in a good-natured mood . . . get the habit of smiling!

"Fresh up"-keep smiling!

When things go wrong and you need to smile, then a chilled bottle of 7-Up is just what you want. As one clean-tasting sip follows another, your spirits rise. You "fresh up." You smile!

All over the country, the demand for 7-Up is soaring. Stock up on this grand family drink at the nearest store displaying a 7-Up sign.

You like it... it likes you

Order a case from your dealer

7up

REG. U.S. PAT. OFF.

Figure 56. 7-Up advertisement for newspapers. April 1945. JWT Archives, Hartman Center, Duke University.

With radiant smiles, pleasant conversation, and good dispositions, women could influence those they saw on a regular basis. For long distance relationships, their cheerful spirits would resonate in letters. Magazines and newspapers offered endless instructions on crafting good letters to men in the military. The Zenith Pen Company advertised its products with the reassuring reminder, "Writing Is Fighting, too." Ethel Gorham devoted an entire chapter in *So Your Husband's Gone to War!* to "The Lost Art of Letter Writing." Couples would see their relationships enhanced more by letters, she argued, than by the few hours spent together on a weekend furlough. But women needed to follow certain letter-writing rules. Gorham told them to avoid "all personal upheavals" including in-law disputes; even if "lonely and upset and vaguely suicidal," she instructed: "Don't put it into written words unless you're prepared to jump out of the window and this is your last message on it all." Husbands in service really did not want to hear home front complaints, she intimated; instead they preferred "newsy" missives filled with details about headlines, books, music, local news, and friends in uniform. Above all, women were to put the "best" of themselves in their writing—"the most charming, most informative, most truly feminine part"—since letters were ultimately "[a] kind of mental, spiritual, companionable seduction," she argued. Eastman Kodak Company encouraged women to enhance their notes with photographs, so that a man in uniform could enjoy "a 'pocketful of home'" wherever he went. While many no doubt followed the prescriptions offered in the popular press, other women chose to be frank, discussing "their fears and frustrations as well as the often harsh realities of life on the homefront." This was one of the most surprising discoveries made by Judy Barrett Litoff and David C. Smith, who collected and archived over thirty thousand letters of American women correspondents during the war. Many women failed to temper their emotions and sugarcoat their news, while many others chose not to write. Naval Reserve officer Ewart Shuler was disappointed that his sweetheart wrote so little, and he mentioned it often in his own frequent missives. Wishing her letters would "start coming in kinda' regular," he complained that he was "doing all the talking."[38]

Morale work depended on millions of women who gave their time and money. Those who cultivated a genuine spirit of volunteerism saw their work bear fruit, even though some were criticized for their approach. Images circulated of the rich snob who spent a few hours a week with the American Women's Voluntary Service (AWVS) but remained oblivious to real sacrifice. A government handbook clarified the organization's purpose as well its diverse membership in many states, where women carried out "real hard work." Across the country the AWVS made strides in several socially sensitive areas. Highlighting its interracial cooperation in local communities, the organization offered classes on home repair and first aid, helped children, and taught women practical wartime skills such as map reading, convoy driving, clinical photography, and Morse Code. The AWVS affected every aspect of wartime culture, sending its members to assist military personnel; distribute ration books; sell war bonds and collect salvage; recruit blood donors, nurses, farm workers and childcare workers; and knit, sew, and recondition clothes for military families and relief agencies. Chapters took pride in their "non-sectarian, non-political, non-profit-making" status to encourage women from many backgrounds to join their ranks. African American women urged one another to support this group whose goal "transcend[ed] any consideration of race, or color, or class, or caste." The AWVS became a place where through their work together, women could understand "each other's problems and shortcomings and consciously or unconsciously, [develop] an appreciation of each other's virtues," Ruby Bryant Yearwood reported. Interracial volunteer activities among women spurred optimism for a more inclusive postwar America while stimulating the growth of similar organizations where women could meet and serve a larger cause.[39]

With morale the purview of women, two groups of young women found themselves in the spotlight during the war—the USO and the All-American Girls Professional Baseball League (AAGPBL). USO recruitment literature encouraged volunteers to consider their work the female equivalent of military service. Their gender-defined actions and activities required particular mental and emotional postures when dealing with soldiers and sailors. As Meghan Winchell has shown, the ideal USO junior hostess's femininity was determined in part by her ability to yield to a serviceman's wishes within proper boundaries of middle-class American womanhood. How these young women presented themselves—not just bodies but minds and spirits as well—would determine the reactions of soldiers and sailors to them, the USO made clear. Patience, general optimism, and fine listening skills were a good hostess's necessary accoutrements. Since many USO sites provided games at their sites, women played ping-pong, checkers, and cards, often yielding to male opponents. As Winchell has argued, such "gendered emotional work" meant women were not to appear too smart or too competitive; to challenge a serviceman's masculinity worked counter to the organization's purpose of morale boosting. A poem distributed at a Madison, Wisconsin, Hostess Training Institute instructed:

You're the girl behind the man behind the gun. You can give our soldier boys a lot of fun.

If you just forget yourself. Put your ego on the shelf. And make sure the hostess' job's well done.

Denying ego became part of a multifaceted package a USO hostess offered in order to enliven U.S. troops. As Winchell argues, "If a hostess made a serviceman happy, then she had done her job, and this, not meeting her own interests, theoretically provided her with satisfaction. . . . Behaving selflessly in an unquestioning manner, moreover, did not threaten the existing gender order."[40]

The cheerful selflessness and wholesome behavior of USO hostesses mirrored the attitudes that AAGPBL founders demanded of their players. Organized in 1943, the AAGPBL recruited its "Ladies of the Diamond" from "Bible Institutes and Sunday School teams" as well as local softball leagues. News coverage highlighted the importance of the players' respectability, indicating that each woman's "character and background" had been "thoroughly investigated by the league" before she could sign a contract. In their off-field training in domestic matters, AAGPBL members sharpened their "conversation techniques" while learning specifically "how to attract the right kind of man," *Time* magazine reported. In their "etiquette" instruction, players learned how to approach the public. Conversation topics and manners figured prominently in making a good impression; players were "not to talk too loudly" and were to avoid "bragging about personal possessions, accomplishments or achievements"—the most "vulgar" pose the young women could assume. They were urged to "win gracefully and modestly and lose gracefully too" and to avoid a "showoff attitude." A haughty, overconfident female athlete was not what the American public wanted, front office sources insisted. AAGPBL players had to keep their "fan" in mind at all times: "After all, he is your customer and he feels that you, as a player, and the team, belong to him." In dealing with autograph hounds, a player needed to be "as friendly and gracious" as possible, since her "personality represent[ed]" her team and the entire league. Maintaining a distance with new acquaintances while also being "polite and considerate" and avoiding "noisy, rough and raucous talk and actions" marked "a truly All American girl." Much of the off-the-field training for AAGPBL players addressed an unspoken worry about female athletes' cultivation of masculinity and the fear that such characteristics might indicate homosexuality. *LIFE* emphasized that several players were married and had children, while "many" others were engaged. An ideal young woman's profile on the home front included heterosexuality, whether she spent her time entertaining service personnel at a USO club or entertaining fans on and off the field.[41]

As the war came to a close, mainstream popular culture portrayed ideal girlfriends and wives as understanding, yielding, even deliberately naïve in their relations to men. Those whose partners had been overseas bore particular responsibilities for making the transition from military to civilian life smooth for their loved ones. A few weeks after V-J Day, an *LHJ* feature—"When Your Soldier Comes Home"—instructed women on how to handle everything from a man's guilt about his wartime activities to his readjustment in a culture where women enjoyed greater status and independence than in the places where he had recently lived. A sweetheart or wife needed to live up to the "idealized version" that he had developed of her over the many months away. While she had become "a perfect being in his imagination," he had been merely human, and his behavior could be attributed to the demands of military life. The narrative was a vehicle to convince American women to overlook their soldiers' dalliances with women abroad. In places where U.S. liberators were welcomed enthusiastically, "your soldier looked pretty good," women were told. If he "liberat[ed] a girl" in the process, his activities came under "the soldier's unwritten code of morals" and therefore were "perfectly excusable." American women were to consider these relationships meaningless to their sweethearts and spouses. Such liaisons served as healthy bases for comparison, the author argued, because "with characteristic American values, he says to himself after the conquest has been completed, 'Thank God my girl back home isn't like that.'"[42]

Such wishful thinking on his part could not diminish the reality that plenty of American women had fulfilled romantic desires and sexual needs in liaisons of their own during the war. A rising rate of infidelity accompanied the "Wartime Marriage Boom," which included over 1.1 million *more* marriages between 1940 and 1943 than the previous years' marriage rates forecast. The U.S. Census Bureau reported in May 1945 that more marriages had occurred "in each of the past four years than in any prior year in the history of the United States." War mobilization had encouraged many couples to marry sooner than they had planned and many others to marry soon after meeting each other. In 1944 a sample survey revealed that more than 2.7 million young, married women had husbands away in the armed services. Women who took control of their own sexuality or appeared independent sexually came under scrutiny at the height of the war but were more closely watched as it drew to a close. In one of her letters home, WAVES enlistee Mary Liskow described a case of "mental homosexuality" at her Oklahoma training station and the subsequent discharge of the two women involved. As a perceived "lesbian threat" in the WAC gained ground, "purges" of suspected lesbians took place. Open challenges to the heterosexual norm or gender crossings considered dangerous in American culture indicated that mainstream media had failed to get its messages through to women. A 1940 textbook on marriage had warned that women who earned and spent as much as men would expect other rights that men enjoyed, concluding that "the right to behave like a man [means] also the right to misbehave as he does. The decay of established moralities [comes] about as a by-product." In *All-Out Arlene*, the protagonist's friend in the WAVES receives a letter from her boyfriend overseas, who signs off: "Be a good girl and remember that the old saying about a sailor having a sweetheart in every port does not go for female sailors." Many Americans saw the erosion of a double standard and women's infidelity as signals of social disorder, dreading their effects on postwar culture.[43]

With social order as high a cultural priority as economic and political order in the waning months of the war, a reinvigorated double standard in the realm of sexual expression and activity permeated society. To prepare for postwar years, *LHJ* recommended, any American woman with a husband overseas would have to consider her "chief rival" not merely a woman in France or Italy (Asian women were not mentioned as possible intimates of U.S. soldiers and sailors); instead, she would have to fight against "the image he has created in his memory of you." Posing a challenge against an internal, emotional, and psychological enemy, *LHJ* concluded, "Your biggest problem is to make the flesh-and-blood woman as interesting to him as that image." Gushing over a photograph his girlfriend had sent to him in the South Pacific, Ewart Shuler claimed that the image grew "more beautiful every day." His expectations reveal the power of a persistent wartime theme—that women had a responsibility to try to match what existed in the mind's eye and imagination. Full awareness and attention to the essentially unknowable would demonstrate the extent of women's fidelity.[44] Men like Shuler worried about their sweethearts' faithfulness, expressing their anxieties in subtle and not so subtle ways. He reminded his girlfriend in more than one letter that she had promised to wait for him, and that only her waiting made his current hardship bearable. Wondering aloud about their respective trust in each other, he assured himself with the entreaty, "I know you'll never let me down." As the months passed, their relationship turned on uncertainties and infidelities. Admitting to an affair with another woman, he nevertheless worried about his girlfriend's faithfulness, demanding to know if she was seeing someone else. When he sent a second photo of himself for her *other* bedside table, he admitted, "So I'll have you surrounded." The sexual containment of a woman he saw slipping away from him spoke to the role of fidelity in wartime romances and postwar desires. Many long distance relationships unraveled over the war years, with the high marriage rates from 1940 to 1944 resulting in the highest divorce rates in U.S. history.[45]

The public's scrutiny of American women's desires, romantic and otherwise, intensified in 1944 and throughout the spring of 1945. The question posed in many offices and living rooms was: What would or should American women want in a postwar world? She would be a demanding consumer of tech goods, it was assumed. Leo Rich's forecast divided the demands for technology along gender lines. Men who had been "soda jerkers, truck drivers, salesmen and students before the war" had become "experts in radar, aviation, or ordnance" and would not be satisfied with antiquated or inefficient equipment on the job, he argued. Women would also have high demands for the mechanical equipment they encountered: "Mollie the machinist and her friends in the war plants will know whether a vacuum cleaner is well made and looks right. Mrs. Housewife, who hasn't had a maid since the war began, will look for labor-saving features—although she'd prefer the maid." JWT's Consumer Panel, based on middle-class households that purchased "85% of *all* consumer goods," pitched women's postwar wishes in such industry magazines as Henry Luce's glossy creation *Fortune*. In mid-1944 the magazine ran advertisements depicting women as demanding domestic operators who had asked for improvements in ovens, refrigerators, and other home appliances. One woman requested a vacuum cleaner that would remove "*all* dog hairs" while another wanted an electric iron with a reliable cord. Domestic wishes ruled over all others in popular media.[46]

Claiming to know what young women wanted in the postwar market, MacFadden magazines reduced it to five points. "Household things" topped the list, with specific requests for electric dishwashers and "roomier refrigerators!" One woman in the ad linked these products to ease but not idleness. New kitchen appliances would not allow women more time for, say, afternoon matinees or university coursework; instead, the middle-class woman preferred "NOT doing housework," she said, so as to have "more time" for her family. In the waning months of the war, domestic skills were emphasized to an even greater extent. Food company pamphlets and kitchen product recipe books focused in particular on mothers' responsibilities for teaching their daughters to cook. They also urged teenage girls to learn to cook sooner rather than later since, as one book pointed out, young men would be even more demanding about their food in the postwar world than they had been before. Cookbook authors offered ways to meet the demands, attracting young women with titles such as "How To Win Favor through Flavor or The Easy Way to be an Angel." The Fawcett publishing empire, which included *True Confessions, Movie Story, Motion Picture*, and *Life Story*, advertised in July 1944, "*[S]he is dreaming dreams*. A white shingled cottage. A streamlined kitchen. The best in work-saving appliances. A whole new wardrobe of clothes. Most of all, she is dreaming of a new home and a better way of life when her man comes home." With a directed and unwavering eye on the postwar markets, Fawcett enticed retailers and advertisers with an overwhelmingly female readership who bought ninety-three million publications a year.[47]

As the preeminent message maker to women during the war, ad agency J. Walter Thompson identified "eternally feminine" interests as: "Romantic tales! Secrets of beauty! Stories about people like her neighbors! The timeless topic of food!" Stimulating "EVERY WOMAN" in America, JWT argued, these themes provided a snapshot of the approach designed to influence women in the waning months of the war. In

1945 Olive Gately instructed those who would speak to American women through advertising to consider what "Mrs. Small-Town America" expected at war's end. Having lived and talked with people who resided in the heartland, Gately set herself up as an expert on the postwar woman. Following a "typical" American mother on a Saturday afternoon shopping trip in Cleveland, she observed: "For herself, she bought nothing. Nor did she so much as cast a sidelong glance at the many enticing wares displayed for her personal glamorizing. Just as it is with most women in America, her family and her home were her main concern." The self-sacrificing mother would command a central place in postwar consumer culture, Gately concluded, and advertisers would be wise to remember that like her, "the majority of Americans" cared more about "home, family and security for the future" than anything else. Gately's ordinary American woman demonstrated an interest in domestic life that would be revered in the coming months and years.[48]

Early in the war Ethel Gorham had speculated about a dismal existence for American women if Nazism prevailed. While arguing that "the most important, difficult and highly skilled work" was that of wife and mother, she noted that it should be work *chosen* by American women rather than forced on them. Nazis would deny conquered women the right to education, Gorham warned, thus separating them from their destinies as modern mothers. In a victorious United States, however, women would have access to the "science of psychology" and other branches of knowledge that would "make the bringing up of children ten times as successful a business as ever before."[49] The real difference rested on whether women would inhabit domestic worlds created by edict in a totalitarian regime or by subtle persuasion in a democratic society. Law and the threat of terror stood against a system of colorful, innocuous home life scenes produced by corporate America and sanctioned by the U.S. government.

If the postwar marketplace promised to offer women the scientific advantages necessary to fulfill their domestic dreams, the postwar workplace did not look quite as receptive to their needs. Many women foresaw what awaited them, and their disillusionment resulted in greater absenteeism and a reluctance to continue in a job market that considered them dispensable. High quit rates in 1944 led the OWI to announce, "In every case reported to date of group layoffs, due to cutbacks or other reasons, a considerable portion of the women separated from their jobs did not seek other employment but simply faded from the labor market." The report looked in particular at war boom areas such as Evansville, Minneapolis, Los Angeles, and San Francisco to explain why women did not seek other work. The "evaporation" was attributed to many reasons, the list topped by the declaration that other available jobs failed to offer "the financial incentive to keep on working." In the Evansville market, "many women" had been "unwilling to accept" jobs in "less essential industries," primarily because the hourly wage rate of around forty cents was one-third of what they had made in industrial work. The OWI report stated that jobs in the retail or service industries probably did not have "enough wartime appeal" to women accustomed to munitions manufacturing.[50]

While some women may have thought they had "done [their] share" and were "suffering from 'war job fatigue,'" others reported "the strain of keeping house and working was either too great, or the attendant problems, like transportation and shopping, too difficult to encourage a second venture." In San Francisco, where in-migration had not kept pace with out-migration of workers by mid-1944, reports mentioned women who wanted "to meet their work and home responsibilities." But more telling was a judgment about Bay Area women's demands for substantive employment opportunities: "Many in-migrant women not suitable for industrial jobs refuse service occupations and insist on a type of work for which they are not fitted." Although veiled, the reference likely referred to the thousands of women of color who had migrated to the area after 1940, most of them from southern states. The report perpetuates stereotypes about workers, even though nearly three years of war production had proven that women of all ages and backgrounds could handle industrial employment. It foreshadows one of basic challenges women would confront on a larger scale in the postwar world—the notion that service work was their natural calling. The OWI report did not blame the U.S. government for making childcare a low priority or for failing to encourage the American public to accommodate working women more fully. Conveniences such as extended hours for stores and laundries never received official sanction or promotion, and recommendations about childcare assistance made by the WMC's Women's Advisory Committee were "ignored" at higher levels by policy makers.[51]

The OWI assigned blame instead to those who had dropped out of the labor market. The nation's greatest reserve pool of workers, nonworking women, continued to show "less receptivity" to recruitment programs and propaganda. Perhaps they realized the hollow promises of skill development for future careers. The OWI report's most stunning incongruity appears in a comment on the long-term effects of the current employment crisis. The "one note of reassurance" was that women understood the limits to which they could go in the American workplace, leading the War Manpower Commission to comprehend "a forecast of the pattern to prevail when the war is over." Outlining a well-ordered, gendered workplace in its conclusions, the OWI noted that "the unobtrusive withdrawal from the labor market of women not usually employed, without pressing for further employment, tends to counterbalance the natural tendency of employers to proffer jobs first to male workers with greater work experience." Many women knew they would not be considered viable competitors for positions sought by men who felt entitled to them; others believed they should not fill good jobs or demand a place in the work-force. So, the home front conundrum remained in 1944: more war workers were needed, and women constituted the best pool of labor; but if women hesitated, American society would benefit in the long run, with a traditionally gendered work culture intact.[52]

In 1945 the looming question for many women was whether they would be able to keep the jobs they had filled during the crisis. Would their winning attitudes have an influence? The new director at the Labor Department's Women's Bureau, Frieda Miller, had been hired to help women who were losing their positions to returning veterans to reintegrate into the American economy. Expressing dismay in a national address, Miller called on women's advocates to confront "those straws in the wind of public opinion that clearly show how it is veering from a period of excessive admiration for women's capacity to do anything, over to the idea, ex-pressed at times with considerable vehemence, that women ought to be delighted to give up any job and return to their proper sphere—the kitchen." Besides the need of many women to work to support their immediate and extended families, Miller pointed out, a recent survey showed that "fully 80%" wanted to remain in the labor market.[53] If women took literally the phrase "for the duration," then they knew that jobs paying them forty-five dollars a week would disappear or be given to returning veterans, despite their desires to continue working. Former African American domestics feared that they would return to positions paying one-tenth of what they had earned in industrial jobs.[54]

In studying women's postwar prospects in industry and the professions, Bryn Mawr College researchers projected that women would probably remain in aircraft and automotive industries in larger numbers than before the war. In "Transpor-tation" women would "continue in lighter jobs and as ticket sellers" but would lose such positions as "conductors, operators, etc." Among federal employees a "sharp immediate decline" in the number of women would eventually give way to an increase in pink-collar work. In jobs identified solely as "Men's Professions" the report bluntly foretold an "uncertain" future for women. Vergil Reed, whose expe-rience combined marketing, consumer research, and a stint in government service as the acting director of the U.S. Census Bureau, argued that local employment opportunities in the postwar era would depend on "the degree to which women stay in industry after the war." He stated at an American Marketing Association meeting in mid-1944, "It is likely that not as many women will want to go back to the home as some people now expect," a trend that he urged "must be taken into account in making postwar plans." He warned his audience not to visualize an expanding industrial sector after the war but instead to consider the need for ser-vice industry workers, a continuation of the current chronic shortage of "service employees." The eleven million returning military personnel would have a great impact on employment, he contended, since they constituted "a restless and mobile" population who would not necessarily "want to settle down where they lived before and go back to their old jobs." The War Department complicated women's postwar employment plans by having male soldiers debate the question, "Do you want your wife to work after the war?" However restless or demanding veterans might have been, most received preference in hiring over women. Even women with wartime work experience saw their opportunities to move into higher echelons in rank or pay disappear.[55]

Women who occupied white-collar positions during the war began to see and feel the squeeze out of career spaces as early as 1944, but by mid-1945 the pressure was relentless. Two magazine essays serve as bookends to illuminate this growing pressure on middle-class women: the first a story directed at the *LHJ*'s wide readership, the other an editorial in *Advertising & Selling* (*A&S*). That the writers of these pieces chose to conceal their identities indicates their awareness of stepping into controversial territory. They spoke on behalf of Americans who yearned for a gendered social order that would include fewer professional women than the war had created. In January 1944 "a successful career wife" told *LHJ* readers that dual career marriages suffered under "terrific strain." A couple's "glossy surface" usually covered many cracks underneath. Women who faced the greatest threats to their home lives were those who truly loved their careers, the author argued, since they could not give their husbands and families "all they deserve." To have one person in a household grappling with ideas, deadlines, and client meetings was enough; the anonymous author asked, "When there are *two* fighters, each needing encouragement; two performers, each demanding an audience? What then?" Should she be more successful, a husband's "male pride" would suffer, and she would have to endure an unbalanced marriage with a "chronically embittered" spouse. Women with a "suicidal hunger for success outside the home" would do much better setting up a home as their "business." The author charged male readers to appeal to women's consumer instincts and "start selling" them on the idea of womanhood, since a man's job was to make a woman feel "so extraordinarily lucky just to be a woman, and a potential wife and mother."[56]

Not as subtle in his responses to women *as women*, the *A&S* writer, identified as "Anonymous," complained about career women who had risen quickly through the ranks and ruined the white-collar workplace. Anonymous was not as appalled by the presence of women as by their attitudes. Believing that they had natural tendencies toward emotional volatility, the author suggested that their elevation to positions of power damaged an office's otherwise congenial atmosphere. Indicting three colleagues in the advertising business, Anonymous concealed their identities with pseudonyms but warned all such career women to "Block That Temperament!" The three scenarios highlighted women who began their jobs on the right track, then got derailed as they grew increasingly more confident and vocal. The first case involved "Explosa," a novice who began in marketing research in 1942, worked hard, and "didn't fool around with office gossip." But after the company hired an office assistant for Explosa, things began to change. After a company executive asked Explosa's assistant to do something for him then wrote the assistant a thank-you note, Explosa told him "not to do a thing like that again." The second scenario featured "Angelina," who impressed everyone because she wrote good copy. Given Angelina's popularity in the office, Anonymous thought "[e]ven after the boys got back there'd be a place for a gal who fitted in as she did." But over time, he reported, Angelina developed an ego, expressed most unbecomingly after an editor changed her ad copy for a new account. Anonymous objected not just to Angelina's indignation at the editorial work but to her manner of expression, complaining that "her voice went into those registers that make radio control room engineers very bald." The third example featured "Astounda," hired as a secretary but soon promoted "because she had brains and was reliable." When an office executive asked the recently promoted Astounda to call his lunch date and cancel it, Astounda retorted, "Isn't that a job for a secretary?"[57]

Anonymous concluded his cautionary tale with a threat to women like the three he had described: "Thousands of fine gals have jumped into business jobs during this wartime emergency and have earned themselves permanent places in fine organizations. But a few have been unable to withstand success. Come peace, dames who go temperamental now, will GO."[58] The writer's unease stemmed not from sharing the white-collar workplace with women or even from seeing them in positions of power. Instead, how they expressed themselves from those positions of authority bothered him most. That both Explosa and Astounda challenged executives' assumptions about the "place" of women in the office—to "help out" whoever needed assistance or to assume clerical duties simply because they were women— was a wrong move, in his opinion. In both situations, their verbal challenges to authority got them into worse trouble since they acted in ways he considered unbecoming their sex. Angelina's tone of voice more than her act of confrontation bothered Anonymous, whose humor disguised an all-too-common barb about women who used their voices with confidence—in a word, they were *shrill*.

Illustrated by a sketch of a woman striding self-assuredly, the essay "Block That Temperament!" reflected a swelling sentiment in American society as postwar plans were in full swing. Women may have found places during the war emergency, but if they believed professional success granted them a wider sense of independence or greater latitude in behavior, they needed to reconsider their illusions.

Passionate opinions could be more usefully channeled toward family and domestic life, popular culture instructed. Where women needed to keep emotions in check was the professional world, Anonymous and others warned. Otherwise, they would find the privileged spots they had occupied under wartime emergency conditions closed forever. Both the *LHJ* article and the *A&S* drama suggested that some American homes and offices had been thrown out of balance; and only a restructuring of the social and economic landscape into traditional prewar patterns would offset additional cultural damage. Nevertheless, such prescriptions invited a few bold critics whose modern voices laid bare the incongruities of white-collar workplace sexism.

Two months after Anonymous issued his threats to ambitious career women, a respondent known to readers only as "A Temperamental Dame" answered him in the pages of *Advertising & Selling*. Identifying herself as someone who hoped to be a successful businesswoman, she challenged his assumption that not handling success well was "a peculiarity of the feminine sex," then she proceeded to interpret the sources of his consternation and unravel his argument. Creating three analogies to match his scenarios, the writer claimed that "Tom," like Angelina, did not enjoy seeing his work edited, but when he threw a tantrum, the boss overlooked it. Then she asked, "Is Explosa necessarily a woman?" Given the situation, she answered, Explosa rather than her assistant should have received a note of gratitude from the executive who used *her* assistant's time for his project. With increasing intensity in her rebuttal the writer summarized the third scenario with a sardonic "Astounda is a heretic—no less. 'Tis unheard of for a woman—no matter what her position— not to be perfectly willing and happy to do little detail jobs for the men when their secretaries are not available. Can you picture Mr. Headlong making his request—I should say 'giving his order'—to another man? Even the one and only office boy in these times might have responded, 'Sorry, sir, that's not what I'm getting paid for.' What's more, the office boy would get away with it."[59] Interpreting each example through the frame of women's experiences in professional positions, the writer laid bare the double standard operating at many levels in the American workplace.

As she concluded her argument, A Temperamental Dame outlined and clarified the tensions in the white-collar world as the war neared its end. If blue-collar workers were being dismissed en masse to open up places for men on the assembly lines, women in professional positions often faced subtler discriminations. The writer encapsulated those aggressions with a bit of prophecy about the overall treatment of American women on the home front, concluding:

> "Block That Temperament" couldn't be a sign that you are making excuses early in
> the game for what most business women are realistic enough to know will happen?

Many women will lose their positions completely or be shoved down the ladder as soon as service men start coming back. Couldn't you just be honest with yourself and admit that the idea of women holding equally responsible positions with men disturbs your staid, stuffy sense of your own importance? It was all right to let women help you out of a bad hole, but—

You admitted in your little dissertation that women have worked hard and proven themselves very capable. What you forgot to say was that in most cases of success, the woman has worked twice as hard and considerably more innate ability was required of her than of a man for the attainment of the same recognition. In very few cases is equal pay received by men and women for equal amount and quality of work turned out. I have seen more than one 4-F put into a position that rightfully belonged to a woman both from a seniority and capability standpoint. Is that what is called "fair play" in business?[60]

The essay reflects the late war pressures on career women to shift their goals and minds away from professional lives. The writer provides a genuine sense that her budding career is near its end, as her dream of becoming a successful professional grows dim. That she and women like her stepped up when asked to contribute disturbs her even more. The postwar culture on the horizon appears a much narrower place for women who had hoped to climb a career ladder as a natural consequence of wartime training and experience. Anonymous no doubt had begun to hope that the ubiquitous moniker "for the duration" would be enforced in his previously comfortable office environment. Finding several ways to ease women out—denying their voices, checking their independent action, challenging their "womanhood" with small tests—would be keys to restoring his prewar world. Women would have to find their level and satisfaction in work elsewhere. Contemporary observer and historian Mary Ritter Beard witnessed the unceasing contemplation about "wage-earning and salaried women" in the closing months of the war, concluding that "the horizon of the future was scanned with anxiety" on the issue. Anxiety reigned because well-paid women challenged a social structure that demanded their acquiescence in realigning gender roles according to more traditional patterns.[61]

At the war's beginning, many readers who saw Margaret Culkin Banning's opening lines in *Women for Defense* no doubt felt spurred by the imperatives, "Women must . . . Women must . . . Women must." The prescriptive tract encouraged disciplined minds, bright spirits, and new habits in order to make the home front work as a smoothly functioning support system for the U.S. military effort. Revealing the ideal contributor to the effort, the image precipitated a slew of others that would emanate from many places recommending to real women how they should think, feel, and act for the duration. From the oversized smiles on fifty-by-fifty-foot billboards to the smallest gestures on four-by-six-inch pamphlets, large and small messages suggested the right attitudes for American women to assume during the crisis. How women responded came through in letters to family, friends, colleagues, lovers, and acquaintances, and in hundreds of other ways—in their decisions to quit jobs before being fired, to challenge recommended career paths, to fulfill sexual needs elsewhere during a partner's absence, to revel in the wartime rhetoric of freedom. Some followed the imperatives, others did not, and still others redrew the boundaries set for them. They grappled with the government's needs, corporate America's enticements, and the culture's demands. They saw femininity and national identity bound tightly together.

American business and its lifeblood, advertising, could not congratulate themselves enough for their wartime accomplishments. Editorials and *aditorials*, they claimed, not only helped to fight and win the war but to provide a solid foundation for business in the postwar world. They carefully measured their contributions, prepared to showcase them when politically expedient. These organizations illustrated their reports with images of workers who had helped to sustain the arsenal of democracy; but the business and trade papers from industries such as steel and aluminum showed men rather than women at work in factories. Rosie, it seems, had disappeared. In the business insider publications, women appeared more often in "domestic" and "commercial" advertisements than in those for industrial enterprises. With the Cold War launched before the Second World War was over, the call for an American home front to be organized along traditional gender lines would securely define the United States against the Soviet Union's communist model, a society where too few distinctions between women and men were made, American pundits and politicians argued.[62] But the glimmer of a different world—one seen only briefly during the years on the home front—would not be forgotten by all Americans. Wartime conditions had allowed many women to sow seeds of opportunity and cultivate them slowly but deliberately. They would employ some of the attitudes required of them during the war—a certain amount of risk taking and a lot of flexibility. Some would secure friends and allies with their cheerfulness and good humor; others would avoid behaviors they considered too emotionally confining. All would confront the model attitudes pitched during the war as necessary for victory, and wonder which ones to keep and which to discard for the peacetime battles ahead.

Making War, Making Women begins with fictional airman Don Corbett hoping to find the ideal American Girl among the flesh-and-blood women on a train. My story ends with a less glamorous character but a real one—an airplane mechanic who left the U.S. Army Separation Center in Fayetteville, North Carolina, in late 1945. On the train home, the twenty-four-year-old veteran wrote, "When I get my $200 mustering out pay I'll buy a piano and take lessons. I'll buy paintings for the house, and go to concerts and ballet, and take Mama and Daddy and William. Occasionally a cold thought squelches my joyful anticipation—am I unrealistic? At Ellington all we talked about was the Utopia awaiting us in civilian life. If I'm honest I admit that life was no Utopia before. Will it be different now? I hope with all my heart to make it better at least." Having realized a few weeks earlier that the GI Bill would not sufficiently fund her dream of owning a small farm, Private Aileen Kilgore had already adjusted her sights on more manageable goals and faced her future with tempered optimism.[1]

It is impossible to know how many American women entertained similar dreams forged from the wartime rhetoric of freedom, democracy, and opportunity. Many no doubt chose to fulfill Don Corbett's vision of them by mimicking what he and others claimed they wanted "to come home to."[2] They had read and seen plenty of ways to work on it. Between 1941 and 1945 the United States fostered a political culture where women's bodies and minds could be used in the service of the war effort. Thousands of government officials, artists, designers, and writers shaped and molded their images of ideal American women for millions of posters, billboards, leaflets, car cards, and print advertisements. They also depicted dangerous, immoral, and dishonest women, warning Americans against those who would weaken the body politic by pursuing their own selfish interests rather than the collective good. Women responded to the government's demands and the culture's requirements in myriad ways.

Perhaps women in the Greatest Generation should be heralded not because they took jobs in heavy industry but gave them up at the end of the war; not because they put on military uniforms and carried out official duties but took off their stripes and chose not to brag about their military service in the postwar years; not because they challenged the culture's expectations and restrictions but played by the official and unofficial rules and grew into the archetypes created for them. But that would oversimplify both the war years and the postwar era, spawning even more grand narratives of extraordinary battlefield courage while rendering almost everyone else invisible.

Anniversaries and commemorations of the Second World War will no doubt continue in the United States, the seventy-fifth anniversary beginning in 2016, the centennial in 2041. What will be the place in these celebrations for American women who built and typed, laundered and bathed, primped and dieted, scrimped and saved, grew Victory Gardens and bought war bonds, painted their faces and posed for cameras in the 1940s? To what extent will the women of the Greatest Generation be remembered as archetypes: the figures imagined and created in corporate boardrooms and at artists' drawing tables, in agency committee meetings and editors' planning sessions, in landladies' boardinghouses and other places where ideas about what women *should be* overshadowed who they were? To what extent will they be overwhelmed by the chimera of nostalgia, turned into relics for contemporary generations to look back on wistfully?

In the last few years, as acquaintances and strangers learned that I was writing a book about American women on the home front, the common enthusiastic response was, "Oh, Rosie the Riveter!" Occasionally I just nodded and smiled, but more often I felt compelled to mention other women, both real and imagined, to complicate the conversation and challenge the customary reactions. Posters, photos, and slogans came up in those chats, as did memories. An occasional conversation turned toward another cultural icon of the war, Alfred Eisenstaedt's photograph of street-level reverie in New York's Times Square on V-J Day, in which a sailor headlocks a nurse in order to get a victory kiss. Published in *LIFE* a few days after the event, the picture became the magazine's most recognizable and frequently reproduced image from its archives. Sculptures of the awkward embrace have been cast and erected in several American cities, and more than a few individuals have claimed to be the famous kissers.

If the combined glee and violence oozing from the picture truly shout "unconditional surrender," the photograph nonetheless comes up short as an embodiment of more complex wartime emotions. A more telling image—a classic memento mori—appeared in *LIFE* in May 1944. The portrait featured an Arizona secretary pondering a skull signed and sent to her by her boyfriend on the Pacific front (fig. 57). What is written on her face? Enigmatic and contemplative, she is the wartime Mona Lisa. The camera shows her to have followed all wartime prescriptions for ideal womanhood. She is well groomed, neatly dressed, with an appropriately painted face and well-manicured nails, a young woman who has taken a

Figure 57. *LIFE*'s caption at the foot of the photograph told readers, "Arizona war worker writes her Navy boyfriend a thank-you note for the Jap skull he sent her." The photograph by Ralph Crane was named "Picture of the Week." *LIFE*, May 22, 1944.

pink-collar government job for the duration. What will be her rewards for having created the woman the wartime culture demanded? Is her posture one of gratitude, as *LIFE* magazine insists in its caption? Or is it bewilderment? Or perhaps, a meditation on her inevitable future? Her postwar years are forecast by the Japanese skull that sits a few inches from her face. Does she realize that her acquiescence, her cheerfulness and fidelity, her sacrifices and smiles and patience, her willingness to write the requisite letters to keep up morale and to play fair in the consumer market, might yield for her a postwar world marked by the remnants and echoes of horrific violence? Will promises of idyllic cottages, sparkling kitchens, sleek appliances, new dresses, and a wealth of other products and gadgets temper the brutishness and fear that will dwell beneath their shiny surfaces? Could the spoils of victory be sweet enough to cover up the psychological damage wrought on both the battlefield and the home front? The answers to these questions bring us closer to the women that the war made, or more aptly, the women that they themselves made out of the mélange of crisis, opportunity, and death.

NOTES

Preface

1. Litoff and Smith, *American Women in a World at War*, xii. Litoff and Smith have collected and edited some thirty thousand wartime letters by women, publishing them in several collections; their work is invaluable to anyone studying women in the 1940s.

Introduction

1. Popkin, *The Journey Home*, 9. *The Journey Home* is based on a train trip that Zelda Popkin took near the end of the war.

2. "Work for Women after the War," September 1, 1944, RG 86, WB-DRWW, Box 206; "The Problem of Postwar Employment for Women," May 1944, RG 211, WMC-FS, Records of May T. Evans, Box 15; Michael C. C. Adams, *The Best War Ever*, 85.

3. This study's focus on sources produced during the war does not discount the remarkable oral history projects that have introduced us to women sharing their memories of the war years. Connie Field's documentary, *The Life and Times of Rosie the Riveter* (1980), is perhaps the best-known film in this genre (and was finally made available on DVD in 2007!). Among the many oral history collections that I hope will launch future cultural studies on the Second World War in American memory are Sherna Berger Gluck's *Rosie the Riveter Revisited* and Cindy Weigand's *Texas Women in World War II*. Westbrook, *Why We Fought*, 58.

4. Graphic Arts Victory Committee, *Guide to Essential Wartime Printing and Lithography* (1943), 27, RG 208, OWI-CC, Box 140. The committee included paper manufacturers and merchants; printing equipment, ink, envelope, and miscellaneous supply manufacturers; typographers, artists, printers, lithographers, letter shops, engravers, electrotypers, and others. It had local branches that supplied government agencies with a talent pool. Quote in Association of National Advertisers, Inc., *News Bulletin* 26 (October 29, 1942). General suspicions were evident in trade papers and journals, with such articles as "If American Business Wants to Run Its Own Show when This War Is Over," 17, 38–45. From Washington, typical antipathy may be seen in Robert Ferry's response to a *Wall Street Journal* article touting advertising's contributions to the war effort—"I am surprised that it has a Washington dateline because it could easily have been written in the inner sanctum of their New York office for the accuracy of it. I suppose it is over-sensitive of me to expect that an article about war advertising should use those three precious initials O-W-I." Ferry to T. S. Repplier, February 14, 1944, RG 208, OWI-CC, Box 151.

5. The three leading magazines in newsstand sales in 1941—*LIFE*, *McCall's*, and *Ladies' Home Journal*—held their positions throughout the war. On their influence, see Gordon E. Cole, "Magazines and Farm Publications," 70.

6. "Women Workers Will Win the War," 1943, RG 211, WMC-ISPD, Files of Allan Wilson, 1942–43, Box 2, which noted that the effort to recruit women for war work became "the *immediate responsibility of the J. Walter Thompson Company*, as consultant advertising agency to the War Manpower Commission and Office of War Information."

7. McDowell, "Recovery Missions," 301; Grosz, *Volatile Bodies*, 23; Bordo, *Unbearable Weight*; Butler, *Bodies That Matter*; Collins, *Fighting Words*, xxiii.

8. Bentley, *Eating for Victory*; Boris, "'You Wouldn't Want One of 'Em Dancing with Your Wife'"; Delano, "Making Up for War"; Hegarty, *Victory Girls, Khaki-Wackies, and Patriotutes*; McGovern, *Sold American*; Meyer, *Creating GI Jane*; Peiss, *Hope in a Jar*; Roeder, *The Censored War*; Westbrook, *Why We Fought*; and Winchell, *Good Girls, Good Food, Good Fun*. All examinations of women and the Second World War begin with the foundational studies published a generation earlier, including Anderson, *Wartime Women*; Campbell, *Women at War with America*; Hartmann, *The Home Front and Beyond*; Honey, *Creating Rosie the Riveter*; and Rupp, *Mobilizing Women for War*.

9. Beard, *Woman as Force in History*, 10. On "agency," see Mary R. Beard to James Putnam, November 10, 1944, in which she asks, "How does this title for my book impress you? . . . It is an exact statement of what I am dealing with" (in Cott, *A Woman Making History*, 254). Lerner, *Why History Matters*, and *Living with History / Making Social Change*.

One. All-American Masks

1. "Cosmetics for Girl Workers Boosting War Production," *Jackson (Miss.) Clarion-Ledger*, December 27, 1942. Researchers at the U.S. Department of Labor Women's Bureau clipped the story for their files, RG 86, WB-DRWW, Box 195.

2. Koehn, "Estée Lauder," 223; "Minimum Civilian Consumer Requirements for Toilet Preparations," [1942], RG 179, WPB-PDF, #533.424.

3. For discussions on the influence of regionalism in the 1930s, see Melosh, *Engendering Culture*, and Bustard, *A New Deal for the Arts*. On the depictions of women in the movies, see Human, "A Woman Rebels," and Haskell, *From Reverence to Rape*. *LIFE*, September 22, 1941, 78–85, discussed in Rupp, *Mobilizing Women for War*, 66.

4. Peiss provides comprehensive coverage on cosmetics use from the late nineteenth century through the 1930s in *Hope in a Jar*; Banta, *Imaging American Women*; see also Thadious Davis's introduction and notes to Nella Larsen's *Passing* (1929); on the acceptance of the painted faces in the 1920s ("provocative but no longer sinful"), see Peiss, *Hope in a Jar*, 142–44, 151–55.

5. *J. Walter Thompson Company News* [Confidential Staff Bulletin], January 10, 1964, 9, JWT-BIO; Abbott, "Doctor? Lawyer? Merchant? Chief?" 43, 154; Scanlon, *Inarticulate Longings*, 217–20. Peiss notes that the competition to "sign up the rich and famous" became "something of a sport" at the JWT agency (*Hope in a Jar*, 140); Blackwelder, *Styling Jim Crow*, 12–13; "individual self-development" quote in Peiss, *Hope in a Jar*, 166.

6. Emphasis mine, although the entire quote is the only statement attributed to Druhmel that is set in bold face type in the advertisement, JWT-DA, Chesebrough-Pond's, Box 16.

7. Goodwin's paraphrase of the poll data, in *No Ordinary Time*, 102; Kennedy, *Freedom from Fear*, 415, in which he cites a 1938 *Fortune* survey revealing that a very small percentage of Americans wanted the United States to accept Jewish refugees from Europe. Anti-Semitic sentiment remained steady during the war; typical feelings were expressed

by ordinary Americans such as Canton, Ohio, dental assistant Josephine Curry in her diary (see Bartson, *In the Shadow of the Hawk*, 439), and "a group of disgruntled wives" to Margaret Hickey, January 18, 1945, RG 211, WMC-WC, Correspondence of Chairman and Executive Secretary, 1942–45, Box 3; see also Yellin's discussion of anti-Semitic, pro-Nazi "Mothers' Movement" groups in the United States, *Our Mothers' War*, 331–41.

8. Kennedy, *Freedom from Fear*, 762–70. Roediger convincingly shows how racial lines had deepened by 1941 as "ethnic" lines (esp. regarding southern European immigrants) blurred, in *Working toward Whiteness*, 24–25, 137, 212–13, 220. "[I]nclusion and exclusion came together during World War II" as turn-of-the-century "new" immigrants who had made themselves "white" by 1940 further distinguished and separated themselves from racial "others," particularly African Americans (137).

9. As early as 1936, FDR had grappled with the issue of potential subversion among Japanese citizens living in Hawaii, suggesting that suspects be identified and "placed in a concentration camp in the event of trouble." Quoted in Okihiro, "An American Story," 50; Evacuation official quoted in Okihiro, "An American Story," 53; Roeder, "Censoring Disorder," 47. For the various racist perceptions of the Japanese during World War II, see Dower, "Race, Language, and War in Two Cultures," 169–201, and Dower, *War without Mercy*.

10. Hereafter referred to as the Ad Council.

11. Carlyle, "How Advertising Went to War"; "JWT Personnel in the Government or Volunteer Services," JWT-BIO, Box 2; Young, *Diary of an Ad Man*. On Young's influence on the business community at this critical moment, see Griffith, "The Selling of America," 388–412.

12. Tearsheet from *McCall's Drug & Toilet Goods Sales Planner*, JWT-DA, Chesebrough-Pond's, Box 16.

13. Young, Lecture #10, 1934, JWT-WS, Box 38.

14. "Ruth Fanshaw Waldo," *Notable American Women*, vol. 4 (n.d.), 715, where she was given credit for the 1942 Pond's "She's Engaged!" campaign, and Ruth F. Waldo, obituary, *Advertising Age*, September 15, 1975 (both clippings in JWT-BIO, Box 21). James Webb Young spoke of a product's ability to play on the "prestige" factor by noting its connection to an "achievement of personality," Lecture #10, JWT-WS, Box 38. On the backgrounds of JWT's Women's Editorial Department in the 1920s and 1930s, see Scanlon, *Inarticulate Longings*, 181–90.

15. Tearsheets, ad texts for the trade, specifically drug stores and other cosmetics retailers, JWT-DA, Chesebrough-Pond's, Box 16.

16. Peiss, *Hope in a Jar*, 176. Scanlon writes that the focus on products created "artificial relationships among women" (*Inarticulate Longings*, 219).

17. On "bridal terror," see Israel, *Bachelor Girl*, 170; Michael C. C. Adams, *The Best War Ever*, 132; Grabill, "The Effect of the Wartime Marriage Boom," 153.

18. See Costello, *Virtue under Fire*, 194–95; Hegarty, *Victory Girls, Khaki-Wackies, and Patriotutes*; and Leder, *Thanks for the Memories*, xiv, 38–40.

19. Tearsheet, February 1942, JWT-DA, Chesebrough-Pond's, Box 16 .

20. Karp, "Selling the Female Industrial Group," 26; Scanlon, *Inarticulate Longings*, 219.

21. *Forecast*, February 1942, 10.

22. Ibid.; "Weinberger Drug Stores' Head," 85.

23. Rupp, *Mobilizing Women for War*, 151; Draft, "Women Workers Will Win the War," [1942], 3, RG 211, WMC-ISPD, Files of Allan Wilson, 1942–43, Box 2.

24. MacFadden Women's Group conducted regular surveys to see who read their magazines, which included *True Romances, Love and Romance,* a..d *Movie Mirror,* among others; on the debate, see *A&S* 35, various issues; Kellar, "Are Women People?" 87.

25. Tearsheet, *Pacific Drug Review,* March 1942. In a 1942 issue of the *National Association of Retail Druggists Journal,* a Texas drug store owner claimed, "Women accept Pond's without a question. National advertising has built up such ready acceptance that Pond's Products are practically sold when we get them." Pond's Cold Cream advertisements appeared in a wide variety of magazines in 1942, including *Good Housekeeping, LHJ, LIFE, Look, Mademoiselle, McCall's, True Story,* and *Vogue.* See insertion schedules in JWT-DA, Chesebrough-Pond's, Box 16; Tearsheet, *National Association of Retail Druggists Journal,* October 4, 1943.

26. Tearsheet, JWT-DA, Chesebrough-Pond's, Box 16.

27. Tearsheets, JWT-DA, Chesebrough-Pond's, Boxes 16 and 17.

28. Mary Anderson, Director of the U.S. Labor Department's Women's Bureau, addressed the issue of night work at a two-day conference. See "Report of Conference on Women in War Industries," April 1943, RG 179, WPB-PDF, 241.11, Box 1016. On the link between nighttime work and alleged promiscuity, see Anderson, *Wartime Women,* chap. 3, and Hegarty, *Victory Girls, Khaki-Wackies, and Patriotutes,* 61–84, 156–57. Tearsheets, JWT-DA, Chesebrough-Pond's, Box 17; Reid, *Slacks and Calluses,* 61; "Women at War," 5.

29. Campbell, *Women at War with America,* 61; McKenna in *Good Housekeeping,* December 1944.

30. Pond's was "backed by 38,274,258 ads . . . reaching practically every woman and girl in the U.S.A." (*Pacific Drug Review,* March 1942); Johnson said, "The war will soon be over and Black vets will soon be coming home, looking for more glamour and more pizzazz than we're running in *Negro Digest*" (Johnson and Bennett, *Succeeding against the Odds,* 153, 113). Regular features in *Negro Digest* included "If I Were a Negro" and "My Most Humiliating Jim Crow Experience," as well as jokes, humorous stories, and reader responses. The journal's popularity across the color line was noted by a USO Mobile Service volunteer, who wrote that the magazine was "more widely read by white people than any other periodical published by Negroes" (*Negro Digest,* February 1944, 100). By 1945 the U.S. Navy was purchasing 2,400 copies per month for distribution; *Negro Digest* was the only African American magazine on the War Department's regular distribution list (*Negro Digest,* August 1945); "Advertising Boom," *Negro Digest,* October 1944, 23–24. For a glimpse at the breadth of the black press during the war, see Potter, *A Reference Guide to Afro-American Publications*; new publications began in several cities, particularly in war boom towns such as Dayton, Ohio, Wilmington, N.C., San Bernardino, Calif., and Houston.

31. Craig, *Ain't I a Beauty Queen?,* 24. For the Columbia University study, see Murray, *The Negro Handbook,* 1946–47, 258–260. The survey covered film, stage, radio, and print media.

32. Megan E. Williams, "The *Crisis* Cover Girl," 200, 202, 206. Circulation figures for *Crisis* vary widely, but they increased dramatically during the war years, from approximately twenty thousand in 1942 to nearly sixty thousand by 1946. For a severe condemnation of the black middle class, see Frazier, *Black Bourgeoisie.*

33. Roi Ottley, "New World A-Coming," excerpted in *Negro Digest,* September 1943, 94; Drake and Cayton, *Black Metropolis,* 496–97; On African American writers' discussions

about the political messages of skin bleaches and whiteners in the 1920s, see Peiss, *Hope in a Jar*, 209.

34. Drake and Cayton, *Black Metropolis*, 498, 499, 503. See Delano's photographic series in Stange, *Bronzeville*. Drake and Cayton note the *combination* of factors composing ideal African American female beauty, including "Caucasoid features and hair that is not kinky" (503 n).

35. A generation later, the NAACP staged the first Miss Black America pageant in Atlantic City, across town from the forty-eighth annual Miss America pageant, notes Craig in *Ain't I a Beauty Queen?*, 3. On color hierarchy, see Deborah Gray White, *Too Heavy a Load*, 159, 293 n, and Giddings, *In Search of Sisterhood*.

36. Peiss, *Hope in a Jar*, 220, 237; see also Sivulka, *Stronger Than Dirt*, 280–81.

37. Anthony, "Two Worlds," 56–57.

38. Megan E. Williams, "The *Crisis* Cover Girl," 200–218; Maxwell, "Glamour Vs. Prejudice," reprinted in *Negro Digest*, January 1944, 6.

39. *Opportunity* 22 (July–September 1944), 127; Honey, *Bitter Fruit*, 29 n, 25. "Differing from white 'cheesecake' shots, attractive African American women were contextualized as college students, professional achievers, or trailblazers for their race," Honey writes (29).

40. *Crisis* 50 (September 1943); Megan E. Williams, "The *Crisis* Cover Girl," 203–7.

41. Smith quoted in Lyons and Finney, *M & M Smith*. A former model commented on the variety of looks the photographers captured. In 1944 one third of the magazine's covers were portraits taken at M. Smith Studios; the next year, the magazine used even more of their work.

42. "Beauty Is a Business," 12, 14; *Crisis* 50 (January 1943), 2; "Women at War," 5; Chivers, "Effects of the Present War," 2; Franklin D. Roosevelt to Lester B. Granger, March 11, 1943, published in *Opportunity* 21 (April 1943): 34 (italics mine); see especially the 1943–45 volumes of *Opportunity*, *Brown American*, and *Negro Digest*.

43. "Beauty Is a Business," 14; Blackwelder, *Styling Jim Crow*, 112–13.

44. OWI, "Women in the War Campaign," (1944), RG 208, OWI-RW, Box 591. The OWI sent monthly guides, many in eleven-by-fourteen-inch format like this one.

45. For Parks's series, see "Ella Watson, U.S. Government Charwoman," at Library of Congress, http://memory.loc.gov/ammem/fsahtml/fachap07.html (accessed March 4, 2010); McEuen, "Exposing Anger and Discontent," 238–60; Ellis, "Esther Bubley," 265–70.

46. "Human Interest Stories, 1942–43," RG 211, WMC-ISPD, Box 2. WMC requested such stories from companies on January 14, 1943.

47. As Megan Williams points out in "The *Crisis* Cover Girl," darker-skinned black women graced *Crisis* covers as laborers engaged in and attentive to their work rather than smiling for a professional photographer in portraiture. The sole exception to this trend during the war years was Aurelia Carter, a welder named "Miss Negro Victory Worker" in 1944; that *Crisis* editors extolled her as "a typical American girl with a fragile, glamorous appearance" and highlighted her prewar work as a milliner and a committee secretary in her church made her an acceptable cover face. See *Crisis* 51 (September 1944): 279. All quotes in U.S. Department of Labor, Women's Bureau, *Negro Women War Workers*, iii, iv.

48. "Negro Migration Trends," in Murray, *The Negro Handbook, 1946–47*, 25–27; see also Daniel, "Going among Strangers," and Lemke-Santangelo, *Abiding Courage*.

49. Costello, *Virtue under Fire*, 43; Vincent quoted in Delano, "Making Up for War," 51; Phillips, *All-Out Arlene*, 51, 11, 134, and on "camp slang," 159–63. Harry Irving [H. I.]

Phillips, a Broadway show writer, was better known for his male antihero, Private Purkey, the protagonist in *Private Papers of Private Purkey* (1941), *Private Purkey in Love and War* (1942), and *Private Purkey's Private Peace* (1945). "You're in the Army Now" was recorded by Abe Lyman and the Californians, November 27, 1940, Bluebird Label, RCA Records.

50. OWI, "Red Makes A Difference Say the Women Marines," RG 208, OWI-RW, Box 589; Emily Yellin mentions the Arden color in *Our Mother's War*, 146. See posters at the Women's Memorial Foundation, Arlington, Virginia.

51. For sake of continuity I use WAC throughout the text to refer to the organization; since a WAC enlistee was known as a Wac, I also use that term. Meyer, *Creating GI Jane*, 35–50.

52. Ad Council, "'Give Us More Wacs . . .' An Urgent Appeal from the Army to You," 31, RG 208, OWI-RW, Box 590; Research Bulletin, "Reference to the Army and Navy in Advertising," Division of Research, National Better Business Bureau, originally published November 1941, revised October 1944, in OAAA-IA, Box 13; Kaplan, Siesel, and Bruck, "Advertising Plan for the Women's Army Corps," [n.d.], 3, RG 208, OWI-RW, Box 590.

53. Appeals in 1917 urged American women to find inspiration in such figures as a rosy-cheeked, red-lipped Joan of Arc and in Howard Chandler Christy's "Honor Roll" devotee. Schlaikjer based his illustration on Wac Helen McConnon, who served in Texas at Ellington Field and in France. On cosmetics use, see OWI Media Guide, 1944.

54. In "Japanese American Beauty Pageants," Malia McAndrew argues that the contestants in camp pageants were described as typically "All-American" and that the events themselves "frequently mirrored small town pageants." Miné Okubo discusses the loyalty process and its "red tape" in her own internment experience in *Citizen 13660*, 177, 205–8. Leisa Meyer recounts an altercation between an AP reporter and WAC officials at a Colorado "swearing-in ceremony" that included some of the first Nisei Wacs. After instructions not to "take pictures or cover the event" the reporter went ahead anyway; WAC officials pressed the Colorado governor to contact AP and tell them to "'back off'" (Meyer, *Creating GI Jane*, 67). Brenda L. Moore, *Serving Our Country*, xii. See OWI-SP for photographs of first African American WAVES; Harry Paxton Howard, "Americans in Concentration Camps," 281, 284, 301–2. Howard noted that it was no coincidence that the most virulently anti-Japanese sentiment was expressed by southern senators, who advocated deportation of the Japanese at some future date after the war ended.

55. Poster Collection, Women's Memorial Foundation, Arlington, Virginia.

56. OWI, "Everything for the Boys but What About the Girls?" *The Women's Page*, September 30, 1944, RG 208, OWI-ND, Box 7; Rosebery, *This Day's Madness*, 67. Reports from military censors who read v-mail, discussed in Costello, *Virtue under Fire*, 62–63; Aileen Kilgore to her parents, March 19, 1944, in Aileen Kilgore Henderson, *Stateside Soldier*, 39.

57. OWI, "Women in the War . . . For the Final Push to Victory," 4–6, RG 208, OWI-RW, Box 587; Ad Council, "'Give Us More Wacs . . .'" 19; Recruitment Booklet, "Your Wardrobe: Uniforms and Accessories," JWT-WW, Box 1.

58. November 3, 1944, and December 4, 1944, in Aileen Kilgore Henderson, *Stateside Soldier*, 108, 121; Betty Bandel's letters home reflect the same attention to the accoutrements of femininity, even though she was higher ranked and several years older than Kilgore. Gifts that she and colleagues exchanged, conversations they enjoyed, and letters they wrote all reveal the importance of a "womanly" appearance while in uniform (see Bugbee, *An Officer and a Lady*); Meyer discusses the backgrounds of Wacs in *Creating GI Jane*, 73; see also Green, *Growing Up in the* WAC.

59. Monahan and Neidel-Greenlee, *And If I Perish*, 28. Page Dougherty Delano analyzes Haskell's title and meaning in "Making Up for War," 54–55 (Haskell quote on page 53).

60. *Crisis* 50 (February 1943): 39, 44; RG 208, OWI-NP, Box 4. Feminist scholar Cynthia Enloe argues that racial integration came about only after many elements came together to reveal serious cultural crisis—including "a particular kind of warfare (long, bloody, geographically dispersed), a policy elite's intense fear of violating public cultural expectations (e.g., the exclusion of white women from the draft) . . . [and] the potential for a strategic alliance between certain women on the outside and certain women on the inside of the state structure" (*Maneuvers*, 217).

61. Advance Information Bulletin, "Immediate Needs for the Care of Our Wounded," March 5, 1945, prepared by Ad Council in cooperation with the OWI, War Dept., Navy Dept., U.S. Public Health Service, VA, and the American Red Cross, JWT-WW, Box 1; "Getting More Nurses for Our Men," February 1945, JWT-WW, Box 1; "Recruit Nurses for the Care of the Wounded," [1947], JWT-WW, Box 1.

62. Delano, "Making Up for War," 33–68, in which she reads the "ideological effects of gendered practices" in wartime American fiction and Hollywood film, with a strong focus on the meanings of lipstick. Applying Luce Irigaray's "emphasis on play and visibility," Delano demonstrates the importance of women's "self-fashioned *presence*" at an important historical moment (61).

63. Gaines, "War, Women, and Lipstick," 43. Peiss discusses the Tangee Company's use of "freedom" and "democracy" in its campaigns in *Hope in a Jar*, 240.

64. Policy draft, June 26, 1942, RG 179, WPB-PDF, #533.45.

65. "Questionnaire on Cosmetics," #1473-B, April 1942, RG 179, WPB-PDF, #533.408.

66. "Cosmetics-Orders" Policy Draft, June 26, 1942, RG 179, WPB-PDF, #533.45; Arthur E. Suffern to Richard A. Lester, June 22, 1942, RG 179, WPB-PDF, #533.405; see Summary Reports, May 26, 1943, and July 15, 1943, RG 179, WPB-PDF, #533.405.

67. Delano, "Making Up for War," 41, 45; *LHJ*, various issues in 1943 and 1944; Gaines, "War, Women, and Lipstick," 43. Delano argues that lipstick "became a code word for gendered ingenuity and perseverance" ("Making Up for War," 66, 57 n); "League History" (http://aagpbl.org/league/history.cfm) and "Charm School" (http://aagpbl.org/league/charm.cfm), All-American Girls Professional Baseball League, National Baseball Hall of Fame Library (accessed March 4, 2010).

68. Tearsheets, JWT-DA, Chesebrough-Pond's, Box 17.

69. Posters at "Venereal Disease," National Library of Medicine, Visual Culture and Public Health Posters, http://www.nlm.nih.gov/exhibition/visualculture/venereal.html#18 (accessed March 4, 2010); Brownmiller, *Femininity*, 163; Hegarty's great title, *Victory Girls, Khaki-Wackies, and Patriotutes*, refers to names given to sexually available women during the Second World War. On "Victory Girls," see Meyer, *Creating GI Jane*, 104; May, *Homeward Bound*, 69–70.

70. Pond's ad for *Mademoiselle* (March 1943), JWT-DA, Chesebrough-Pond's, Box 17.

71. On the early wrangling between U.S. government agencies and advertising, see Wayne Coy to Archibald MacLeish, January 24, 1942, and George A. Barnes to Felix Belair, January 27, 1942, RG 208, OWI-OFF, Box 12; Office of Facts and Figures, "Outline for the Coordination of Government War Graphics," June 1, 1942, 1, RG 208, OWI-OFF, Box 27; Office of Facts and Figures, "Outline for OFF Visual Arts Production," [summer 1942], RG 208, OWI-OFF, Box 27.

72. Office of Facts and Figures, "Outline for the Coordination of Government War Graphics," June 1, 1942, RG 208, OWI-OFF, Box 27.

73. Paul West to Ken Dyke, September 24, 1942, RG 208, OWI-CC, Box 140; Paul West to Henry A. Wallace, October 7, 1942, RG 208, OWI-CC, Box 140. See other correspondence in RG 208, OWI-CC, Boxes 140–41, 151; e.g., Robert Ferry to T. S. Repplier, February 14, 1944.

74. "Girl of 'Just Average' Looks Can Be a Knockout if She Likes."

75. Rupp, *Mobilizing Women for War*, 155–60; Delano, "Making Up for War," 45; Thanks to my colleague, Ken Slepyan, for drawing my attention to this particular image in the rich collection of wartime *New Yorker* cartoons; Tearsheet, "The Saleswoman Observes," October 1944, JWT-DA, Chesebrough-Pond's, Box 17.

76. Koehn, "Estée Lauder," 224. The figure of $700 million includes fragrances as well as facial preparations. Darnton, "4800 Call It Home"; Hirose, "What Postwar Products Do Women Want?" 29.

Two. Tender Hands and Average Legs

1. War Manpower Commission, Campaign Plan Manuscript, "Women Workers Will Win the War," 1943, RG 211, WMC-ISPD, Files of Allan Wilson 1942–43, Box 2; "Fawcett's Winning War Girl," *A&S* 36 (February 1943): 138.

2. *Saturday Evening Post*, August 21, 1943, 81.

3. Sivulka, *Stronger Than Dirt*, 182; Janello and Jones, *The American Magazine*. On pulp's successes, see Dorothy Ducas to Ken Dyke, September 3, 1942, RG 208, OWI-CC, Box 141. On the function of fiction in women's magazines as well as the working class readership of *True Story* and readers' purchasing power, see Scanlon, *Inarticulate Longings*, 138–39, 220. On romantic tropes in particular, see Radway, *Reading the Romance*.

4. "Fawcett's Winning War Girl."

5. Alsop and McBride, *Arms and the Girl*, excerpted in Litoff and Smith, *American Women in a World at War*, 168.

6. "Sales Forces Get Substitute Lines," *A&S* 35 (June 1942): 53. After 1933, as more Americans trusted banks to keep their money safe, the industry expanded and women employees filled a good number of the new positions. James, "Women at Work," 40; Hawks, "Women's Bank"; Tearsheets, *Banking*, March 1943, April 1943, and March 1945, JWT-DA, Eastman Kodak, Boxes 10 and 11.

7. "Sales Forces Get Substitute Lines," 53; Tearsheets, *Banking*, March 1945, JWT-DA, Eastman Kodak, Box 11.

8. Leff, "The Politics of Sacrifice," 1314; Scanlon, *Inarticulate Longings*.

9. Tearsheet, Ad #5721-A, *McCall's*, October 1942, JWT-DA, Lever Bros., Box 35.

10. Tearsheet, Ad #6744-A, *McCall's*, April 1943, JWT-DA, Lever Bros., Box 36. Robert Westbrook argues that propaganda produced by the U.S. government and corporate America urged Americans on the home front and battle fronts "to support the war effort as a duty they owed to the family that raised them, the family they were themselves raising, the family they would someday raise, and/or, somewhat more abstractly, to the family as a social institution" (*Why We Fought*, 50).

11. Costello, *Virtue Under Fire*, 192–209.

12. Peeler, *The Illuminating Mind in American Photography*. Weston had several models who became his lovers, but his photographs of Wardell are the best examples of the dis-

memberment to which I refer here. On Bourke-White's isolation of elements, see McEuen, *Seeing America*, 197–249. Coward quoted in Walters, *Material Girls*, 56. Walters situates Coward's contention inside a larger discussion of contemporary advertising's messages to women: "Women are urged to think of their bodies as 'things' that need to be molded, shaped, or remade into a male conception of female perfection. The fragmentation of the female body into parts that should be 'improved' or 'worked on' often results in women having a self-hating relationship with their bodies" (56).

13. The reiteration of such seemingly mundane activity bears out feminist philosopher Judith Butler's explanation of gender construction through performativity, wherein body management is not just an ongoing project but comprises applications that are normalized over time. And, as Butler notes, it is also "the reiterative and citational practice by which discourse produces the effects that it names" (*Bodies That Matter*, 2).

14. See, e.g., JWT-DA, Lever Bros., Boxes 37 and 38; "The Mood Has Changed," *Harper's Bazaar*, September 1944, 67, in Walker, *Women's Magazines*, 198–99; Ad Council, "The chipped teacup," sponsored by the Magazine Publishers of America, *Vogue*, 1944, available at Duke University Libraries, Digital Collections, Ad*Access, http://library.duke.edu/digitalcollections/adaccess.w0004/pg.1/ (accessed March 4, 2010).

15. Ad for *Cosmopolitan* magazine, *A&S* 37 (August 1944): 43.

16. Marion Stegeman to her mother, April 16, 1943, in Litoff and Smith, *We're in This War, Too*, 115; Bandel to her mother, December 4, 1942, in Bugbee, *An Officer and a Lady*, 51; Phillips, *All-Out Arlene*, 4; "Your Wardrobe," in "Be a Marine . . . Free a Marine to Fight," pamphlet [1943], 21, JWT-WW. Box 1; "Red Makes a Difference Say the Women Marines," undated typescript draft, RG 208, OWI-RW, Box 589; "Advise [*sic*] on Organization of Women Marines," typescript report, [n.d.], JWT-WW. JWT initiated the campaign to recruit women marines, and the agency surveyed the public several times in 1943 to determine "public attitude" toward women in service; Ad Council, "'Give Us More Wacs . . .'"31; "How a Woman Should Wear a Uniform," *Good Housekeeping*, August 1942.

17. Meyer, *Creating GI Jane*, 66; Delano, "Making Up for War," 53.

18. "Charm School," All-American Girls Professional Baseball League Web site.

19. "Victory Song," All-American Girls Professional Baseball League, National Baseball Hall of Fame Library, http://www.aagpbl.org/league/song.cfm (accessed March 4, 2010).

20. Peiss, *Hope in a Jar*, 190, 195, 245–46; *LIFE*, January 27, 1941; *LIFE*, February 3, 1941. For the *LIFE* covers, see March 10, 1941, May 19, 1941, and November 24, 1941.

21. *Philadelphia Evening Bulletin* advertisement, *A&S* 35 (June 1942): 35; "Cosmetics-Orders" Policy draft, June 26, 1942, RG 179, WPB-PDF, #533.45; Toiletries & Cosmetics Committee, Summary Report, May 26, 1943, RG 179, WPB-PDF, #533.405. The WPB Toiletries & Cosmetics Committee had no female members.

22. See, e.g., Proctor & Gamble, "Recipes for Good Eating," 1944, in NDP, Box 6; Mac-Fadden Women's Group ad, *A&S* 38 (May 1945): 75.

23. *LIFE*, August 7, 1941; *LIFE*, January 18, 1943.

24. Koppes and Black, *Hollywood Goes to War*, 167; on ticket sales, see Roberts, "You Must Remember This," 174; Sklar, *Movie-Made America*, 250; Dick discusses female moviegoers in *Star-Spangled Screen*, 177; Koppes and Black, "What to Show the World," 167.

25. See, e.g., posters for David O. Selznick's 1944 classic, *Since You Went Away*, starring Claudette Colbert, Jennifer Jones, and Shirley Temple.

26. Place, "Women in Film Noir," 47; Dickos, *Street with No Name*, 156–62.

27. Kershner's story recounted in Colman, *Rosie the Riveter*, 68–69; Hawes, "Let's Ration the Clothes Problem," 338; "Milady Can't Crack 'Hair Today and Gone Tomorrow' Now."

28. LeRoy W. Jeffries, "Step Up, Lady—Want a War Job?" *Opportunity* (April 1943), 39–40; "Dear Bill," 7. The photograph accompanying the text, oddly, shows a woman at her desk, pen in hand, with darkly lacquered nails. Jane Gaines mentions lack of constraints on office workers in "War, Women, and Lipstick," 44.

29. *Crisis* 51 (March 1944) and (June 1944); Lyons and Finney, *M & M Smith*.

30. Meyerowitz, *Women Adrift*; Peiss, *Cheap Amusements*.

31. Benson, *Counter Cultures*, 128–30; Israel, *Bachelor Girl*, 85–88; Clement, *Love for Sale*, 69. Clement notes that "treating" had disappeared by the 1940s, "replaced by a less specific set of economic and sexual assumptions embedded in the practice of dating" (238).

32. Kasson, *Amusing the Million*, 42. See Peiss, *Cheap Amusements*, 129–38, on the differences between the major parks' effects on culture; 48 and 88 on female workers and dancing; and 156 on the voyeurism of early movies. For "dance mad" quote, see Riordan, *Inventing Beauty*, 86. The Ziegfeld Follies ran from 1907 to 1931 and reappeared briefly in the mid-1930s. In 1922 Ziegfeld publicity initiated the motto, "The Glorified American Girl" (Mizejewski, *Ziegfeld Girl*, 111). For a history of earlier erotic images, see Banta, *Imaging American Women*, 634.

33. Roach, "Social Symbolism of Women's Dress," 420; McEuen, *Seeing America*, 167–86.

34. Riordan, *Inventing Beauty*, 143. Joanne Meyerowitz notes that as early as the publication of its second issue (in late 1936), *LIFE* magazine "included cheesecake photos of women in bathing suits" ("Women, Cheesecake, and Borderline Material," 29 n.15).

35. *LIFE*, January 20, 1941, 29; Israel, *Bachelor Girl*, 170; Hartmann, *The Home Front and Beyond*, 164.

36. "Pretty Los Angeles Schoolgirls Slide and Scramble at Hockey," *LIFE*, April 7, 1941, 102–04; "Femininity was a high priority" for the All-American Girls Professional Baseball League organizers (see "League History," All-American Girls Professional Baseball League Web site).

37. *LIFE*, June 2, 1941, 62–63. *LIFE* would exhibit a much more famous set of "decapitated" legs when it featured the actress Betty Grable in a similar way. See "Betty Grable's Legs," 82, as well as Westbrook's discussion in "'I Want a Girl,'" 613 n.17; Meyerowitz, "Women, Cheesecake, and Borderline Material," 9–35.

38. "Beauties at Atlantic City Have Splendid Backgrounds," *LIFE*, September 15, 1941, 38–39.

39. *LIFE*, September 15, 1941, 39. Schofield points out that competition rules stated that only "white" women could participate ("Miss America, Rosie the Riveter, and World War II," 53–66).

40. "'Tatuta Maru' Brings What May Be Last Silk from Japan," *LIFE*, August 11, 1941, 30; Scherman, *LIFE Goes to War*, 153; "Reporter 'Strips' for Victory," *Washington Times Herald*, February 3, 1943, collected in RG 179, WPB-GRIE, Scrapbooks, Box 2.

41. Tearsheet #4679, 1942, JWT-DA, Lever Bros., Box 34. The small-print text is diminished by the graphic image and its accompanying cartoon bubble.

42. Buszek, *Pin-Up Grrrls*, 11. Robert Westbrook interprets Rockwell's painting of "Roosevelt's most controversial" of the four freedoms as "the defense of the familial surfeit" (*Why We Fought*, 48). For a history of the years leading up to FDR's famous statement, see Donohue, *Freedom from Want*.

43. Buszek paraphrases Finch's theory in *Pin-Up Grrrls*, 11; Meyerowitz, "Women, Cheesecake, and Borderline Material," 17.

44. Koppes, "Never Underestimate the Power of a Woman," 66–68.

45. *A&S* 37 (November 1944): 80.

46. JWT-DA, Lever Bros., Box 37, 1944.

47. Buszek, *Pin-Up Grrrls*, 207, 210 (Bob Hope quote); Meyerowitz, "Women, Cheesecake, and Borderline Material."

48. Buszek's evidence led her to conclude that "not all pin-ups" were "for the iconic or masturbatory uses of a heterosexual male soldier" ("Of Varga Girls and Riot Grrrls"). Buszek argues that through the years pin-ups of various kinds, including the Varga Girls, provided women with "models for expressing and finding pleasure in their sexual subjectivity" (*Pin-Up Grrrls*, 12; quotes at 187, 208).

49. Barthes, *Camera Lucida*, 76. The power of documentary photography in the 1930s had helped to create this attachment to and belief in still pictures. I'm not suggesting that the American public was naïve about photo manipulation—viewers were well aware of such doctoring, as revealed in the case of U.S. government documentarian Arthur Rothstein. Yellin opens chapter 2 of *Our Mothers' War* with the Grable quote (73). "I have a lot of the snapshots of you stuck up alongside my bunk," Ewart Shuler wrote to Annie Faye Ross, September 29, 1945, SCHS.

50. Several legends about the origin and history of the famous pose exist; most biographical sources date it to 1943, as did *LIFE* magazine that year.

51. "Betty Grable's Legs," 86.

52. Westbrook, "'I Want a Girl,'" 600. As Westbrook points out, the U.S. war in the Pacific was a "race" war that enhanced Grable's popularity among military personnel there. Westbrook also notes *Time* magazine's revelation that "soldiers preferred Grable to other pin-ups 'in direct ratio to their remoteness from civilization'" (599).

53. Adams and Donovan, *Animals and Women*; on objectification, fragmentation, and consumption, see Carol J. Adams, "The Rape of Animals, the Butchering of Women."

54. Carol J. Adams, "The Sexual Politics of Meat"; see also Butler, *Bodies That Matter*, on constraints that become normalized over time; "Betty Grable's Legs," 82; D'Emilio and Freedman, *Intimate Matters*.

55. "Betty Grable's Legs," 82; Ewart Shuler to Annie Faye Ross, September 22, 1945, SCHS; Buszek, *Pin-Up Grrrls*, 224.

56. "Betty Grable's Legs," 83, 84. Although Westbrook does not analyze the images in the *LIFE* feature, he notes that they are "a superb example of the presentation in advertising and other mass media of women as *disassembled body parts*", 613 n.17 (emphasis mine).

57. "Grable's Baby," *LIFE*, May 8, 1944, 32; Yellin, *Our Mothers' War*, 98; *Photoplay* quoted in Westbrook, "'I Want a Girl,'" 605.

58. Warren, quoted at University of San Diego Department of History, World War II Timeline—1943, "Betty Grable," http://history.sandiego.edu/gen/ww2Timeline/betty grable.html (accessed April 22, 2010). The discussion noted here is the only point at which I engaged in oral history for the project. Although brief, the informal comments about Betty Grable made by my mother, father, mother-in-law, and father-in-law struck me in their uniformity, which is why I chose to include them (Stanton and Stanton interview; McEuen and McEuen interview). My first question in each conversation was "What do you remember about Betty Grable?" followed by "What do you think accounted for her

popularity during the war?" In none of the conversations did I show photographs of Grable; all comments were based on memories.

59. Buszek, *Pin-Up Grrrls*, 215. Page Dougherty Delano notes that the U.S. Army publication *Yank* "replaced pictures of women warplant workers with cheesecake photos" as early as September 1942 ("Making Up for War," 66 n.62).

60. See photos in "*LIFE* Goes to a Swing Shift Dance," *LIFE*, January 19, 1942, 86–89.

61. As Winchell argues, the USO "fashioned itself as the chief source of wholesome sexual companionship for servicemen in the United States" (*Good Girls, Good Food, Good Fun*, 111).

62. Riordan, *Inventing Beauty*, 143; "Charm School," All-American Girls Professional Baseball League Web site; "A Book of Facts about the WAC," 1944, JWT-WW, Box 1; Tearsheet, "Serve your Country in the 'war job with a future,'" sponsored by Eastman Kodak Company, JWT-WW, Box 1; HEF.

63. Popkin, *The Journey Home*, 28–44. Mark Carnes discusses fiction's ability to capture "aesthetic truth" in *Novel History*, 25. Susan Gubar analyzes the brutalities suffered by female characters at the hands of servicemen in postwar fiction in "'This Is My Rifle, This Is My Gun,'" 251–55.

64. Quoted in Israel, *Bachelor Girl*, 149; Costello, *Virtue under Fire*, 262. May mentions a similar sentiment recommended by a marriage counselor in *Homeward Bound*, 81.

Three. Pleasant Aromas and Good Scents

1. U.S. Department of Labor, Women's Bureau, *Progress Report on Women War Workers' Housing*; hereafter cited as WB *Progress Report*.

2. Bordo, *Unbearable Weight*, 27. In "Feminism, Foucault and the Politics of the Body," Bordo borrows the idea of "overseer" from the Foucaultian framework of modern power and interprets it from a feminist perspective, reiterating that outside coercion is not as forceful as that emanating from the self (253).

3. I use the term LUX to refer to LUX soap for laundry (as it was used in the 1940s) and to distinguish the product from Lux Toilet Soap. Both products were manufactured by Lever Brothers, which ranked third in magazine advertising expenditures during the war, just behind second-ranked Proctor & Gamble and top-ranked General Motors; between 1941 and 1945, those expenditures increased 214.67 percent. See Adkins Covert, "Consumption and Citizenship," 336, table 6.

4. Harriet Elliott, "Woman's Part in Defense Plans," speech typescript/press release copy, October 22, 1940, RG 179, WPB-PDF, 241.11, Box 1016.

5. "Women Workers Will Win the War," typescript, 1, RG 211, WMC-ISPD, Files of Allan Wilson, 1942–43, Box 2; Dorothy Ducas to Ken Dyke, September 3, 1942, and Ken Dyke to Keith Kane, September 5, 1942, RG 208, OWI-CC, Box 141. In this correspondence, they discuss magazine "tip sheets" distributed by the agency and the extent to which magazines were implementing the government's suggestions about the kinds of stories to run. Also, the OWI Magazine Section's "War Jobs for Women" (November 1942), a forty-five-page booklet sent to all magazine editors with suggestions for stories about "womanpower," made clear that women would determine their fate in the war: "Since America continues to be a land of initiative, the final catalogue of the jobs that women do

in this war will be what women make it"; Beard, *Woman as Force in History*, 28; "Women Workers Will Win the War," 2.

6. Minutes, June 16, 1943, RG 211, WMC-WC, Summary Minutes, Box 1; Thomas, *Riveting and Rationing in Dixie*, 12–14 (Thomas points out that the "call for married women who were residents of war production areas to take jobs was largely a way of limiting the migration to defense centers" [12–13]); Anderson, *Wartime Women*, 85, 79. Anderson identifies Detroit as having the worst living conditions of the three home front boom cities she compares in her study—Baltimore, Seattle, and Detroit. See also Rosebery, *This Day's Madness*, 43–45, and Hall, "Crisis at Hampton Roads."

7. Dorothy Ducas to Ken Dyke, September 3, 1942, RG 208, OWI-CC, Box 141.

8. Honey, *Creating Rosie the Riveter*, 49, 72–85; Rosebery, *This Day's Madness*, 111; "Life in Washington Isn't Bitter, Recruiting Stenographers Say," *Atlanta Constitution*, September 2, 1942. See also voluminous newspaper clippings on the problem in RG 86, WB-DRSB, Box 3.

9. Telephone interview report, Sara Buchanan and FPHA official, October 7, 1942, WB-DRSB, Box 3; WB *Progress Report*.

10. Hagner, "No Housing Problem Here!"

11. Peiss, *Cheap Amusements*, 73–75. See McCandless, *The Past in the Present*, and Lowe, *Looking Good*, on college residential life for women. Telephone interview report, Sara Buchanan, August 10, 1942, RG 86, WB-DRSB, Box 3; interview report, Sara Buchanan, September 2, 1942, RG 86, WB-DRSB, Box 3.

12. Peiss, *Cheap Amusements*, 72–73; Meyerowitz, *Women Adrift*, 121, 70–74.

13. Helen Duey Hoffman (Director, Washington Housing Association) to Sara L. Buchanan, November 12, 1942, RG 86, WB-DRSB, Box 2. Similar complaints were made a generation earlier by Chicago women who resisted "homes that restricted their independence, curbed their initiative, and invaded their privacy," writes Meyerowitz (*Women Adrift*, 79); Women's Bureau, "Wartime Reminders to Women Who Work," leaflet, January 1943, RG 86, WB-DRSB, Box 2. Although the brochure title suggests its audience is workers, the text offered sections of equal length to lessors and lessees. Last quote from Peiss, *Cheap Amusements*, 74.

14. Interview report, Sara Buchanan, October 3, 1942, RG 86, WB-DRSB, Box 3. David Brinkley discusses the housing crisis for African Americans in *Washington Goes to War*, 236–37; Johnson and Bennett, *Succeeding against the Odds*, 119; Landis, *Segregation in Washington*.

15. Boris, "'You Wouldn't Want One of 'Em Dancing with Your Wife,'" 86, 79, 87; see Sivulka, *Stronger Than Dirt*, 100–106, on the western ideologies connecting cleanliness and morality.

16. Boris, "'You Wouldn't Want One of 'Em Dancing with Your Wife,'" 93–97.

17. Interview report, Sara Buchanan, October 3, 1942. James Grossman illuminates the phenomenon of middle-class blacks' resentments and treatment of newly arrived rural African Americans in Chicago in the early twentieth century in *Land of Hope*, 123–60. Chivers, "Effects of the Present War," 1. On class division within African American communities, see Deborah Gray White, *Too Heavy a Load*, and Megan E. Williams, "The *Crisis* Cover Girl"; for its history in Washington, D.C., specifically, see Jacqueline M. Moore, *Leading the Race*.

18. Lemke-Santangelo, *Abiding Courage*; "Dear Bill," 7.

19. "Young unattached" was the descriptor used in the WB *Progress Report* to define the group most often discriminated against by boardinghouse keepers. See also Rosebery, *This Day's Madness*, 42–45, on housing shortages for war workers nationwide.

20. Minutes, April 15, 1943, RG 211, WMC-WC, Summary Minutes, Box 1; "immorality" quote, Helena Weil to Esther Franklin (AAUW), [1943], RG 86, WB-DRSB, Box 4; Housing Questionnaire response, RG 86, WB-DRSB, Box 5; Housing Questionnaire responses from various cities in Indiana, Louisiana, Michigan, Missouri, Nebraska, New York, North Carolina, Oklahoma, Tennessee, Texas, Virginia, and Wyoming, RG 86, WB-DRSB, Boxes 4 and 5.

21. Mrs. Fair Minded, "The Awful Type of People That Clutter Up a House," collected in RG 86, WB-DRSB, Box 3.

22. Housing Questionnaire, RG 86, WB-DRSB, Box 4. Question 7 read, "Are householders reluctant to accept women as roomers? For what reasons?" The final analysis of the answers collated with other WB-DRSB evidence, was published in WB *Progress Report*, which concluded, "Quite generally, women are not desired as roomers, for reasons that are fairly uniform in character over the country," 5. Mrs. Fair Minded, "The Awful Type of People"; "anything but themselves" quote in Rosebery, *This Day's Madness*, 111. The WB *Progress Report* also included "cooking" as a "privilege" alongside washing and ironing, even though the evidence on which the final report was based clearly shows that women's kitchen use was a minor inconvenience compared with their laundering. See Housing Questionnaire responses, RG 86, WB-DRSB, Boxes 4 and 5.

23. D. W. Vanderwater to OAAA Members, August 24, 1943, OAAA-IA; Margaret Ford's comments in interview report, Sara Buchanan, September 2, 1942; Flyer, "Boarding Homes for Women War Workers," WB, Special Bulletin No. 11, January 1943; WB *Progress Report*, 4.

24. Women's Bureau, "Wartime Reminders to Women Who Work"; Banghart quote in Brinkley, *Washington Goes to War*, 233; other quotes in Brinkley, 244.

25. Housing Questionnaire response, RG 86, WB-DRSB, Box 4; Women's Bureau, "Wartime Reminders to Women Who Work," 3.

26. Solinger, *Pregnancy and Power*, 80; Hegarty, "Patriot or Prostitute," 114, in which she notes that "romance magazines reinforced a connection between 'loose' sexual morals and the working class." See also Hegarty, *Victory Girls*, 61–84, and Boris, "'You Wouldn't Want of 'Em Dancing with Your Wife,'" on black women's efforts to "reproduce themselves" as neater and cleaner than whites (94–96).

27. Laundering and bathing constitute important operations in determining gender status, and in the case of American women during the Second World War, the extent to which they could be considered feminine. Here I have used Judith Butler's definition of "performativity" as a framework for understanding young women on the American home front; that is, I have analyzed their engagement in continual and seemingly mundane activities (laundering and bathing), which by the nature of their repetition conceal their larger cultural significance. As Butler explains in *Bodies That Matter*, "Performativity is neither free play nor theatrical self-presentation; nor can it be simply equated with performance. Moreover, constraint is not necessarily that which sets a limit to performativity; constraint is, rather, that which impels and sustains performativity. Performativity is thus not a singular 'act' for it is always a reiteration of a norm or set of norms, and to the extent that it acquires an act-like status in the present, it conceals or dissimulates the conventions

of which it is a repetition" (241). In explicating the role of performativity in constructing gender, Butler states, "The 'performative' dimension of construction is precisely the forced reiteration of norms. In this sense, then, it is not only that there are constraints to performativity; rather, constraint calls to be rethought as the very condition of performativity" (94–95); all work to consolidate "the heterosexual imperative," Butler argues (2).

28. See campaign designs for numerous clients, JWT-DA. Tawnya Adkins Covert shows that ads for personal hygiene products were second only to food advertisements in *LHJ* during the war years ("Consumption and Citizenship," 332, table 3).

29. "Cosmetics-Orders" Policy draft, June 26, 1942, RG 179, WPB-PDF, #533.45. Sivulka argues that by the 1920s daily bathing and the use of "large quantities of soap" had become commonplace in the United States (*Stronger Than Dirt*, 299).

30. Helen Lansdowne Resor, Stockholder's Affidavit, March 20, 1924, JWT-BIO, Box 15. Also, *J. Walter Thompson Company News* [Confidential Bulletin for Staff Members], January 10, 1964 [Helen L. Resor obituary]; Resor quote is from the March 1924 affidavit. For an understanding of Resor's place in the first generation of advertising women, see Peiss, *Hope in a Jar*, 117–26, and Scanlon, *Inarticulate Longings*, 174–81 (quote on 175–76).

31. Abbott, "Doctor? Lawyer? Merchant? Chief?" 45. Although Resor isn't identified in the article, the long detailed description of a certain advertising woman's career leaves no doubt as to its subject; Resor was not the sole creator of endorsement advertising, but she is credited with changing its "whole tone" by seeking women of high socioeconomic status to publicly support certain products. "Vital Role in Lux Advertising Development Held by Mrs. Resor," *J. Walter Thompson Company News* [Confidential Bulletin for Staff Members], January 10, 1964, 9, 11. Peiss discusses other early cases of endorsement advertising by high society women, notably ad pioneer Helen Woodward's securing the support of one famous matron for a product *before* the product was manufactured, in *Hope in a Jar* (116–17).

32. Sivulka discusses the evolution of the Hollywood–Lux relationship in *Stronger Than Dirt*, 195.

33. JWT-DA, Lever Bros., Boxes 33–39.

34. Koppes and Black, "What to Show the World," 157–68.

35. Kilgore to her parents, June 7, 1944, in Aileen Kilgore Henderson, *Stateside Soldier*, 73; Mary Cugini to Dena Cugini, January 27, 1945, in Litoff and Smith, *We're in This War, Too*, 109; "A Book of Facts about the WAC," 16; Meyer, *Creating GI Jane*, 153–56.

36. JWT-DA, Lever Bros., Box 34; Brownmiller, *Femininity*, 151; Price and Shildrick, *Feminist Theory and the Body*, 3.

37. Sivulka, *Stronger Than Dirt*, 109–10; Hegarty, "Patriot or Prostitute," 129 n.9; Clement, *Love for Sale*, 258.

38. Etymology for "dainty" from *Merriam-Webster's Eleventh Collegiate Dictionary* (2003): [ME *deinte*, fr. AF *deinté*, fr. L *dignitat-*, *dignitas* dignity, worth] (14th c); Boris, "'You Wouldn't Want One of 'Em Dancing with Your Wife'"; Hoy, *Chasing Dirt*, 165.

39. Sivulka, *Stronger Than Dirt*, 255, 256–71. Sivulka reproduces several turn-of-the-century ad campaigns that made promises to neutralize or eliminate dark or black skin. The characters in the ads find happiness, love, or social mobility after using such products.

40. Women's Bureau, "Wartime Reminders to Women Who Work," 3.

41. JWT used the stereotypical soldier outline in particular markets as early as fall of 1942. Ad #4549-F (1942), JWT-DA, Lever Bros., Box 33; JWT-DA, Chesebrough-Pond's, Box

16. Pulp fiction magazines published similar stories with "happy" endings for protagonists who had been sufficiently patriotic.

42. See, e.g., JWT-DA, Lever Bros., Boxes 35 and 37.

43. Anderson, *Wartime Women*, 77; "In Marriage, It's a Man's Market," *New York Times Magazine* (June 17, 1945); "Somebody's after Your Man!" *Good Housekeeping*, August 1945. Even earlier, guides such as Steven Hart and Lucy Brown's *How to Get Your Man and Hold Him* (1944), proved popular. See also Hartmann, *The Home Front and Beyond*, 164–65.

44. Ad #6526A, JWT-DA, Lever Bros., Box 36.

45. Hill, *Advertising to the American Woman*, 121; Marchand, *Advertising the American Dream*, 344; Hoy, *Chasing Dirt*, 147–48, 153–54, 162–63. On domestic efficiency, see Cowan, *More Work for Mother*, 172–91, and Rutherford, *Selling Mrs. Consumer*. On laundry's reputation as "the great domestic dread," see Strasser, *Never Done*, 104–24.

46. Tearsheets, JWT-DA, Lever Bros., Box 34.

47. "Unifying a Nation: World War II Posters from the New Hampshire State Library," http://www.nh.gov/nhsl/ww2/ (accessed March 7, 2010); George A. Barnes to Felix Belair, January 27, 1942, RG 208, OWI-OFF, Box 12; Winchell, *Good Girls, Good Food, Good Fun*, 96.

48. Ads #5333 and #5334 (1942), JWT-DA, Lever Bros., Box 34.

49. Ad #5037 (May 1942) and other tearsheets, JWT-DA, Lever Bros., Box 34.

50. Darnton, "4800 Call It Home"; Esther Bubley, LC-FSA-OWI, Lot 763.

51. WPB regulations and OPA rules prompted conscientious consumption, an idea sold by official propaganda creators. See all JWT wartime accounts, OAAA correspondence, and wartime runs of *LIFE, LHJ*, and *Saturday Evening Post* for the variety and frequency of messages.

52. Ad #6538 (1943), JWT-DA, Lever Bros., Box 36.

53. Tearsheets, JWT-DA, Lever Bros., Box 39; Heilbrun, *Writing a Woman's Life*, 27–28. From a medieval fair maiden's rescue from oblivion to a nineteenth-century "true" woman's move from the home of one patriarch (her father) to that of another patriarch (her husband), the narrative arc reached its height with a woman's marriage.

54. Tearsheet, March 1945, JWT-DA, Lever Bros., Box 39; Friedan, *The Feminine Mystique*.

55. Rohter, "Dear Donna"; Westbrook, "'I Want a Girl.'"

Four. Proper Attire and Streamlined Silhouettes

1. Gammon, "The Consumer Viewpoint," 30.

2. For working women's clothing in the early twentieth century, see Peiss, *Cheap Amusements*, 62–67. For fashion in subsequent decades, see Saville, "Dress and Culture in Greenwich Village"; Hannel, "The Influence of American Jazz on Fashion"; Warner, "The Americanization of Fashion"; Lurie, *The Language of Clothes*, 212–29.

3. In 1863 actress and abolitionist Fanny Kemble noted that "the figures of some of the women" she observed were "handsome"; "figure" definition from *Oxford English Dictionary*, Compact Ed., 1971, 996.

4. While I recognize that men who dressed in drag also bought clothing designed for women, I have limited my discussion in this chapter to women since the U.S. government and mainstream advertising industry directed their initiatives toward them.

5. On streamlining, see Meikle, *Twentieth-Century Limited*, 101–9, and McEuen, *Seeing America*, 225–30. Witt notes the "widespread U.S. cultural investment in black female fat" in *Black Hunger*. Mizejewski, *Ziegfeld Girl*, 6; Seid, *Never Too Thin*, 102. In *Fat History*, social historian Peter Stearns reveals the 1940s to be at the center of the "misogynist phase" in American society's perception and treatment of women's bodies. According to Stearns, the "misogynist phase" began in the 1920s and ran through the 1960s. "American Designers," *LIFE*, May 8, 1944, 64; Martha Parker, "Trim Figure," 37.

6. Mitchell, *Gone With the Wind*, 1; McDowell, "Recovery Missions," 298. African American women, as Doris Witt points out, have been represented overwhelmingly in discourses about food and U.S. identities "in specular form as the naturalized fat body" (*Black Hunger*, 191). Seid reads the Scarlett O'Hara character as an antebellum figure (*Never Too Thin*, 67). The exhibition of delicacy in an upper-class white woman in the antebellum South was preferred behavior, but my reading of *GWTW* is in the context in which it was written rather than set, i.e., the 1930s. In this context, the novel's readership would have been aware of, if not directly affected by, the Great Depression and widespread hunger and unemployment. That U.S. government policy addressed such matters on a large scale for the first time through President Franklin Roosevelt's New Deal initiatives made food availability and consumption a public issue. Joan Jacobs Brumberg's classic study of anorexia nervosa, *Fasting Girls*, examines the connections between women's food consumption in a society that has traditionally viewed "displays of appetite" in young women as dangerous.

7. This chapter does not take dieting as a subject for analysis; it focuses instead on women's bodies in relation to clothing. I approach food consumption as a national issue, stressing conservation and other strategies introduced to prevent inflation.

8. NYDI appeal quoted in Ten Eyck, "Feminine Styles Inspired by War." The NYDI campaign was attributed to JWT's James Webb Young. Buckland, "Promoting American Designers, 1940–44," 105. Buckland discusses Mayor Fiorello LaGuardia's active involvement to make his city the center of the American fashion world and a postwar rival for Paris (109–10).

9. Ten Eyck, "Feminine Styles Inspired by War." However their dispositions might have changed, English women still had to abide by clothing restrictions under the British Utility Scheme, commonly known as CC41 (Civilian Clothing 1941).

10. Full page advertisement, *Women's Wear Daily*, January 7, 1942. Fashion magazines used this imagery early in the war. See, e.g., the cover of *Vogue*, July 1, 1942.

11. *New York Times* ad text in Buckland, 115; Clipping [Dec. 1941], collected in JWT-DA, N–Z, Box 2.

12. *Women's Wear Daily*, January 23 and 21, 1942; Crawford, "Says Fashion Advance Can't Cease in War"; Tearsheet, *Town & Country*, February 1942, JWT-DA, NYDI, Box 1; Ten Eyck, "Feminine Styles Inspired by War." See Welters and Cunningham, *Twentieth-Century American Fashion*, 3, on *Godey's Lady's Book* editor Sarah Josepha Hale's advice to women about clothing.

13. L-85 was titled the Women's and Children's Apparel Order.

14. Farrell-Beck and Gau, *Uplift*, 98; *LIFE*, April 20, 1942, 63–71; Alexis Sommaripa to Roland S. Vaile, May 1, 1942, RG 179, WPB-PDF, #546.215; *LIFE*, April 20, 1942.

15. Marcus, "American Fashion Comes of Age," 22; Ethel Gorham, *So Your Husband's Gone to War!* 130–31.

16. H. Stanley Marcus to Clearance Committee, [April 1942], RG 179, WPB-PDF, #546.215; pajamas were limited to one pocket. H. Stanley Marcus to Clearance Committee, [April 1942], RG 179, WPB-PDF, #546.215; Alexis Sommaripa to Roland S. Vaile, May 1, 1942, RG 179, WPB-PDF, #546.215, in which he contended that it would be "inconsistent not to restrict the consumption of fabrics in nightgowns."

17. Marcus to Clearance Committee, [April 1942], RG 179, WPB-PDF, #546.215. Order L-116 on "feminine lingerie" was not revoked until October 1946, a very late decision on materials restriction. Herbert Rose to William J. Kerlin, October 22, 1946, RG 179, WPB-PDF, #546.215; Marcus to Clearance Committee [April 1942], RG 179, WPB-PDF, #546.215.

18. Chase quoted in Buckland, "Promoting American Designers, 1940–44," 112; *LIFE*, April 20, 1942, 70–71; Marcus, "American Fashion Comes of Age," 22.

19. See numerous examples in JWT-WW, Box 1, and RG 208, OWI-RW, Box 590; "Your Wardrobe," in "Be a Marine . . . Free a Marine to Fight," JWT-WW, Box 1; "Red Makes a Difference Say the Women Marines," typescript, RG 208, OWI-RW, Box 589; Costello, *Virtue under Fire*, 44; tearsheets, *Collier's*, May 13, 1944, *Photoplay*, June 1944, JWT-WW, Box 2; Ad Council, "'Give Us More Wacs . . .'"; Hampton, "Negro Women and the WAAC," 55.

20. May, "Rosie the Riveter Gets Married," 135; USMCWR recruitment brochure, JWT-WW, Box 1. The deliberate use of quotation marks throughout the USMCWR literature suggests the need to have women think differently about the camp they would attend, to set aside their mental images of boot camp for men, and perhaps even imagine their own training as, to use a contemporary term, *boot camp lite*. A section of Camp Lejeune, North Carolina, had been reserved for them, where they could enjoy the perks of civilian life, since it included "hairdressing shop, laundry, tailor shop, church" as well as a soda fountain and library for their use. The USMCWR pamphlet assured women they would have a "chance to relax" with such activities as swimming, sailing, and other sports as well as "amateur theatricals" (10).

21. The large "V" in the shape of a check mark was balanced by a rounded loop of the "g" in Vargas's signature. Buszek shows that women read *Esquire* as regularly as men did (*Pin-Up Grrrls*, 207–8).

22. Meyer, *Creating GI Jane*, 153–54; Kilgore to her parents, February 8, 1944, in Aileen Kilgore Henderson, *Stateside Soldier*, 8, 17; Eunice McConnell to her parents, February 25, 1943, in Litoff and Smith, *We're in This War, Too*, 95.

23. Floyd to Betty Bandel, November 29, 1942, in Bugbee, *An Officer and a Lady*, 46–47; Kilgore to her parents, April 5, 1944, in Aileen Kilgore Henderson, *Stateside Soldier*, 48 (she informed them that 48 was "the only size available").

24. On segregated clothing distribution, see Earley, *One Woman's Army*, 25.

25. In *The Best War Ever* Michael C. C. Adams offers a concise look at the cultural costs of wartime regulations (153). He draws on and describes William H. Whyte's "organization culture" (*The Organization Man* [1956]) as "a trend toward bureaucracy, conformity, and standardization in everything from clothing to values to political candidates." Paul Fussell also provides a view of the absurdities that surfaced in U.S. government bureaucracy during World War II in his study *Wartime*.

26. "How a Woman Should Wear a Uniform," 36–37; *Women's Wear Daily*, January 23, 1942.

27. On the making of the masculine soldier, see Jarvis, *The Male Body at War*; Floyd to Betty Bandel, November 29, 1942, in Bugbee, *An Officer and a Lady*, 46–47, 195 n.31.

One of the public's fears about the corps' integration into the U.S. Army was that women soldiers, like their male counterparts, would be issued condoms in fulfillment of official army policy, thus encouraging sexual activity. See Meyer, *Creating GI Jane*, on the 1943 rumor campaign against Wacs (33–50), and on the "lesbian threat" (148–78). Meyer writes, "Laws addressing gender disguise and women's adoption of male dress are far more relevant in analyzing the cultural construction of lesbianism historically than are sodomy laws" (149). On cross-dressing and culture, see Hoffert, "Gender, Identity, and Sexuality (1600–1975)," 392–95; Garber, *Vested Interests*; and Butler, *Gender Trouble*. On fashion and gender boundaries, see Wilson, *Adorned in Dreams*, 117. Brownmiller, *Femininity*, 82.

28. Hobby quoted in Meyer, *Creating GI Jane*, 155; Kilgore to her parents, May 10, 1944, in Aileen Kilgore Henderson, *Stateside Soldier*, 64; Ad Council, "'Give Us More Wacs . . .'"; OWI Media Guide, "Women in the War," 1944; also, "How Direct Mail and Printed Literature Can Help Recruit Womanpower for the Final Push to Victory," June 12, 1944, RG 208, OWI-RW, Box 587. In OWI documents the follow-up line about uniform appearance was the reminder that service women "should never be shown smoking or drinking alcoholic beverages." "A Book of Facts about the WAC"; Tearsheets, *Collier's*, May 13, 1944; *Photoplay*, June 1944, JWT-WW, Box 2.

29. Ayling, *Calling All Women*, 60, 59. Ayling's work, like many wartime appeals, was officially sponsored propaganda published by a trade press rather than a Washington war agency or the GPO.

30. Ethel Gorham, *So Your Husband's Gone to War!* 41, 136; Winchell, *Good Girls, Good Food, Good Fun*, 71.

31. "The Mood Has Changed," *Harper's Bazaar*, September 1944, 67, in Walker, *Women's Magazines*, 198–99; Broch quoted in Fussell, *Uniforms*, 14.

32. On the slow acceptance of trousers for women, see Lurie, *The Language of Clothes*, 224–26; Wilson, *Adorned in Dreams*, 162; Farrell-Beck and Gau, *Uplift*, 87; *LIFE*, April 20, 1942, 63–71; see Ann Rosener's work for the FSA-OWI at Library of Congress, "America from the Great Depression to World War Two," http://memory.loc.gov/ammem/fsahtml/ fahome.html (accessed March 8, 2010).

33. "Business Papers on the Wartime Business Front," *A&S* 35 (May 1942).

34. Hornaday, "Curtiss-Wright St. Louis Plant Lightens Jigs"; "Fashions at Boeing," RG 211, WMC-ISPD, Human Interest Stories, 1942–43, Box 1; untitled report, September 1942, RG 86, WB-DRWW, Box 204; D. H. Davenport [Employment and Occupational Outlook Branch, U.S. Labor Dept] to Roy E. Stryker, August 25, 1942, LC-FSA-OWI, Lot 12024, Office Files, Box 2; "Women Workers Will Win the War," February 1943, 12, RG 211, WMC-ISPD, Files of Allan Wilson, 1942–43.

35. War Manpower Commission, "America at War Needs Women at Work," [1943], 7, JWT-WW, Box 1; U.S. Department of Labor, Women's Bureau, "Report of Conference on Women in War Industries," April 1943, 47, in RG 179, WPB-PDF, 241.11, Box 1016, hereafter cited as WB *War Industries Conference Report*. See, in particular, comments by Margaret Ackroyd regarding her experiences in Rhode Island.

36. "Girls in Slacks at War Plants Hail Tampax," *American Weekly*, 1942, available at Duke University Libraries, Digital Collections, Ad*Access, http://library.duke.edu/ digitalcollections/adaccess.BH0173/pg.1/ (accessed July 8, 2009); Ethel Gorham, *So Your Husband's Gone to War!* 138–39.

37. *Los Angeles Times* promotion in *A&S* 36 (February 1943): 144; Reid, *Slacks and Calluses*, 70, 178; see also Clement, *Love for Sale*, and Milkman, *Gender at Work*.

38. Reid, *Slacks and Calluses*, 67, 17, 69; feminist critic Sandra Gilbert commends Bowman's account for showing that "while the wearing of slacks *de*feminized women factory workers, paradoxically it also eroticized them" (introduction to *Slacks and Calluses*, ix); see Grantham, "The South and Congressional Politics," 27, and Honey, *Bitter Fruit*, 129, on racial tensions and violence against women of color during the war.

39. "Charm School," All-American Girls Professional Baseball League Web site; Costin, *South Bend Tribune*, March 3, and July 6, 1943. I want to thank Kristin Fitch for directing me to Costin's work.

40. Faderman, *Odd Girls and Twilight Lovers*, 125–26; Hegarty, "Patriot or Prostitute," 113, on "the ultimate promiscuity."

41. Vicki Howard, *Brides, Inc.*, 168; Hartmann, *The Home Front and Beyond*, 164; Rosebery, *This Day's Madness*, 103.

42. Brownmiller, *Femininity*, 95.

43. Farrell-Beck and Gau, *Uplift*, 91–92; Griffiths, "The Little Woman Looks at the Substitutes," 106; Summary Report, "Corset and Brassiere Industry Advisory Committee Meetings," June 15, 1943, RG 179, WPB-PDF, #546.2205. One of the seventeen industry representatives was a woman; two of the ten WPB representatives were women.

44. On rubber drives, see "Cuties," *Washington Times Herald*, May 29, 1942; "Everyday Movies," *News*, July 3, 1942; and other collected materials in RG 179, WPB-GRIE, Scrapbooks, Box 1; also Ayling, *Calling All Women*, 179–81; Rosebery, *This Day's Madness*, 61–63; "Off with Garters and—Er—Girdles, Girls," *Washington Times Herald*, June 16, 1942, RG 179, WPB-GRIE, scrapbooks, Box 1.

45. Seid, *Never Too Thin*, 83; McEuen, *Seeing America*, 221–33; Meikle, *Twentieth-Century Limited*, 29–38; Brumberg, *Fasting Girls*, 239–40. In *Fasting Girls* Brumberg argues that smoothness of bodily form became even more an issue after Coco Chanel introduced a substantially dropped waistline and shorter hem in the mid-1920s (what became recognizable as the "flapper" costume). See also Brumberg, "Beyond Meat and Potatoes," 271–81. Vassarette ad in *LIFE*, April 1941, 18; *Corset and Underwear Review*, 1942, quoted in Farrell-Beck and Gau, *Uplift*, 100.

46. Seid, *Never Too Thin*, 102; *A&S* 36 (May 1943); Cades, "Change Your Food but Keep Your Figure," 76–77.

47. *McCall's* Washington newsletter, quoted in Lingeman, *"Don't You Know There's a War On?"* 121. "The war of attrition against hips and thighs began in the Forties," writes Brownmiller (*Femininity*, 48). Amendments were passed on L-116 in order to accommodate bigger girls and bigger teens with "Teen Age Chubby Sizes," which included larger trouser and top lengths and trouser leg circumferences (J. S. Knowlson, "Amendment No. 1 to General Limitation Order L-116," May 1942, RG 179, WPB-PDF, #546.215).

48. Award-winning advertisement sponsored by Northwest Airlines, designed by Batten, Barton, Durstine & Osborne, Inc., in *A&S* 38 (March 1945): [n.p.]; Phillips, *All-Out Arlene* (1943), 8; Mary Cugini to Dena Cugini, January 27, 1945, and March 1945, in Litoff and Smith, *We're in This War, Too*, 109, 111; Kilgore to her parents, February 4, 1944, in Aileen Kilgore Henderson, *Stateside Soldier*, 7. Soon after a women's army was formed, mess officers at the first officer's camp at Fort Des Moines "worried over the feminine appetite" since as one said, "women are daintier eaters than men" (reported in Rosebery, *This Day's*

Madness, 81). Kilgore to her parents, February 5, 1944, February 10, 1944, and February 17, 1944, in Aileen Kilgore Henderson, *Stateside Soldier*, 8, 14, 19. At one point she went to the base doctor to find out about her dramatic weight loss (fifteen pounds) and constant fatigue, which she finally chalked up to long days as a mechanic. Somerville, May 21, 1943, in *Dear Boys*, 94; Pearl "Perla" Gullickson to Fred "Hal" Halverson, August 20, 1943, in Litoff and Smith, *We're in This War, Too*, 103; Marion Stegeman to her mother, May 31, 1943, in Litoff and Smith, *We're in This War, Too*, 116.

49. "Dear Bill," 15, 7; General Mills, "Your Share: How to Prepare Appetizing, Healthful Meals with Foods Available Today" (1943), NDP, 1940s, Box 7; Reid, *Slacks and Calluses*, 63, 66. Hackshaw, "What My Job Means to Me," 52.

50. "Women at War," *Brown American* (Summer 1943), 4; Hughes, "Soul, Black Women, and Food," 273.

51. *Crisis* 51 (July 1944): 221. Although Maureen Honey notes that magazines directed at African American audiences steered away from "cheesecake" photographs, *Crisis* put many beauty pageant winners on its covers and in its pages during the war years. See Honey, *Bitter Fruit*, Introduction.

52. "Sigma Chi Chapter at Georgia Picks Its Sweetheart for Year," *LIFE*, November 3, 1941, 53–56. Winners of the annual Modern Venus competition may be found in various editions of *Pandora*, the University of Georgia Yearbook; Seid, *Never Too Thin*, 97.

53. Brumberg, *Fasting Girls*, 249; Brumberg notes, "During the Great Depression and World War II, in times of scarcity, voluntary food refusal had little efficacy as an emotional strategy and anorexic girls were a relative rarity in American clinical practice" (10). Bentley, *Eating for Victory*, 103.

54. For "discriminating women," see the John Gerber Company, OAAA-PSN, Chronological Series, Box CH1. Carson, "Short and Low," 26; on Rosenstein, see "American Designers," 64; Martha Parker, "Trim Figure," 37.

55. Brumberg draws on examples from mid- to late nineteenth-century America to make her case, but her framework may be applied to the war years, given the shifting grounds on which young women stood regarding sexuality, marriage, work opportunities, and wartime necessity. Brumberg's overwhelming message is that young women could be heard "through denial of appetite" ("The Appetite as Voice," 174). "Girl of 'Just Average' Looks Can Be a Knockout if She Likes."

56. Popkin, *The Journey Home*, 14.

57. Thelma Thurston Gorham, "Negro Army Wives," 21–22; MacLennan, "Gypsy Wives, Army Style," 19; McEuen, "Exposing Anger and Discontent," 238–60; Perrett, *Days of Sadness, Years of Triumph*, 347. In popular culture, the predominant image of the military wife was a male soldier's spouse, even though the women's military services allowed married women to enlist. Personal stories and letters reveal that young enlisted women often met fellow service personnel and formed relationships with them. But married military women were rarely represented in government propaganda or popular literature.

58. "The Impact of War on Advertising," 16; Gould, "First Reader Cuisine," 12–13, 53; Grocer-Consumer Anti-Inflation Campaign, #6148, Newspaper Ad No. 7 (1944), JWT-WW, Box 2; "vital arms" quote in "The Impact of War on Advertising," 16; Amy Bentley discusses the role of the Home Front Pledge in *Eating for Victory* (36–38).

59. Ad designs, JWT-WW, Box 2; Brumberg, "Beyond Meat and Potatoes," 279, 278; *Gourmet*, July 1944, 57. On the extent of "rackets against wives and mothers of servicemen," see

"Vultures on the Home Front," *Woman's Home Companion*, promoted in *A&S* 37 (August 1944): 16–17.

60. Chester Bowles, Letter to Advertisers, August 23, 1944; also, "Copy Ideas and Roughs," 1944, JWT-WW, Box 2.

61. Shoe Retailers Industry Advisory Committee, Proceedings Transcript, July 30, 1942, RG 179, WPB-PDF, #545.1005. The Shoe Retailers Advisory Committee included ten men "Representing Industry," twelve men "Representing Government (WPB)" and five "Others" as voices for government; Roland Vaile to Civilian Supply Committee, August 3, 1942, RG 179, WPB-PDF, #545.109, Box 1808; L. B. Sheppard (WPB Leather & Shoe Branch) to Footwear Rationing Branch, OPA, February 12, 1943, RG 179, WPB-PDF, #545.109; On Perkins's opening address at March 1943 "Women in War Industries" Conference, see WB *War Industries Conference Report*, 1. The poor quality of shoes created a booming business for both second-hand stores and shoe repair shops; and magazines ran regular features on how to preserve footwear. See, e.g., Rosebery, *This Day's Madness*, 188; and issues of *Business Week* and *Time*, 1943.

62. Women's Millinery Advisory Committee Summary Report, April 27, 1943, RG 179, WPB-PDF, #546.2305; Ethel Gorham, *So Your Husband's Gone to War!* 134; Gammon, "The Consumer Viewpoint," 30, 126. Gammon described wartime hats as varying "widely between feathered thimbles, hors d'oeuvre platters, flowered coal hoods in miniature, windmills and Aunt Susan's doilies," bitterly asking, "Where is the in-between? Who can say that any of them are becoming to the majority of women?"

63. WB *War Industries Conference Report*, 42, 47.

64. Scherman, *LIFE Goes to War*, 142. On Lake's influence, see Koppes and Black, *Hollywood Goes to War*, 12; Lingeman, *"Don't You Know There's a War On?"* 158; and Rosebery, *This Day's Madness*, 78–79. Rosener series, "Safe Clothes for Women War Workers," March 1943, at Library of Congress, "America from the Great Depression to World War Two," LC-USE623-D-009138, Lot 1885, http://memory.loc.gov/ammem/fsahtml/fahome.html (accessed March 11, 2010); press release, March 12, 1943, WMC-ISPD, Files of Mary White, Box 3; Koehn, "Estée Lauder," 223.

65. Women's Bureau, "Safety Caps for Women in War Factories," Special Bulletin No. 9, October 1942, RG 86, WB-DRSB, Box 2; Women's Bureau, "Safety Caps for Women Machine Operators," Supplement to Special Bulletin No. 9, 1943, RG 86, WB-DRSB, Box 1.

66. James W. Smith to Mary Anderson, August 17, 1942, RG 86, WB-DRSB, Box 1; Reid, *Slacks and Calluses*, 24–25, 154–63.

67. Griffiths, "The Little Woman Looks at the Substitutes," *A&S* 36 (August 1943): 106; Lingeman, *"Don't You Know There's a War On?"* 119; Ethel Gorham, *So Your Husband's Gone to War!* 129; Rosebery, *This Day's Madness*, 99–102, 148; Ewart Shuler to Annie Faye Ross, November 1, 1944, SCHS, in which he tells her his ship's store has "a lot of silk stockings" and he'd like to send her some pairs but needs to know her size.

68. Perrett, *Days of Sadness, Years of Triumph*, 135; tearsheets, 1942, April 1944, JWT-DA, Lever Bros., Boxes 34 and 37; Bandel to Mother, July 30, 1943, in Bugbee, *An Officer and a Lady*, 113; Kilgore to her parents, February 8, 1944, December 12, 1944, September 15, 1945, in Aileen Kilgore Henderson, *Stateside Soldier*, 8, 123, 215; Kilgore also promised her mother that she'd try to find some nylon hosiery on her next trip to Houston (Kilgore to her parents, November 20, 1945).

69. Gardner, "Hiding the Scars," 312; Warner's ad quoted in Farrell-Beck and Gau, *Uplift*, 83; *Corset and Underwear Review* quoted in Riordan, *Inventing Beauty*, 101. Some of the more modern and "natural" brassiere designs came from Southern California makers, such as Beautee-Fit Brassiere Company (Los Angeles) and Hollywood-Maxwell; *Vogue*, September 1, 1944.

70. Sklar, *Movie-Made America*, 173–74; "Hays Office Cracks Down on Cinema's Sweater Set," LIFE, April 14, 1941, 32–33; LIFE, May 5, 1941, 6; Seid, *Never Too Thin*, 98; Turner announced "no more sweaters," in LIFE, October 13, 1941, 26.

71. Untitled report, September 1942, RG 86, WB-DRWW, Box 204, OWI Correspondence; Lingeman, *"Don't You Know There's a War On?"* 157–58; Rosebery, *This Day's Madness*, 78.

72. Farrell-Beck and Gau, *Uplift*, 98; Riordan, *Inventing Beauty*, 102–3. Brassiere designers weren't without their critics, among them Margaret Gammon, who begged for a garment to "hook or clip in front" so "you could see what you were doing" (Gammon, "The Consumer Viewpoint," 126); Bazin, "Entomology of the Pin-Up Girl," 158–62. Westbrook doesn't agree with Bazin and uses Betty Grable's popularity among servicemen as evidence that female legs still held sway over breasts as the main site of the male gaze during the Second World War ("'I Want a Girl,'" 599, 613). Rosen, *Popcorn Venus*, 1, 282.

73. Perrett, *Days of Sadness, Years of Triumph*, 394–95; Rosebery, *This Day's Madness*, 57–59; *The Star*, November 22, 1942, RG 179, WPB-GRIE, Scrapbooks, Box 2; "Sleek Outfits for Shapely Minority Spread Glamor on Southern Beaches," LIFE, January 13, 1941, 55; Los Angeles County Museum of Art, "A Century of Fashion, 1900–2000."

74. "V for Voluptuous," 90; "Fashion Warfare: Los Angeles Boosts Fund to Sell City as Style Capital of the World," *Business Week*, March 25, 1944, 48; Buckland, "Promoting American Designers, 1940–44," 108; 1945 manual quoted in Wilson, *Adorned in Dreams*, 124; Ewart Shuler to Annie Faye Ross, October 15, 1945, SCHS.

75. Minutes, Shoe Retailers Advisory Committee, Feb 16, 1943, April 16, 1943, and June 1943, RG 179, WPB-PDF, #545.109 and #545.1005; K. W. Marriner (Director of Textile, Clothing & Leather Bureau) to J. A. Krug, January 18, 1945, RG 179, WPB-PDF, #545.1041; Buckland, "Promoting American Designers, 1940–44," 117; Gammon, "The Consumer Viewpoint," 126, 30. Gammon sought to speak for women who had a host of specific complaints about wartime apparel and general dissatisfaction with the standard clothing imposed on women by male designers.

76. Phillips, *All-Out Arlene*, 126–27.

77. Kilgore to her parents, November 25, 1945, in Aileen Kilgore Henderson, *Stateside Soldier*, 235; Bandel to her mother, July 4, 1945, in Bugbee, *An Officer and a Lady*, 182–83.

78. Popkin, *The Journey Home*, 99; Ethel Gorham, *So Your Husband's Gone to War!* 109.

Five. Sacrifice and Agreeability

1. Dorothy Parker, "Miss Brass Tacks of 1943," manuscript, RG 208, OWI-CC, Box 151.

2. Mary Brewster White to Robert Ferry, April 26, 1943, RG 208, OWI-CC, Box 151. White says at the end of her memo: "[A]nyone who can read English should read this piece. But, for the sake of international diplomatic relations, it should not be reprinted in any other language, as it makes the American woman look like a first class idiot." *Mademoiselle* published Parker's essay in May 1943 with the author's original title; *Readers Digest* editors

chose "Are We Women or Are We Mice?" for its July 1943 issue; Albert Z. Carr to Robert R. Ferry, April 29, 1943, RG 208, OWI-CC, Box 151.

3. Carewe, "Where's the Woman's Angle in This War?" 23.

4. *Woman's Home Companion Cook Book*, x; Kerr Glass Manufacturing Corporation, "Food for Victory," 1942, NDP, 1940s, Box 4; Kerr Glass Manufacturing Corporation, *Kerr Home Canning Book*, 1943, NDP, 1940s, Box 4; Aunt Jenny quote in Lever Brothers, "Good Cooking Made Easy," 1942, NDP, 1940s, Box 6; Amy Bentley discusses the relationship of women to desserts and "sweets" in *Eating for Victory*, 102–13.

5. Banning, *Women for Defense* (1942), quoted in Litoff and Smith, *American Women in a World at War*, 5; Ayling, *Calling All Women*, 31, 177.

6. U.S. Department of Labor, Women's Bureau, "Report of Conference on Women in War Industries," April 1943, 47, in RG 179, WPB-PDF, 241.11, Box 1016, hereafter cited as WB *War Industries Conference Report*.

7. "Meet the Berckmans," 38, 39, 41.

8. MacArthur narrative, Boeing report, RG 211, WMC-ISPD, Human Interest Stories, Box 1.

9. Elaine Tyler May provides a clear sense of the abrupt shifts in public opinion, first during the Depression then again during the war, about women (especially married women) working (*Homeward Bound*, 58–75); Federal Shipbuilding and Dry Dock Company, typescript, [n.d.], RG 211, WMC-ISPD, Human Interest Stories, Box 2; *Evansville Courier and Press* clipping, Feb 28, 1943, collected in RG 211, WMC-ISPD, Human Interest Stories, Box 5; design commentary, WMC Poster #11, April 1944, HEF, Box 1.

10. Mary Brewster White to Dorothy Ducas, April 19, 1943, quoting from a "confidential report," RG 208, OWI-CC, Box 151; U.S. Department of Labor, Women's Bureau, *Negro Women War Workers*, 11; "Survey of the Months," *Opportunity* 21 (July 1943): 124.

11. Rosenberg, "Womanpower and the War," 35, 36.

12. Granger, "Women Are Vital to Victory," 36; Baker, "To a Brown Lady," n.p.

13. Hackshaw, "What My Job Means to Me," 52–53; Clark, "Negro Woman Worker, What Now?" 84–85.

14. Johnson, "What My Job Means to Me," 50–51.

15. U.S. Department of Labor, Women's Bureau, *Negro Women War Workers*, 11.

16. Elmer W. Henderson, "Negroes in Government Employment," 121, 142–43.

17. Ayling, *Calling All Women*, 151; Nancy Cott discusses Philip Wylie's influence in *A Woman Making History*, 268–69; Hoover, "Mothers . . . Our Only Hope," 45–46; see posters in JWT-WW, Box 2; Candee, "Women in Defense Industry," 47–48. Candee reported that in locales where recent population explosions strained resources, school personnel "resent[ed] the lack of availability of parents to help with their children and their apparent willingness to let the agencies do the worrying." On the "general mood of alarm" over employed mothers and family disintegration, see Michel, "American Women and the Discourse of the Democratic Family in World War II," 162–67.

18. OAAA-IA, Box 14; *Outdoor Advertising: A Channel of Communication in the War Effort* (1944), OAAA-IA, Box 13.

19. Somerville, *Dear Boys*, 207; "A Mother's Faith," *Redbook*, March 1943, reprinted in *Opportunity* 21 (April 1943): 80.

20. JWT-WW, Box 2; JWT-DA, Scott Paper Company, Box 7; Rosebery, *This Day's Madness*, 189; military nurse recruitment campaigns, March 1945, JWT-WW, Box 1; "How Direct

Mail and Printed Literature Can Help Recruit Womanpower for the Final Push to Victory," June 12, 1944, RG 208, OWI-RW, Box 587.

21. "How Direct Mail and Printed Literature Can Help Recruit Womanpower for the Final Push to Victory."

22. JWT-WW, Box 2; May, *Homeward Bound*, 89; Ayling, *Calling All Women*, 29–31; "Women Line Up 6th Events," *Minute Man* 4, October 1, 1944, 10, OAAA-IA, Box 12; Bert Holloway, Lockheed Aircraft, Burbank, RG 211, WMC-ISPD, Human Interest Stories, 1942–43, Box 1.

23. May, *Homeward Bound*, 68; Bandel to her mother, July 30, 1943, in Bugbee, *An Officer and a Lady*, 121; Thelma Thurston Gorham, "Negro Army Wives," 21–22.

24. JWT-WW, Box 2; "The More Women at War the Sooner We'll Win," typescript, February 15, 1944, RG 208, OWI-RW, Box 587; Rhea Radin to Sophie Nack, February 16, 1944, RG 208, OWI-RW, Box 587; Verda Barnes to Sophie Nack, February 15, 1944, RG 208, OWI-RW, Box 587. Barnes noted that women who wanted to leave the workforce now might need to rejoin it later in life and therefore needed the valuable training being offered currently. "How Direct Mail and Printed Literature Can Help Recruit Womanpower for the Final Push to Victory."

25. U.S. Cadet Nurse Corps series, sponsored by Eastman Kodak Company, appeared in *Collier's*, May 13, 1944, *Look*, April 1944, et al., JWT-WW, Box 2; military nurse recruitment campaigns, March 1945, JWT-WW, Box 1; OAAA-IA, Boxes 13 and 14; Phillips, *All-Out Arlene*, 162, 113.

26. OAAA-IA, Box 13; Somerville, May 21, 1943, and September 3, 1943, in *Dear Boys*, 94, 142; Macy, "Negro Women in the WAC," 14.

27. Dorothy Muni to Betty Bandel, May 6, 1943, in Bugbee, *An Officer and a Lady*, 102; Marion Stegeman to Mrs. H. J. Stegeman, April 24, 1943, quoted in Litoff and Smith, "'Writing Is Fighting, Too,'" 449; Wac quoted in Costello, *Virtue under Fire*, 54; Mary Cugini to Dena Cugini, February 10, 1945, Mary Cugini to Ginnie and Dena, July 2, 1945, and Mary Cugini to Dena, March 12, 1946, in Litoff and Smith, *We're in This War, Too*, 110, 112–113; Bandel to mother, June 25, 1944, in Bugbee, *An Officer and a Lady*, 155.

28. Government Policies and Agencies Campaigns, JWT-WW, Boxes 1 and 2; Banning, *Women for Defense* (1942), quoted in Litoff and Smith, *American Women in a World at War*, 5; *Outdoor Advertising: A Channel of Communication in the War Effort* (July 1942), [n.p.], OAAA-IA, Box 13; War Food Administration, Poster #6, "Home Front Pledge," 1944, OAAA-IA, Box 12.

29. Frigidaire Division of GMC, "101 Refrigerator Helps," 1944, 21, 26–27, NDP, 1940s, Box 1; McGovern, *Sold American*, 327–52; see, e.g., Rutherford, *Selling Mrs. Consumer*.

30. General Mills, "Your Share: How to Prepare Appetizing, Healthful Meals with Foods Available Today" (1943), NDP, 1940s, Box 7.

31. Tearsheet, 1944, JWT-DA, Kraft, Box 37; "Home Canners Text Book," sponsored by Boston Woven Hose & Rubber Company, 1943, NDP, 1940s, Box 4; Corn Products Refining Company, "How to Can Finer Fruits and Save Sugar," ca. 1944, NDP, 1940s, Box 5; Ad Council memo, April 1945, OAAA-IA, Box 12. See also Hayes, *Grandma's Wartime Kitchen*, 52–55.

32. Bandel to her mother, March 21, 1944, in Bugbee, *An Officer and a Lady*, 151; *McCall's* reference in *A&S* 36 (March 1943): 72; Frances Harriet Williams, "A Woman Looks at Her Government," 73, 94. On wartime queues, see Rosebery, *This Day's Madness*, 110.

33. Gray, "America's Womanpower," 68–70; U.S. Department of War, *You're Going to Employ Women*; Candee, "Women in Defense Industry," 49.

34. Clark, "Negro Woman Worker, What Now?" 84; Greene, "They Prepare for 'A New Nation,'" 76; Clark, "Negro Woman Worker, What Now?" 93.

35. Ethel Gorham, *So Your Husband's Gone to War!* 117; Mary Cugini to Dena Cugini, February 10, 1945, in Litoff and Smith, *We're in This War, Too*, 110; Anita Colby, "That Romantic Look," *Photoplay* 30 (December 1943), quoted in May, *Homeward Bound*, 66.

36. Tearsheets, April 1945, JWT-DA, 7-Up, Box 1.

37. Tearsheets, 1945, JWT-DA, 7-Up. Box 4.

38. Litoff and Smith, "'Writing Is Fighting, Too,'" 442n, 437n; Ethel Gorham, *So Your Husband's Gone to War!* 187–99; tearsheets for *Good Housekeeping, National Geographic, The New Yorker*, JWT-DA, Eastman Kodak—Consumer, Boxes 12 and 13; Litoff and Smith, "'Writing Is Fighting, Too,'" 442; Ewart Shuler to Annie Faye Ross, October 3, 1944; October 25, 1944, SCHS.

39. Ewart Shuler to Annie Faye Ross, March 13, 1945, SCHS, in which he mentions Max Shulman's wartime book, *Feather Merchants*, a lampoon of the civilian war effort. One passage describing a women's club program on the nature of military organization satirizes the program's emphasis on military uniform colors. Also, Wac Aileen Kilgore referred to women civilians as "Feather Merchants," March 26, 1944 and April 30, 1944, in Aileen Kilgore Henderson, *Stateside Soldier*, 44, 59; Ayling, *Calling All Women*, 100; Yearwood, "Women Volunteers Unite to Serve," 89; see also Gladys P. Graham, "The Salvation Army Servicemen's Club Today and Tomorrow," [1945], LC-NAACP, No. 21.

40. Winchell, *Good Girls, Good Food, Good Fun*, poem at 87, quote at 89.

41. "Ladies of the Diamond," 74; "Girls' Baseball," 64–65; *Time*, July 31, 1944; "Charm School," All-American Girls Professional Baseball League Web site.

42. "When Your Soldier Comes Home," 59–60.

43. Costello, *Virtue under Fire*; Bérubé, *Coming Out under Fire*; Grabill, "The Effect of the Wartime Marriage Boom," 153; Liskow to her parents, January 3, 1944, in Litoff and Smith, *We're in This War, Too*, 63; Meyer, *Creating GI Jane*, 176–78; Reuben Hill and Howard Baker, eds., *Marriage and the Family* (Boston: D.C. Heath & Co., 1940), 587–88, quoted in May, *Homeward Bound*, 69 n.25; Phillips, *All-Out Arlene*, 171. Some 6,579,000 marriages were recorded between 1940 and 1943, Grabill notes.

44. "When Your Soldier Comes Home," 60; Ewart Shuler to Annie Faye Ross, February 26, 1945, SCHS.

45. Winchell, *Good Girls, Good Food, Good Fun*, 163; Ewart Shuler to Annie Faye Ross, various letters from October 13, 1944 to October 15, 1945, SCHS.

46. Harry Crawford to OAAA Members, March 1, 1944, OAAA-IA, Box 12; Rich, "The Public Expects Progress," 36; tearsheets, JWT-DA, JWT, Box 6. For the increased focus on consumption, see Adkins Covert, "Consumption and Citizenship."

47. *A&S* 38 (May 1945): 75; See NDP, 1940s, Boxes 7, 8, and 10; *A&S* 37 (July 1944): 112.

48. Tearsheets, 1944, JWT-DA, RCA, Box 3; Gately, "Let's Give Our Copy the Fresh-Air Treatment," 50–52, 112–14; Westbrook, *Why We Fought*, 38–65.

49. Ethel Gorham, *So Your Husband's Gone to War!* 223.

50. OWI, Press Release, August 23, 1944, RG 208, OWI-ND, Box 7.

51. Ibid; see also "The Contribution of Women to the Wartime Economy," typescript, August 1943, RG 211, WMC-FS, Records of May T. Evans, Box 15. Laundry work was the

most common example listed in these reports and many others. See Lemke-Santangelo, *Abiding Courage*, 2, for migration numbers from southern states. The WMC Women's Advisory Committee members agreed that their recommendations on working women's issues were met with "indifference," with the most glaring example in the arena of childcare assistance; minutes, May 12, 1943, RG 211, WMC-WC, Summary Minutes, Box 1.

52. OWI, Press Release, August 23, 1944, RG 208, OWI-ND, Box 7.

53. Miller, "War and Postwar Adjustments of Women Workers," speech transcript, December 5, 1944, RG 211, WMC-FS, Records of May T. Evans, 1942–45, Box 15; Miller, "Negro Women Workers," 207.

54. Pidgeon, *A Preview as to Women Workers in Transition*; also, RG 211, WMC-FS, Records of May T. Evans, 1942–45, Boxes 15 and 16.

55. James, "Women at Work," 142, 144; Vergil Reed, American Marketing Association speech transcript, May 2, 1944, JWT-WS, Box 28; Beard, *Woman as Force in History*, 27.

56. "You Can't Have a Career and Be a Good Wife," *LHJ*, January 1944, in Walker, *Women's Magazines*, 71–75.

57. Anonymous, "Block That Temperament!" 82.

58. Ibid.

59. A Temperamental Dame, "Hell Hath No Fury," 68.

60. Ibid.

61. See speeches and correspondence of Frieda S. Miller, 1944–1946, WB-DRWW, Boxes 175 and 176; Beard, *Woman as Force in History*, 27.

62. Associated Business Publications, "A Guide to Effective Wartime Advertising: A Record of the Kind of Problems Met and Handled by Business Paper Editors and Advertisers during World War II," originally published in 1942 and followed by three supplements; this brief edition, a postwar publication, OAAA-IA, Box 13. See also JWT-DA and JWT-Trade Advertisements for examples of these measurements. Elaine Tyler May refers to the "domestic containment" of women in the postwar years, *Homeward Bound*, 91.

Epilogue

1. Kilgore to her parents, December 8, 1945, in Aileen Kilgore Henderson, *Stateside Soldier*, 239–40.

2. Rohter, "Dear Donna."

BIBLIOGRAPHY

Manuscript Collections

John W. Hartman Center for Sales, Advertising and Marketing History. Rare Book, Manuscript, and Special Collections Library. Duke University.

HEF   H. E. Fisk Collection of War Effort Mobilization Campaigns, ca. 1941–45.
JWT-BIO   J. Walter Thompson Advertising Agency Archives. Biographical Information.
JWT-DA   J. Walter Thompson Advertising Agency Archives. Domestic Advertisements.
JWT-WS   J. Walter Thompson Advertising Agency Archives. Writings and Speeches.
JWT-WW   J. Walter Thompson Advertising Agency Archives. World War II Advertising.
NDP   Nicole Di Bona Peterson Collection of Advertising Cookbooks.
OAAA-IA   Outdoor Advertising Association of America Archives. Issues and Activities Series.
OAAA-PSN   Outdoor Advertising Association of America Archives. Photos, Slides, and Negatives Series.

Library of Congress. Prints & Photographs Division. Washington, D.C.

LC-FSA-OWI Farm Security Administration–Office of War Information.
LC-NAACP   Lot 13103. National Association for the Advancement of Colored People. Photographs of African American Women in the Military Services.

National Archives and Records Administration. Archives II. College Park, Maryland.

OWI-CC   RG 208. U.S. Office of War Information. Records of the Office of the Director of War Programs. Records of the Chief, Bureau of Campaigns.
OWI-ND   RG 208. U.S. Office of War Information. Records of Natalie Davisen, Program Manager for Home Front Campaigns, 1943–45.
OWI-NP   RG 208. U.S. Office of War Information. Negro Press.
OWI-OFF   RG 208. U.S. Office of War Information. Files of Office of Facts and Figures.
OWI-RW   RG 208. U.S. Office of War Information. Records of Recruitment of Women.
OWI-SP   RG 208. U.S. Office of War Information. Still Photographs.
WB-DRSB   RG 86. U.S. Department of Labor. Women's Bureau. Division of Research. Special Bulletins, 1940–44.
WB-DRWW   RG 86. U.S. Department of Labor. Women's Bureau. Division of Research. Records: Women Workers in World War II.

WB-GC	RG 86. U.S. Department of Labor. Women's Bureau. Division of Research. General Correspondence.
WMC-FS	RG 211. U.S. War Manpower Commission. Field Service.
WMC-ISPD	RG 211. U.S. War Manpower Commission. Information Service. Program Division.
WMC-WC	RG 211. U.S. War Manpower Commission. Women's Advisory Committee.
WPB-PDF	RG 179. U.S. War Production Board. Policy Documentation File.
WPB-GRIE	RG 179. U.S. War Production Board. General Records. Records of Informational and Educational Programs.

South Carolina Historical Society. Charleston, South Carolina.

SCHS   Shuler, Ewart Arnold. Letters to Faye, 1944–1946.

Magazines

A&S (Advertising & Selling) 35–38 (1941–45)
Brown American (1940–45)
The Crisis: A Record of the Darker Races (1939–45)
LHJ (Ladies' Home Journal) (1942–45)
LIFE Magazine (1941–45)
Negro Digest (1942–45)
Opportunity: Journal of Negro Life (1939–45)
Southern Frontier (1942–45)

Electronic and Media Sources

All-American Girls Professional Baseball League. National Baseball Hall of Fame Library. http://aagpbl.org/.
Library of Congress. "America from the Great Depression to World War Two: Black-and-White Photographs from the FSA-OWI, 1935–1945." http://memory.loc.gov/ammem/fsahtml/fahome.html.
National Library of Medicine. "Venereal Disease." Visual Culture and Public Health Posters. http://www.nlm.nih.gov/exhibition/visualculture/venereal.html.
"Unifying a Nation: World War II Posters from the New Hampshire State Library." http://www.nh.gov/nhsl/ww2/.

Other Sources

Primary

Abbott, Harriet. "Doctor? Lawyer? Merchant? Chief? Which Shall She Be? Woman's New Leadership in Business." *LHJ*, July 1920, 45, 164.
Alsop, Gulielma Fell, and Mary F. McBride. *Arms and the Girl: A Guide to Personal Adjustment in War Work and War Marriage.* New York: Vanguard Press, 1943.
"American Designers." *LIFE*, May 8, 1944, 63–69.
Anonymous. "Block That Temperament!" *A&S* 38 (March 1945): 82.

Anthony, Helen Bayne. "Two Worlds." *Opportunity* 21 (April 1943): 56–57.

A Temperamental Dame. "Hell Hath No Fury." *A&S* 38 (May 1945): 68.

Ayling, Keith. *Calling All Women*. New York: Harper & Brothers, 1942.

Baker, Joseph V. "To a Brown Lady." *Brown American* (Fall 1943): n.p.

Bartson, Lester J. *In the Shadow of the Hawk: An Intimate Chronicle of World War II and One Woman's Search for Meaning*. Lanham, Md.: University Press of America, 2004.

Beard, Mary Ritter. *Woman as Force in History: A Study in Traditions and Realities*. New York: Collier Books, 1946. Reprint. New York: Macmillan, 1976.

"Beauty Is a Business." *Brown American* (Winter–Spring 1944): 12–14.

"Betty Grable's Legs." *LIFE*, June 7, 1943, 82–86.

Bugbee, Sylvia J., ed. *An Officer and a Lady: The World War II Letters of Lt. Col. Betty Bandel, Women's Army Corps*. Hanover, N.H.: University Press of New England, 2004.

Cades, H. R. "Change Your Food but Keep Your Figure." *Woman's Home Companion*, June 1943, 76–77.

Candee, Beatrice. "Women in Defense Industry." *Opportunity* 21 (April 1943): 46–49, 86–87.

Carewe, Sylvia. "Where's the Woman's Angle in This War?" *A&S* 35 (August 1942): 23.

Carlyle, James. "How Advertising Went to War." *Nation's Business*, November 1944.

Carson, R. "Short and Low: Newest Fashion Is the Short Evening Dress." *Collier's*, January 15, 1944, 26.

Chivers, Walter. "Effects of the Present War upon the Status of Negro Women." *Southern Frontier*, December 1943, n.p.

Clark, Ida Coker. "Negro Woman Worker, What Now?" *Opportunity* 22 (April–June 1944): 84–85, 93.

Cole, Gordon E. "Magazines and Farm Publications." *A&S* 35 (February 1942): 69–74.

Crawford, M. D. C. "Says Fashion Advance Can't Cease in War." *Women's Wear Daily*, December 18, 1941.

Darnton, Eleanor. "4800 Call It Home." *New York Times*, August 22, 1943.

Davis, Elmer, and Byron Price. *War Information and Censorship*. Washington, D.C.: American Council of Public Affairs, 1943.

"Dear Bill." *Brown American* (Summer 1943): 7, 15.

Drake, St. Clair, and Horace R. Cayton. *Black Metropolis: A Study of Negro Life in a Northern City*. New York: Harcourt Brace & Company, 1945.

Earley, Charity Adams. *One Woman's Army: A Black Officer Remembers the* WAC. College Station: Texas A & M Press, 1989.

"Fashion Warfare: Los Angeles Boosts Fund to Sell City as Style Capital of the World." *Business Week*, March 25, 1944, 48.

Gammon, Margaret H. "The Consumer Viewpoint." *A&S* 37 (February 1944): 30, 126.

Gately, Olive P. "Let's Give Our Copy the Fresh-Air Treatment." *A&S* 38 (January 1945): 50–52, 112–14.

Giles, Neil. *Punch in, Susie! A Woman's War Factory Diary*. New York: Harper & Brothers, 1943.

"Girl of 'Just Average' Looks Can Be a Knockout if She Likes." *Washington Post*, September 28, 1942.

"Girls' Baseball." *LIFE*, June 4, 1945, 64–65.

Gorham, Ethel. *So Your Husband's Gone to War!* Garden City, N.Y.: Doubleday, Doran and Company, 1942.

Gorham, Thelma Thurston. "Negro Army Wives." *Crisis* 50 (January 1943): 21–22.

Gould, Lawrence. "First Reader Cuisine." *Gourmet,* July 1944, 12–13, 53.

Grabill, Wilson H. "The Effect of the Wartime Marriage Boom." *A&S* 38 (May 1945): 153.

"Grable's Baby." *LIFE,* May 8, 1944, 32.

Granger, Lester B. "Women Are Vital to Victory." *Opportunity* 21 (April 1943): 36.

Gray, Albert. "America's Womanpower." *A&S* 36 (May 1943): 68–70.

Green, Blanche. *Growing Up in the* WAC: *Letters to My Sister, 1944–1946.* New York: Vantage, 1987.

Greene, Marjorie E. "They Prepare for 'A New Nation.'" *Opportunity* 22 (April–June 1944): 76.

Griffiths, Janice. "The Little Woman Looks at the Substitutes." *A&S* 36 (August 1943): 106.

Hackshaw, Leotha. "What My Job Means to Me." *Opportunity* 21 (April 1943): 52–53.

Hagner, Anne. "No Housing Problem Here!" *Washington Post,* September 28, 1942.

Hampton, Elizabeth C. "Negro Women and the WAAC." *Opportunity* 21 (April 1943): 54–55, 93.

Hart, Steven, and Lucy Brown. *How to Get Your Man and Hold Him.* New York: Dover, 1944.

Hawes, Elizabeth. "Let's Ration the Clothes Problem." *Independent Woman,* November 1942, 335, 338.

Hawks, Josephine. "Women's Bank." *The Daily Oklahoman,* November 29, 1942.

Henderson, Aileen Kilgore. *Stateside Soldier: Life in the Women's Army Corps, 1944–45.* Columbia: University of South Carolina Press, 2001.

Henderson, Elmer W. "Negroes in Government Employment." *Opportunity* 21 (July 1943): 118–21, 142–43.

Hirose, Arthur P. "What Postwar Products Do Women Want?" *A&S* 37 (January 1944): 29–30, 106.

Honey, Maureen, ed. *Bitter Fruit: African American Women in World War II.* Columbia: University of Missouri Press, 1999.

Hoover, J. Edgar. "Mothers . . . Our Only Hope." *Woman's Home Companion,* January 1944. In *Women's Magazines, 1940–1960: Gender Roles and the Popular Press,* edited by Nancy A. Walker, 44–47. Boston: Bedford/St. Martin's, 1998.

Hornaday, Mary. "Curtiss-Wright St. Louis Plant Lightens Jigs to Attract Women Workers." *Christian Science Monitor,* August 4, 1942.

Howard, Harry Paxton. "Americans in Concentration Camps." *Crisis* 49 (September 1942): 281–84, 301–2.

"How a Woman Should Wear a Uniform." *Good Housekeeping,* August 1942. In *Women's Magazines, 1940–1960: Gender Roles and the Popular Press,* edited by Nancy A. Walker, 35–37. Boston: Bedford/St. Martin's, 1998.

"If American Business Wants to Run Its Own Show When This War Is Over." *Printer's Ink* 198 (January 16, 1942): 17, 38–45.

"The Impact of War on Advertising: Report on Advertising and Sales Management." *A&S* 35 (January 1942): 13–20.

James, Parker. "Women at Work: Is the Double-Pay Envelope a Permanent Trend?" *A&S* 38 (September 1945): 40, 136–44.

Johnson, Hortense. "What My Job Means to Me." *Opportunity* 21 (April 1943): 50–51.

Karp, A. Lawrence. "Selling the Female Industrial Group." *A&S* 35 (March 1942): 26.

Kellar, Charlotte. "Are Women People?" *A&S* 35 (September 1942): 87.

Koppes, Dwight W. "Never Underestimate the Power of a Woman." *A&S* 37 (October 1944): 66–68.

"Ladies of the Diamond." *Time*, June 14, 1943, 74.

Landis, Kenesaw M. *Segregation in Washington: A Report of the National Committee on Segregation in the Nation's Capital*. Chicago: Allied Printing, 1948.

Litoff, Judy Barrett, and David C. Smith, eds. *American Women in a World at War: Contemporary Accounts from World War II*. Wilmington, Del.: Scholarly Resources, Inc., 1997.

———. *Since You Went Away: World War II Letters from American Women on the Home Front*. New York: Oxford University Press, 1991.

———. *We're in This War, Too: World War II Letters from American Women in Uniform*. New York: Oxford University Press, 1994.

MacLennan, N. "Gypsy Wives, Army Style." *New York Times Magazine*, December 27, 1942, 19.

Macy, J. Noel. "Negro Women in the WAC." *Opportunity* 23 (January–March 1945): 14.

Marcus, H. Stanley. "American Fashion Comes of Age." *New York Times Magazine*, September 13, 1942, 22.

Maxwell, Elsa. "Glamour Vs. Prejudice." *New York Post*, November 16, 1943.

McEuen, James Bruce, and Peggy S. McEuen. Interview by author. September 20, 2005.

"Meet the Berckmans: The Story of a Mother Working on Two Fronts." *LHJ*, October 1942. In *Women's Magazines, 1940–1960: Gender Roles and the Popular Press*, edited by Nancy A. Walker, 37–44. Boston: Bedford/St. Martin's, 1998.

"Milady Can't Crack 'Hair Today and Gone Tomorrow' Now—It Usually Takes Week to Get in Beauty Parlor." *Evansville Courier and Press*, February 28, 1943.

Miller, Frieda S. "Negro Women Workers." *Opportunity* 23 (October–December 1945): 207.

Mitchell, Margaret. *Gone with the Wind*. New York: Macmillan Company, 1936.

Mrs. Fair Minded. "The Awful Type of People That Clutter Up a House." *Washington News*, May 20, 1943.

Murray, Florence, ed. *The Negro Handbook, 1946–47*. New York: Current Books, 1947.

National Museum of American History, Smithsonian Institution. "July 1942: United We Stand." Exhibit. March 22–October 27, 2002.

Newman, Dorothy K. *Employing Women in the Shipyards*. No. 192-6. Bulletin of the Women's Bureau, Department of Labor. Washington, D.C.: GPO, 1944.

Okubo, Miné. *Citizen 13660*. New York: Columbia University Press, 1946. Reprint. Seattle: University of Washington Press, 1983.

Parker, Dorothy. "Are We Women or Are We Mice?" *Readers Digest*, July 1943, 71–72.

Parker, Martha. "Trim Figure." *New York Times Magazine*, November 12, 1944, 37.

Phillips, H. I. *All-Out Arlene: A Story of the Girls behind the Boys behind the Guns*. Garden City, N.J.: Doubleday, Doran and Co., 1943.

Pidgeon, Mary Elizabeth. *A Preview as to Women Workers in Transition from War to Peace*. Special Bulletin No. 18 of the Women's Bureau. Washington, D.C.: GPO, 1944.

Popkin, Zelda. *The Journey Home*. Philadelphia: J. P. Lippincott, 1945.

Reid, Constance Bowman. *Slacks and Calluses: Our Summer in a Bomber Factory*. Illustrated by Clara Marie Allen. 1944. Reprint, with an introduction by Sandra M. Gilbert. Washington, D.C.: Smithsonian Institution Press, 1999.

Rich, Leo. "The Public Expects Progress." *A&S* 37 (July 1944): 36.

Rosebery, Mercedes. *This Day's Madness: A Story of the American People against the Background of the War Effort.* New York: Macmillan, 1944.

Rosenberg, Anna M. "Womanpower and the War." *Opportunity* 21 (April 1943): 35.

Somerville, Keith Frazier. *Dear Boys: World War II Letters from a Woman Back Home.* Edited by Judy Barrett Litoff and David C. Smith. Jackson: University of Mississippi Press, 1991.

Stanton, Edward F., Jr., and Rose E. Stanton. Interview by author. Laguna Niguel, California. July 26, 2005.

Ten Eyck, Alice. "Feminine Styles Inspired by War." *Journal of Commerce (New York),* January 21, 1942.

U.S. Department of Labor. Women's Bureau. *Negro Women War Workers.* Bulletin No. 205. Washington, D.C.: GPO, 1945.

———. *Progress Report on Women War Workers' Housing: April 1943.* Special Bulletin No. 17. Washington, D.C.: GPO, 1944.

U.S. Department of War. *You're Going to Employ Women.* Washington, D.C.: U.S. Department of War, 1943.

U.S. Office of War Information. *American Handbook.* Washington, D.C.: Public Affairs Press, 1945.

———. *A Handbook of the United States of America: Pertinent Information about the United States and the War Effort.* Produced by the Features Division, News and Features Bureau, Overseas Branch. London: Hutchinson & Co., 1943.

"V for Voluptuous." *Newsweek,* September 6, 1943, 90.

"Weinberger Drug Stores' Head Sees Young-Woman Market a Profitable One to Cultivate." *Chain Store Age,* September 1942, 85.

"When Your Soldier Comes Home." *LHJ,* October 1945. In *Women's Magazines, 1940–1960: Gender Roles and the Popular Press,* edited by Nancy A. Walker, 56–62. Boston: Bedford/St. Martin's, 1998.

White, Barbara A. *Lady Leatherneck.* New York: Dodd, Mead & Co., 1945.

Williams, Frances Harriet. "A Woman Looks at Her Government." *Opportunity* 21 (April 1943): 73, 94.

Woman's Home Companion Cook Book. New York: Collier & Son, 1942.

"Women at War." *Brown American* (Summer 1943): 4–5.

Yearwood, Ruby Bryant. "Women Volunteers Unite to Serve." *Opportunity* 21 (April 1943): 89.

Young, James Webb. *Diary of an Ad Man: The War Years, June 1, 1942–December 31, 1943.* Chicago: n.p., 1946.

Secondary

Adams, Carol J. "The Rape of Animals, the Butchering of Women." In *The Sexual Politics of Meat: A Feminist-Vegetarian Critical Theory,* 50–73. Tenth Anniversary Edition. New York: Continuum, 1999.

———. "The Sexual Politics of Meat." Speech delivered at Transylvania University. Lexington, Kentucky. May 16, 2005.

Adams, Carol J., and Josephine Donovan, eds. *Animals and Women: Feminist Theoretical Explorations.* Durham, N.C.: Duke University Press, 1995.

Adams, Michael C. C. *The Best War Ever: America and World War II.* Baltimore: Johns Hopkins University Press, 1994.

Adkins Covert, Tawnya. "Consumption and Citizenship during the Second World War: Product Advertising in Women's Magazines." *Journal of Consumer Culture* 3 (November 2003): 315–42.

Anderson, Karen. "Last Hired, First Fired: Black Women Workers during World War II." *Journal of American History* 69 (1982): 82–97.

———. *Wartime Women: Sex Roles, Family Relations, and the Status of Women during World War II.* Westport, Conn.: Greenwood Press, 1981.

Banta, Martha. *Imaging American Women: Idea and Ideals in Cultural History.* New York: Columbia University Press, 1987.

Barthes, Roland. *Camera Lucida.* Translated by Richard Howard. New York: Hill & Wang, 1981.

Bazin, André. "Entomology of the Pin-Up Girl." In *What Is Cinema?* edited by André Bazin, 158–62. Berkeley: University of California Press, 1971.

Benson, Susan Porter. *Counter Cultures: Saleswomen, Managers, and Customers in American Department Stores.* Urbana: University of Illinois Press, 1987.

Bentley, Amy. *Eating for Victory: Food Rationing and the Politics of Domesticity.* Urbana: University of Illinois Press, 1998.

Bérubé, Allan. *Coming Out under Fire: The History of Gay Men and Women in World War Two.* New York: Free Press, 1990.

Blackwelder, Julia Kirk. *Styling Jim Crow: African American Beauty Training during Segregation.* College Station: Texas A & M University Press, 2003.

Blum, John. *V Was for Victory: Politics and Culture during World War II.* New York: Harcourt Brace Jovanovich, 1976.

Bordo, Susan. "Feminism, Foucault and the Politics of the Body." In *Feminist Theory and the Body: A Reader,* edited by Janet Price and Margrit Shildrick, 246–57. New York: Routledge, 1999.

———. *Unbearable Weight: Feminism, Western Culture, and the Body.* Berkeley: University of California Press, 1993.

Boris, Eileen. "'You Wouldn't Want One of 'Em Dancing with Your Wife': Racialized Bodies on the Job in World War II." *American Quarterly* 50 (March 1998): 77–108.

Brinkley, David. *Washington Goes to War.* New York: Knopf, 1988.

Brownmiller, Susan. *Femininity.* New York: Fawcett Columbine, 1984.

Brumberg, Joan Jacobs. "The Appetite as Voice." In *Food and Culture: A Reader,* edited by Carole Counihan and Penny Van Esterik, 159–79. New York: Routledge, 1997.

———. "Beyond Meat and Potatoes: A Review Essay." *Food and Foodways: Explorations in the History and Culture of Human Nourishment* 3 (1989): 271–81.

———. *Fasting Girls: The Emergence of Anorexia Nervosa as a Modern Disease.* Cambridge, Mass.: Harvard University Press, 1988.

Buckland, Sandra Stansbery. "Promoting American Designers, 1940–44: Building Our Own House." In *Twentieth-Century American Fashion,* edited by Linda Welters and Patricia A. Cunningham, 99–121. New York: Berg, 2005.

Bustard, Bruce. *A New Deal for the Arts.* Washington, D.C.: National Archives and Records Administration, 1997.

Buszek, Maria Elena. "Of Varga Girls and Riot Grrrls: The Varga Girl and WWII in the Pin-Up's Feminist History." http://www.spencerart.ku.edu/collection/print/vargas/buszek.shtml (accessed March 3, 2010).

———. *Pin-Up Grrrls: Feminism, Sexuality, Popular Culture.* Durham, N.C.: Duke University Press, 2006.

Butler, Judith. *Bodies That Matter: On the Discursive Limits of "Sex."* New York: Routledge, 1993.

———. *Gender Trouble: Feminism and the Subversion of Identity.* New York: Routledge, 1990.

Campbell, D'Ann. *Women at War with America: Private Lives in a Patriotic Era.* Cambridge, Mass.: Harvard University Press, 1984.

Carnes, Mark. *Novel History: Historians and Novelists Confront America's Past (And Each Other).* New York: Simon & Schuster, 2001.

Chinn, Sarah E. "'Liberty's Life Stream': Blood, Race, and Citizenship in World War II." In *Technology and the Logic of American Racism: A Cultural History of the Body as Evidence,* edited by Sarah E. Chinn, 93–140. New York: Continuum, 2000.

Clement, Elizabeth Alice. *Love for Sale: Courting, Treating, and Prostitution in New York City, 1900–1945.* Chapel Hill: University of North Carolina Press, 2006.

Collins, Patricia Hill. *Fighting Words: Black Women and the Search for Justice.* Minneapolis: University of Minnesota Press, 1998.

Colman, Penny. *Rosie the Riveter: Working Women on the Home Front in World War II.* New York: Crown Publishers, 1995.

Costello, John. *Virtue under Fire: How World War II Changed Our Social and Sexual Attitudes.* Boston: Little, Brown and Co., 1985.

Cott, Nancy F., ed. *A Woman Making History: Mary Ritter Beard through Her Letters.* New Haven, Conn.: Yale University Press, 1991.

Cowan, Ruth Schwartz. *More Work for Mother: The Ironies of Household Technology from the Open Hearth to the Microwave.* New York: Basic Books, 1983.

Coward, Rosalind. *Female Desires: How They Are Sought, Bought and Sold.* New York: Grove Press, 1985.

Craig, Maxine Leeds. *Ain't I a Beauty Queen? Black Women, Beauty, and the Politics of Race.* New York: Oxford University Press, 2002.

Dabakis, Melissa. "Gendered Labor: Norman Rockwell's 'Rosie the Riveter' and the Discourses of Wartime Womanhood." In *Gender and American History since 1890,* edited by Barbara Melosh, 182–204. New York: Routledge, 1993.

Daniel, Pete. "Going among Strangers: Southern Reactions to World War II." *Journal of American History* 77 (December 1990): 886–911.

Davis, Thadious. Introduction to *Passing,* by Nella Larsen. 1929. Reprint. New York: Penguin Books, 1997.

Delano, Page Dougherty. "Making Up for War: Sexuality and Citizenship in Wartime Culture." *Feminist Studies* 26 (Spring 2000): 33–68.

D'Emilio, John, and Estelle B. Freedman. *Intimate Matters: A History of Sexuality in America.* New York: Perennial, 1989.

Dick, Bernard F. *The Star-Spangled Screen: The American World War II Film.* Lexington: University of Kentucky Press, 1996.

Dickos, Andrew. *Street with No Name: A History of the Classic American Film Noir.* Lexington: University Press of Kentucky, 2002.

Donohue, Kathleen G. *Freedom from Want: American Liberalism and the Idea of the Consumer.* Baltimore: Johns Hopkins University Press, 2003.

Dower, John W. "Race, Language, and War in Two Cultures: World War II in Asia." In *The War in American Culture: Society and Consciousness during World War II,* edited by Lewis A. Erenberg and Susan E. Hirsch, 169–201. Chicago: University of Chicago Press, 1996.

———. *War without Mercy: Race and Power in the Pacific War.* New York: Pantheon Books, 1986.

Ellis, Jacqueline. "Esther Bubley: FSA Documentarist." *History of Photography* 20 (August 1996): 265–70.

Enloe, Cynthia. *Maneuvers: The International Politics of Militarizing Women's Lives.* Berkeley: University of California Press, 2000.

Faderman, Lillian. *Odd Girls and Twilight Lovers: A History of Lesbian Life in Twentieth-Century America.* New York: Penguin, 1992.

Farrell-Beck, Jane, and Colleen Gau. *Uplift: The Bra in America.* Philadelphia: University of Pennsylvania Press, 2002.

Finkle, Lee. *Forum for Protest: The Black Press during World War II.* Cranbury, N.J.: Associated University Presses, Inc., 1975.

Fox, Frank. *Madison Avenue Goes to War: The Strange Military Career of American Advertising, 1941–1945.* Provo, Utah: Brigham Young University Press, 1996.

Frankenberg, Ruth. *White Women, Race Matters: The Social Construction of Whiteness.* Minneapolis: University of Minnesota Press, 1993.

Frazier, Edward Franklin. *Black Bourgeoisie.* Glencoe, Ill.: Free Press, 1957. Reprint. New York: Free Press, 1997.

Friedan, Betty. *The Feminine Mystique.* New York: Norton, 1963.

Fussell, Paul. *Uniforms: Why We Wear What We Wear.* Boston: Houghton Mifflin, 2002.

———. *Wartime: Understanding and Behavior in the Second World War.* Oxford: Oxford University Press, 1990.

Gaines, Jane. "War, Women, and Lipstick: Fan Mags in the Forties." *Heresies* 18 (1985): 42–47.

Garber, Marjorie. *Vested Interests: Cross-Dressing and Cultural Anxiety.* New York: Routledge, 1991.

Gardner, Kirsten E. "Hiding the Scars: History of Breast Prostheses after Mastectomy since 1945." In *Beauty and Business: Commerce, Gender, and Culture in Modern America,* edited by Philip Scranton, 309–27. New York: Routledge, 2001.

Garvey, Ellen Gruber. *The Adman in the Parlor: Magazines and the Gendering of Consumer Culture, 1880s to 1910s.* New York: Oxford University Press, 1996.

Giddings, Paula. *In Search of Sisterhood: Delta Sigma Theta and the Challenge of the Black Sorority Movement.* New York: William Morrow, 1988.

Gluck, Sherna Berger. *Rosie the Riveter Revisited: Women, the War, and Social Change.* Boston: Twayne, 1987.

Goodwin, Doris Kearns. *No Ordinary Time: Franklin and Eleanor Roosevelt: The Home Front in World War II.* New York: Simon & Schuster, 1994.

Grantham, Dewey W. "The South and Congressional Politics." In *Remaking Dixie: The Impact of World War II on the American South,* edited by Neil R. McMillen, 21–32. Jackson: University of Mississippi Press, 1997.

Griffith, Robert. "The Selling of America: The Advertising Council and American Politics, 1942–1960." *Business History Review* 157 (Autumn 1983): 388–412.

Grossman, James. *Land of Hope: Chicago, Black Southerners, and the Great Migration.* Chicago: University of Chicago Press, 1989.

Grosz, Elizabeth. *Volatile Bodies: Toward a Corporeal Feminism.* Bloomington: Indiana University Press, 1994.

Gubar, Susan. "'This Is My Rifle, This Is My Gun': World War II and the Blitz on Women." In *Behind the Lines: Gender and the Two World Wars,* edited by Margaret Randolph Higonnet, Jane Jenson, Sonya Michel, and Margaret Collins Weitz, 227–59. New Haven, Conn.: Yale University Press, 1987.

Hall, Phyllis A. "Crisis at Hampton Roads: The Problems of Wartime Congestion, 1942–1944." *Virginia Magazine of History and Biography* 101 (July 1993): 405–32.

Hannel, Susan L. "The Influence of American Jazz on Fashion." In *Twentieth-Century American Fashion,* edited by Linda Welters and Patricia A. Cunningham, 57–77. New York: Berg, 2005.

Hartmann, Susan. *The Home Front and Beyond: American Women in the 1940s.* Boston: Twayne, 1982.

Haskell, Molly. *From Reverence to Rape: The Treatment of Women in the Movies.* New York: Holt, Rinehart and Winston, 1974.

Hayes, Joanne Lamb. *Grandma's Wartime Kitchen: World War II and the Way We Cooked.* New York: St. Martin's Press, 2000.

Hegarty, Marilyn E. "Patriot or Prostitute? Sexual Discourses, Print Media, and American Women during World War II." *Journal of Women's History* 10 (Summer 1998): 112–36.

———. *Victory Girls, Khaki-Wackies, and Patriotutes: The Regulation of Female Sexuality during World War II.* New York: New York University Press, 2008.

Heilbrun, Carolyn G. *Writing a Woman's Life.* New York: Norton, 1988.

Higonnet, Margaret Randolph, Jane Jenson, Sonya Michel, and Margaret Collins Weitz, eds. *Behind the Lines: Gender and the Two World Wars.* New Haven, Conn.: Yale University Press, 1987.

Hill, Daniel Delis. *Advertising to the American Woman, 1900–1999.* Columbus: Ohio State University Press, 2002.

Hoffert, Sylvia D. "Gender, Identity, and Sexuality (1600–1975)." In *A History of Gender in America: Essays, Documents and Articles,* 392–423. Upper Saddle River, N.J.: Prentice Hall, 2003.

Hollander, Anne. *Sex and Suits: The Evolution of Modern Dress.* New York: Knopf, 1994.

Honey, Maureen. *Creating Rosie the Riveter: Class, Gender, and Propaganda during World War II.* Amherst: University of Massachusetts Press, 1984.

Howard, Vicki. *Brides, Inc.: American Weddings and the Business of Tradition.* Philadelphia: University of Pennsylvania Press, 2006.

Hoy, Suellen. *Chasing Dirt: The American Pursuit of Cleanliness.* New York: Oxford University Press, 1995.

Hughes, Marvalene H. "Soul, Black Women, and Food." In *Food and Culture: A Reader,* edited by Carole Counihan and Penny Van Esterik, 272–80. New York: Routledge, 1997.

Human, Julie. "A Woman Rebels? Gender Roles in 1930s Motion Pictures." *Register of the Kentucky Historical Society* 98 (Autumn 2000): 405–28.

Israel, Betsy. *Bachelor Girl: The Secret History of the Single Girl in the Twentieth Century.* New York: Harper Collins, 2002.

Janello, Amy, and Brennon Jones. *The American Magazine.* New York: Henry N. Abrams, 1991.

Jarvis, Christina. *The Male Body at War: American Masculinity during World War II.* DeKalb: Northern Illinois University Press, 2004.

Johnson, John H., and Lerone Bennett Jr. *Succeeding against the Odds.* New York: Warner Books, 1989.

Kasson, John. *Amusing the Million: Coney Island at the Turn of the Century.* New York: Hill and Wang, 1978.

Kennedy, David M. *Freedom from Fear: The American People in Depression and War, 1929–1945.* New York: Oxford University Press, 1999.

Koehn, Nancy. "Estée Lauder: Self-Definition and the Modern Cosmetics Market." In *Beauty and Business: Commerce, Gender, and Culture in Modern America,* edited by Philip Scranton, 217–53. New York: Routledge, 2001.

Koppes, Clayton R., and Gregory D. Black. *Hollywood Goes to War: How Politics, Profits, and Propaganda Shaped World War II Movies.* New York: Free Press, 1987.

———. "What to Show the World: The Office of War Information and Hollywood, 1942–1945." In *Hollywood's America: United States History through Its Films,* edited by Steven Mintz and Randy Roberts, 157–68. St. James, N.Y.: Brandywine Press, 1993.

Lears, T. J. Jackson. *Fables of Abundance: A Cultural History of Advertising in America.* New York: Basic Books, 1994.

Leder, Jane Mersky. *Thanks for the Memories: Love, Sex, and World War II.* Westport, Conn.: Praeger, 2006.

Leff, Mark. "The Politics of Sacrifice on the American Home Front in World War II." *Journal of American History* 77 (March 1991): 1296–1318.

Lemke-Santangelo, Gretchen. *Abiding Courage: African American Migrant Women and the East Bay Community.* Chapel Hill: University of North Carolina Press, 1996.

Lerner, Gerda. *Living with History / Making Social Change.* Chapel Hill: University of North Carolina Press, 2009.

———. *Why History Matters: Life and Thought.* New York: Oxford University Press, 1998.

Lingeman, Richard. *"Don't You Know There's a War On?" The American Homefront, 1941–45.* New York: G. P. Putnam's Sons, 1970.

Litoff, Judy Barrett, and David C. Smith. "'Will He Get My Letter?' Popular Portrayals of Mail and Morale during World War II." *Journal of Popular Culture* 23 (Spring 1990): 21–43.

———. "'Writing Is Fighting, Too': The World War II Correspondence of Southern Women." *Georgia Historical Quarterly* 76 (Summer 1992): 436–57.

Los Angeles County Museum of Art. "A Century of Fashion, 1900–2000." Exhibit. May 23, 2002–January 6, 2003.

Lowe, Margaret A. *Looking Good: College Women and Body Image, 1875–1930.* Baltimore: Johns Hopkins University Press, 2003.

Lurie, Alison. *The Language of Clothes.* New York: Random House, 1981.

Lyons, Heather, and Nikky Finney. *M & M Smith: For Posterity's Sake.* Videocassette. Lexington, Ky.: Little City Productions, 1995.

Marchand, Roland. *Advertising the American Dream: Making Way for Modernity.* Berkeley: University of California Press, 1985.

May, Elaine Tyler. *Homeward Bound: American Families in the Cold War Era.* New York: Basic Books, 1988.

———. "Rosie the Riveter Gets Married." In *The War in American Culture: Society and Consciousness during World War II,* edited by Lewis A. Erenberg and Susan Hirsch, 128–43. Chicago: University of Chicago Press, 1996.

McAndrew, Malia. "Japanese American Beauty Pageants and Minstrel Shows: A Cultural Analysis of Two Arkansas Internment Camps during World War II." Paper presented at the Eighth Southern Conference on Women's History. Columbia, South Carolina. June 5, 2009.

McCandless, Amy Thompson. *The Past in the Present: Women's Higher Education in the Twentieth-Century American South.* Tuscaloosa: University of Alabama Press, 1999.

McDowell, Deborah E. "Recovery Missions: Imaging the Body Ideals." In *Recovering the Black Female Body: Self-Representations by African American Women,* edited by Michael Bennett and Vanessa D. Dickerson, 296–318. New Brunswick, N.J.: Rutgers University Press, 2001.

McEuen, Melissa A. "Exposing Anger and Discontent: Esther Bubley's Portrait of the Upper South during World War II." In *Searching for Their Places: Women in the South across Four Centuries,* edited by Thomas H. Appleton Jr. and Angela Boswell, 238–60. Columbia: University of Missouri Press, 2003.

———. *Seeing America: Women Photographers between the Wars.* Lexington: University Press of Kentucky, 2000.

McGovern, Charles F. *Sold American: Consumption and Citizenship, 1890–1945.* Chapel Hill: University of North Carolina Press, 2006.

McMillen, Neil R., ed. *Remaking Dixie: The Impact of World War II on the American South.* Jackson: University of Mississippi Press, 1997.

Meikle, Jeffrey. *Twentieth-Century Limited: Industrial Design in America, 1925–1939.* Philadelphia: Temple University Press, 1979.

Melosh, Barbara. *Engendering Culture: Manhood and Womanhood in New Deal Public Art and Theatre.* Washington, D.C.: Smithsonian Institution Press, 1991.

Merryman, Molly. *Clipped Wings: The Rise and Fall of the Women Airforce Service Pilots (WASPs) of World War II.* New York: New York University Press, 1998.

Meyer, Leisa D. *Creating GI Jane: Sexuality and Power in the Women's Army Corps during World War II.* New York: Columbia University Press, 1996.

Meyerowitz, Joanne. *Women Adrift: Independent Wage Earners in Chicago, 1880–1930.* Chicago: University of Chicago Press, 1988.

———. "Women, Cheesecake, and Borderline Material: Responses to Girlie Pictures in the Mid-Twentieth-Century U.S." *Journal of Women's History* 8 (1996): 9–35.

Michel, Sonya. "American Women and the Discourse of the Democratic Family in World War II." In *Behind the Lines: Gender and the Two World Wars,* edited by Margaret Randolph Higonnet, Jane Jenson, Sonya Michel, and Margaret Collins Weitz, 154–67. New Haven, Conn.: Yale University Press, 1987.

Milkman, Ruth. *Gender at Work: The Dynamics of Job Segregation by Sex during World War II.* Urbana: University of Illinois Press, 1987.

Mizejewski, Linda. *Ziegfeld Girl: Image and Icon in Culture and Cinema*. Durham, N.C.: Duke University Press, 1999.

Monahan, Evelyn M., and Rosemary Neidel-Greenlee. *And If I Perish: Frontline U.S. Army Nurses in World War II*. New York: Random House, 2003.

Moore, Brenda L. *Serving Our Country: Japanese American Women in the Military during World War II*. New Brunswick, N.J.: Rutgers University Press, 2003.

Moore, Jacqueline M. *Leading the Race: The Transformation of the Black Elite in the Nation's Capital, 1880–1920*. Charlottesville: University of Virginia Press, 1999.

Okihiro, Gary Y. "An American Story." In *Impounded: Dorothea Lange and the Censored Images of Japanese American Internment*, edited by Linda Gordon and Gary Y. Okihiro, 47–84. New York: W. W. Norton, 2006.

Peeler, David P. *The Illuminating Mind in American Photography: Stieglitz, Strand, Weston, Adams*. Rochester, N.Y.: University of Rochester Press, 2001.

Peiss, Kathy. *Cheap Amusements: Working Women and Leisure in Turn-of-the-Century New York*. Philadelphia: Temple University Press, 1986.

———. *Hope in a Jar: The Making of America's Beauty Culture*. New York: Metropolitan Books, 1996.

Perrett, Geoffrey. *Days of Sadness, Years of Triumph: The American People, 1939–1945*. Madison: University of Wisconsin Press, 1973.

Place, Janey. "Women in Film Noir." In *Women in Film Noir*, edited by E. Ann Kaplan, 47–68. New ed. London: British Film Institute, 1998.

Potter, Vilma Raskin. *A Reference Guide to Afro-American Publications and Editors, 1827–1946*. Ames: Iowa State University Press, 1993.

Price, Janet, and Margrit Shildrick, eds. *Feminist Theory and the Body: A Reader*. New York: Routledge, 1999.

Radway, Janice A. *Reading the Romance: Women, Patriarchy, and Popular Literature*. Chapel Hill: University of North Carolina, 1984.

Riordan, Teresa. *Inventing Beauty: A History of the Innovations That Have Made Us Beautiful*. New York: Broadway Books, 2004.

Roach, Mary Ellen. "The Social Symbolism of Women's Dress." In *The Fabrics of Culture: The Anthropology of Clothing and Adornment*, edited by Justine M. Cordwell and Ronald A. Schwarz, 415–22. New York: Mouton Publishers, 1979.

Roberts, Randy. "You Must Remember This: The Case of Hal Wallis' *Casablanca*." In *Hollywood's America: United States History through Its Films*, edited by Steven Mintz and Randy Roberts, 169–77. St. James, N.Y.: Brandywine Press, 1993.

Roeder, George. *The Censored War: American Visual Experience during World War Two*. New Haven, Conn.: Yale University Press, 1993.

———. "Censoring Disorder: American Visual Imagery of World War II." In *The War in American Culture: Society and Consciousness during World War II*, edited by Lewis A. Erenberg and Susan E. Hirsch, 46–70. Chicago: University of Chicago Press, 1996.

Roediger, David R. *Working toward Whiteness: How America's Immigrants Became White: The Strange Journey from Ellis Island to the Suburbs*. New York: Basic Books, 2005.

Rohter, Larry. "Dear Donna: A Pinup So Swell She Kept G.I. Mail." *New York Times*, May 25, 2009, A1.

Rosen, Marjorie. *Popcorn Venus: Women, Movies, and the American Dream*. New York: Coward, McCann, and Geoghegan, 1973.

Rupp, Leila J. *Mobilizing Women for War: German and American Propaganda, 1939–1945*. Princeton, N.J.: Princeton University Press, 1978.

Rutherford, Janice Williams. *Selling Mrs. Consumer: Christine Frederick and the Rise of Household Efficiency*. Athens: University of Georgia Press, 2003.

Saville, Deborah. "Dress and Culture in Greenwich Village." In *Twentieth-Century American Fashion*, edited by Linda Welters and Patricia A. Cunningham, 33–55. New York: Berg, 2005.

Scanlon, Jennifer. *Inarticulate Longings: The Ladies' Home Journal, Gender, and the Promises of Consumer Culture*. New York: Routledge, 1995.

Scherman, David E., ed. *LIFE Goes to War*. New York: Pocket Books, 1977.

Schofield, Mary Anne. "Miss America, Rosie the Riveter, and World War II." In *"There She Is, Miss America": The Politics of Sex, Beauty, and Race in America's Most Famous Pageant*, edited by Darcy Martin and Elwood Watson, 53–66. New York: Palgrave, 2004.

Scranton, Philip, ed. *Beauty and Business: Commerce, Gender, and Culture in Modern America*. New York: Routledge, 2001.

Seid, Roberta Pollack. *Never Too Thin: Why Women Are at War with Their Bodies*. New York: Prentice Hall, 1989.

Sivulka, Juliann. *Stronger Than Dirt: A Cultural History of Advertising Personal Hygiene in America, 1875 to 1940*. Amherst, N.Y.: Prometheus Books, 2001.

Sklar, Robert. *Movie-Made America: A Social History of American Movies*. New York: Random House, 1975.

Solinger, Rickie. *Pregnancy and Power: A Short History of Reproductive Politics in America*. New York: New York University Press, 2005.

Stange, Maren. *Bronzeville: Black Chicago in Pictures, 1941–43*. New York: New Press, 2003.

Stearns, Peter N. *Fat History: Bodies and Beauty in the Modern West*. New York: New York University Press, 2002.

Strasser, Susan. *Never Done: A History of American Housework*. New York: Pantheon, 1982.

Thomas, Mary Martha. *Riveting and Rationing in Dixie: Alabama Women and the Second World War*. Tuscaloosa: University of Alabama Press, 1987.

Walker, Nancy A., ed. *Women's Magazines, 1940–1960: Gender Roles and the Popular Press*. Boston: Bedford/St. Martin's, 1998.

Walters, Suzanna Danuta. *Material Girls: Making Sense of Feminist Cultural Theory*. Berkeley: University of California Press, 1995.

Warner, Patricia Campbell. "The Americanization of Fashion: Sportswear, the Movies and the 1930s." In *Twentieth-Century American Fashion*, edited by Linda Welters and Patricia A. Cunningham, 79–98. New York: Berg, 2005.

Washburn, Patrick Scott. *A Question of Sedition: The Federal Government's Investigation of the Black Press during World War II*. New York: Oxford University Press, 1986.

Weigand, Cindy. *Texas Women in World War II*. Lanham, Md.: Rowman and Littlefield, 2003.

Welters, Linda, and Patricia A. Cunningham, eds. *Twentieth-Century American Fashion*. New York: Berg, 2005.

Westbrook, Robert B. "'I Want a Girl Just Like the Girl That Married Harry James': American Women and the Problem of Political Obligation in World War II." *American Quarterly* 42 (December 1990): 587–614.

————. *Why We Fought: Forging American Obligations in World War II*. Washington, D.C.: Smithsonian Institution Press, 2004.

White, Deborah Gray. *Too Heavy a Load: Black Women in Defense of Themselves, 1894–1994*. New York: W. W. Norton, 1999.

Williams, Megan E. "The *Crisis* Cover Girl: Lena Horne, the NAACP, and Representations of African American Femininity, 1941–1945." *American Periodicals* 16 (2006): 200–218.

Wilson, Elizabeth. *Adorned in Dreams: Fashion and Modernity*. Berkeley: University of California Press, 1987.

Winchell, Meghan K. *Good Girls, Good Food, Good Fun: The Story of* USO *Hostesses during World War II*. Chapel Hill: University of North Carolina Press, 2008.

Winkler, Allan M. *The Politics of Propaganda: The Office of War Information, 1942–45*. New Haven, Conn.: Yale University Press, 1978.

Witt, Doris Smith. *Black Hunger: Food and the Politics of U.S. Identity*. New York: Oxford University Press, 1999.

Wolcott, Victoria W. *Remaking Respectability: African American Women in Interwar Detroit*. Chapel Hill: University of North Carolina, 2001.

Yellin, Emily. *Our Mothers' War: American Women at Home and at the Front during World War II*. New York: Free Press, 2004.

INDEX

Page numbers in *italics* refer to illustrations.

immigrants, 10, 73–74, 104, 110, 117, 134–35
Independent Woman, 72
industrial safety, 4, 56, 57, 150, 166–71, *168*, *169. See also* slacks; Women's Bureau [U.S. Department of Labor]

James, Harry, 89
Japanese Americans, 10, 38, *40*, 40–41, 224n54
Johnson, John H., 21, 105, 222n30
J. Walter Thompson Advertising Agency (JWT): female copywriters at, 112; growth of, 8, 112; relationship to U.S. government information campaigns, 10–11, 20–21, 220n6; women consumers and, 3, 8–9, 112, 123, *199*, 205. *See also* LUX advertisements; Lux Toilet Soap advertisements; Pond's Cold Cream advertisements

Koppes, Dwight, 82

labor mobilization. *See* defense industry
Ladies' Home Journal, 17, 82, 181, 197, 202–3, 204, 209
Lady Is Willing, The, 113
Lake, Veronica, 167–68, *168*
Lerner, Gerda, 4
Lever Brothers, 112, 123. *See also* LUX advertisements; Lux Toilet Soap advertisements
LIFE: circulation, 75; defense plant safety featured in, 167–68; heterosexuality promoted in, 75–76; Hollywood depicted in, 70, *71*, 89, 167, *168*, 172–73; popularity among African Americans, 21; wartime clothing depicted in, 140, 150, 172–73; women depicted in, 7, 68, 72, 75–78, 86–90, 215, *216*
lipstick: advertisements, 47–48, *49*; "dangerous" women and, 48–50; defense workers and, 45; home front rationing and, 45–47; role in women's beauty routines, 45–47
Litoff, Judy Barrett, xii, 200
Lockheed Aircraft, 6, 28, 33–34, *34*, 168, 191

Los Angeles Times, 153
LUX advertisements: directed at young unmarried women, 101, 124, *125*, 125–27; for dishwashing, 61–64, *62*; for laundry, 79, *80*, *84*, 123, 124–27, *127*, 128–32
Lux Toilet Soap advertisements: and cleanliness, 101; endorsed by actresses, 112–15, *114*, 117, 118–20, *119*, *122*; gender-specific campaigns, 120–21; themes in, 112–15, 116–17, 118–20

MacFadden Women's Group, 69, 205, 222n24
Madam C. J. Walker Company, 8, 29–30
magazines, xi, 11, 84–85; confessional genre, 56–57, 58; cosmetics advertising and, 7, 47–48; documentary photography and, xi, 75, 79–80, 81; fashion genre, 139–140; middle-class women and, 22–23, 61, 64, 101, 178, 187, 205; movies and, 47, 70, 71–72; Office of War Information (OWI) and, 30–32, *31*; weight control advice in, 158. See also *LIFE*
Marcus, H. Stanley, 138–39
marriage: fear of "man shortage," 14, 20, 121; fidelity in, 48, 63, 202–3; high rates of, 203; long distance relationships and, 200, 202–4; sexual double standard in, 202–4; short engagements and, 11, 203; social order and, 155, 202–4; as theme in advertising, 8, 15, 61, 123, 126
Marshall, George C., 66
McCall's, 23, 55, 61, 158, 196
McDowell, Deborah, 3, 135
McPeek, Francis, 105, 106
men, 120, 129–32, 198. *See also* military men
Meyer, Leisa, 143, 237n27
Meyerowitz, Joanne, 81, 228n34, 231n13
middle-class women: club membership of, 13; contrasted with working-class women, 110; morale work and, 200–3; postwar domesticity and, 209; self-starvation of, 161–63; sexualization of, 4, 61, 77–78, 83, 98–99
migration, 35, 100–3, 106–7, 132, 207